ROUTLEDGE LIBRARY EDITIONS: 19TH CENTURY RELIGION

Volume 15

ORGANIZED FREETHOUGHT

ORGANIZED FREETHOUGHT
The Religion of Unbelief in
Victorian England

SHIRLEY A. MULLEN

LONDON AND NEW YORK

First published in 1987 by Garland Publishing, Inc.

This edition first published in 2018
by Routledge
2 Park Square, Milton Park, Abingdon, Oxon OX14 4RN

and by Routledge
711 Third Avenue, New York, NY 10017

Routledge is an imprint of the Taylor & Francis Group, an informa business

© 1987 Shirley A. Mullen

All rights reserved. No part of this book may be reprinted or reproduced or utilised in any form or by any electronic, mechanical, or other means, now known or hereafter invented, including photocopying and recording, or in any information storage or retrieval system, without permission in writing from the publishers.

Trademark notice: Product or corporate names may be trademarks or registered trademarks, and are used only for identification and explanation without intent to infringe.

British Library Cataloguing in Publication Data
A catalogue record for this book is available from the British Library

ISBN: 978-1-138-06800-1 (Set)
ISBN: 978-1-315-10089-0 (Set) (ebk)
ISBN: 978-1-138-07120-9 (Volume 15) (hbk)
ISBN: 978-1-138-07133-9 (Volume 15) (pbk)
ISBN: 978-1-315-11470-5 (Volume 15) (ebk)

Publisher's Note
The publisher has gone to great lengths to ensure the quality of this reprint but points out that some imperfections in the original copies may be apparent.

Disclaimer
The publisher has made every effort to trace copyright holders and would welcome correspondence from those they have been unable to trace.

Organized Freethought
The Religion of Unbelief in Victorian England

Shirley A. Mullen

Garland Publishing, Inc.
New York and London 1987

Copyright © 1987 Shirley A. Mullen
All rights reserved

Library of Congress Cataloging-in-Publication Data

Mullen, Shirley A. (Shirley Annette), 1954–
  Organized freethought : the religion of unbelief in Victorian England / Shirley A. Mullen.
    p. cm.—(Modern European history)
    Thesis (Ph.D.)—University of Minnesota, 1985.
    Bibliography: p.
    Includes index.
    ISBN 0-8240-7825-X (alk. paper)
    1. Free thought—England—History—19th century. 2. England—Religion—19th century.
I. Title. II. Title: Organized free thought.
III. Series.
B2765.G7M84   1987
211'.4'0942—dc19   87-26032

All volumes in this series are printed on acid-free, 250-year-life paper.

Printed in the United States of America

TABLE OF CONTENTS

Introduction	Organized Freethought in Summary and in Context	1
I	Child as Father of the Man	22
II	Orthodoxy: Immoral and Untrue	55
III	Personalities, Posturing, and Principles	107
IV	Choosing a Creed and a Cause	147
V	Orthodoxy "Out-Orthodoxed"	185
Conclusion		230
Appendix		241
Bibliography		249
Index		262

Religious faith was a solemn matter in Victorian England: So was religious doubt.[1] That this is no longer true in England cannot be attributed to a failure of zeal on the part of either the "faithful" or the "doubtful." To the extent that the missionaries of either side were directly responsible for the eventual absence of their items of business from the agenda of national concern, it was a matter of their addressing the wrong questions or failing to understand the nature of the questions. Equally significant in the eclipse of fervent organizational commitment to dogmatic consideration of religious issues was the social and intellectual transformation that made the traditional categories of serious religious debate on truth simply irrelevant. Which of the two factors--the increasingly secular cultural milieu or the growing irrelevance of dogmatic theology--caused the other could be much debated with little fruitful result. Each side's reading of the situation would of necessity be largely a function of presuppositions about such matters as the nature of truth, the nature of man, and the inter-relationship of ideas and action. Perhaps the fairest approach one can take, based on historical evidence, is to observe that the two trends developed side by side, and to suggest that each was related to the other as both cause

---

[1] "Religion" or "religious" in this dissertation will be used in the sense of "a belief system held to with ardor and faith." (Webster's New Collegiate Dictionary)

and effect during the course of the nineteenth century. That weighty
belief and weighty non-belief went hand in hand in an age of faith in
the possibility of metaphysical certainty is difficult to dispute. That
both are generally perceived to be anachronistic in the second half of
the twentieth century is without question.

Thus, doubt was important to the Victorians in a way that we in the
twentieth century find difficult to understand, precisely because faith
was important. There were at least three varieties of religious doubt
in nineteenth-century England. There was the doubt of the intellectuals
such as Mary Ann Evans (George Eliot), Thomas Huxley, Frances W. Newman,
and Matthew Arnold. For them, the "crisis of faith" was a slow, often
reluctantly undertaken, often painful, journey to the conclusion that
they could not maintain their own intellectual integrity and continue to
affirm faith in traditional Christian orthodoxy when its historical and
rational apologetics appeared to be succumbing to the onslaught from
rational humanitarian ethical considerations, geological evidence, and
higher criticism of scripture.

There was the "unconscious" doubt--the apathetic irreligion of much
of the urban working classes, born of the perceived or practical
irrelevance of organized religion to their daily existence. This was
the doubt that frightened the Establishment in the 1820's into building
more churches for the masses, and that alarmed the faithful in the
1850's when the 1851 Church Census recorded that, on Census Sunday, only
about one-half of able-bodied Englishmen, and far less than half of
able-bodied working class citizens, attended church, even once,
anywhere. Horace Mann's analysis suggested, not so much that the

working classes had deliberately adopted "unbelief," as that religion simply did not fit into their way of life.[2]

There was the proselytizing doubt of working class radicalizers, who consciously and deliberately sought to "convert" England from the Christian faith. Often with the same techniques, institutions, and dogmatic conviction as the orthodox Christians they denounced, these freethinkers proclaimed the gospel of freedom from enslavement to the political-religious Establishment that threatened to keep the working classes forever in intellectual, political, social, and economic bondage and deprivation. It is with the third of these varieties, "organized freethought," that this study is primarily concerned.[3]

Unlike the masses of apathetic non-believers, these doubters consciously, deliberately, and zealously advocated the righteousness of choosing to live free from burdens imposed by a demanding ecclesiastical establishment, supported by an unknowable, if existent, deity. Unlike the intellectuals, the organized freethinkers argued that the soundness of disbelief was good news. The intellectuals, who tended to be from

---

[2]Census of Great Britain, 1851, Religious Worship in England and Wales. Sessional Papers, House of Commons, 1852-53. LXXXIX, 1852, pp. 162-63. Such an analysis is supported by Kenneth Inglis, Churches and the Working Classes in Victorian England (London: Routledge and Kegan Paul, 1963), and R. A. Soloway, Prelates and People--Ecclesiastical Social Thought in England 1783-1852 (London: Routledge and Kegan Paul, 1969).

[3]Naming this movement is difficult. "Freethought" incorporates a broader range of people and chronology than the term "atheist," and thus includes all the phases of the movement from 1840-1870. Nevertheless, it does not communicate the dogmatic character, nor the anti-theistic flavor of most freethought. The adjective "organized" also is mild for parts of the movement, but it does suggest the regimentation of doctrine and zeal associated with these sectors of freethought, while accommodating less militant variations as well.

the upper strata of society, were, as a matter of vested interest, often as concerned about the potential political, social, and ethical upheaval of society that might conceivably follow widespread realization of the shortcomings of orthodoxy, as they were certain that orthodoxy, as established, did in fact fall short of being orthodox, that is, it did not rightly conform to reality. To those advocating disbelief, the masses had only to gain by the realization that social morality could exist apart from Christian doctrine, and that the existing social and political order, buttressed as it was by Christian doctrine and institutions, did not have the sanction of the Cosmos.

Having theoretically separated the organized freethinkers by definition from the intellectuals and the "unconscious secularists," the practical problem remains of deciding which actual persons and groups should properly be placed within this category. Furthermore, one must determine a time frame that would be an appropriate chronological boundary for consideration of the propagandizing freethinkers.

The problem of determining who might be classed as an organized freethinker is created largely by the fact that few men devoted their whole attention at any time to promoting freethought. Various freethinkers were involved in many of the interest groups of Victorian society such as the Anti-Persecution Union formed to defend the free press, the better-known Chartist organizations, the Owenite Rational Society, the Northern Reform Union, the Sunday League, the Political Reform League, the Committee for the Abolition of the Taxes on Knowledge, and various Cooperative societies. Besides their concerns at home, the freethinkers actively promoted foreign liberal and national causes through men, propaganda, and financial support. George Jacob Holyoake, for example, idolized Mazzini, and was responsible for recruiting Englishmen for Garibaldi's legion. For freethinkers, their beliefs allowed for, and even fostered, a broad range of commitments. Nevertheless, to confuse any of these extra movements with "organized freethought" would be wrong. Besides having many commitments at any one time, the freethinkers moved in and out of strong concern for proselytizing during the course of their lifetimes. Bradlaugh often minimized his atheism during political campaigns. Both Holyoake and Bradlaugh came to tone down their once dogmatic assertion of materialism as they became older.

For the purposes of this study, I have adopted as representative of organized freethought, six periodicals and the editors and contributors associated with these periodicals to the extent of their commitment to the magazines. The periodicals include _Oracle of Reason_, (1841-43); _Movement_, (1843-45); _Herald of Progress_, (1845-46); _Investigator_, (1854-59); _National Reformer_, (1860-90); and _Reasoner_, (1846-61, 1865, 1871-72). Thus, though its boundaries are blurred, organized freethought, represented by this cluster of periodicals, was a real movement with generally definable characteristics and goals. Committed in the long run to working class reform, freethinkers believed that correct metaphysical and theological thinking was a prerequisite.

This study will deal with the years 1840-1870. It was in 1839 that the Central Board of Robert Owen's Rational Society demanded that their missionaries exclude theological matters from their sermons and discussions. These topics upset too many potential Socialists.

This decision angered a number of the missionaries, including G. J. Holyoake, who believed that correct theological views were central to the Rational Society's message. Though Holyoake continued to belong to the Rational Society after 1839, he and several other missionaries continued promoting atheism on their own. It was in 1841 that Charles Southwell started the caustically atheistic **Oracle of Reason**. With the exception of the **National Reformer**, the six periodicals noted had life spans that fell roughly within the thirty year period 1840-70.[4] In 1870, Bradlaugh and Holyoake met to debate the question of the centrality of atheism to "Secularism." In other words, was a particular theological stance essential to, or inherent in, a philosophy of daily living that focused on this world as known and knowable through reason and experience? Holyoake said, "No." Bradlaugh said, "Yes." After 1870, Bradlaugh and Holyoake each increasingly went his own way. The National Secular Society, Bradlaugh's London-based organization, derived much of its animation from the drama associated with Bradlaugh's parliamentary career in the 1880's. Holyoake devoted more time to the provinces and the cause of Cooperativism. Both the National Secular Society and the atheist cause in general were torn by personality

---

[4] Holyoake revived the **Reasoner** briefly both in 1865 and in 1871-72. In the 1870's, Holyoake's followers were associated with the **Secular World**, the **Secular Review**, and the **Secularist**. All were self-consciously devoted to promoting Holyoake's religion of this world-- Secularism. In adopting this "positivist" and articulated world view, they are visionaries of a different sort than the iconoclasts of the earlier era.

conflicts, and disagreement over strategies and policies.[5] Atheism *qua* atheism became more and more irrelevant to the cause of British working class reform, for reasons to be discussed in the course of this study. Despite spurts of activity associated with specific issues such as birth control in the late 1870's and Bradlaugh's parliamentary campaign in the 1880's, organized freethought, as an articulated and comprehensive world view, was most viable in the middle years of the nineteenth century. As the century progressed, other groups, especially the Socialists, promised more tangible benefits to the working classes, and cared little that members subscribe to any particular theological position. 1840-70 provides then, not an absolute, but an appropriate, time frame in which to look at the branch of Victorian doubt that was actively committed to working class reform and that was convinced that the possibility of right action was contingent upon prior conviction of right thinking, particularly on theological matters.

---

[5] I have chosen not to deal with Annie Besant, for though she associates with the atheists prior to 1870, her primary significance comes from her prominence in the Knowlton trial in the 1870's, her partnership in the 1880's and 1890's with Bradlaugh in the Freethought Publishing Company, and her departure from atheism to socialism in 1884, and finally to Theosophy in the late 1890's.

In much the same way, the dissertation will not concern itself with the growth of Positivism in England, except as it was a tangential theme in Holyoake's writing during the late 1850's and 1860's. Positivism was a nineteenth-century transplant from France, unlike organized freethought which had been nurtured in the English Radical and Owenite traditions. Though there were similarities in doctrine and style between the Positivist "churches," and the Atheist/Secularist gatherings, Positivism remained primarily a "faith" of the intellectuals. Organized freethought was distinctively working class-- at least ostensibly.

It would be false to argue that the organized freethinkers were of major significance in Victorian England. Though they did have a wider exposure through lecturing and debating than might be suggested by membership rolls of the local atheist societies or subscription lists to the various periodicals, the movement's impact was marginal at best. Because they were on the fringes of much successful social and political reform agitation, and because England was more "secular" in 1900 than in 1800, it would be easy to credit the organized freethinkers with too much. One must guard against the fallacy of post hoc ergo propter hoc. More accurately understood, organized freethinkers were simply in harmony--at least ostensibly--with the direction in which Victorian society was headed, for reasons often quite apart from the work of these unbelievers.

Nonetheless, the organized freethinkers were not without significance in Victorian England. But it is as a symptom of what was happening, rather than as a cause, that this movement can best be understood. The organized freethinkers embodied the epistemological, metaphysical, and sociological confusion of a society whose Weltanschauung is in transition. They had rejected orthodoxy, but still believed in truth. They propagated new ideas, but in old-style categories, and with old-style methods. They claimed to be addressing and representing the working classes, but made every effort to rise above their social status. In impiously berating theology while exalting rigid morality, in fiercely advocating free thought while dogmatically insisting on the righteousness of their particular vision of reality, in seeking to maintain the edifice of Victorian values of constitutionalism, freedom, individualism, and self-help, while seeking to demolish the foundations perceived by the Establishment to have made the structure possible--the organized freethinkers graphically illustrate contradictions inherent in a society in conflict with itself. Somewhat less abstractly, the organized freethinkers were a sort of bridge between the thinking of the intellectuals and that of the masses. They were not original thinkers, but "translated" high culture Enlightenment ideology into low culture. Furthermore, the movement is interesting for its effort to link thought and action. Unbelief was rarely, if ever, treated as an end in itself by the propagandists. It was a means to material progress. Right thinking existed that right doing might follow.

Aside from a theoretical justification for the inherent worth of studying the organized freethinkers, there are practical considerations as well. The proselytizers, who tended to be of working class origin, have been much less studied than the higher class intellectuals, whose "crisis of faith" has been perceived to be of much greater importance in setting the tone for Victorian belief. Unlike the atheists by default, for whom unbelief was a non-issue, the organized freethinkers have left written materials that make a study of their struggles and concerns practical. Finally, study of this movement is essential to do justice to several of its main characters. G. Kitson Clark notes in *The Making of Victorian England* the tendency for historians to focus on past causes that have succeeded, or that are understandable to their own mindsets.[6] Perhaps this explains the fact that Charles Bradlaugh is best known for his political struggle to enter Parliament as an avowed atheist without taking the Oath, and that George Jacob Holyoake is remembered for his work in the Cooperative movement. Judging in terms of time and energy expended upon them, Bradlaugh's and Holyoake's theological/philosophical interests were equally as important to them as their political and socio-economic concerns. They are not less part of Victorian history for being less in line with our own thought patterns.

Existing studies of the organized freethinkers have tended to be primarily biographical,[7] or autobiographical.[8] Several of the works are written by contemporaries and reflect deep ideological and personal loyalties.[9] Only recently have efforts been made to arrive

---

[6] G. Kitson Clark, The Making of Victorian England (Cambridge, Mass.: Harvard University Press, 1962), p. 24.

[7] See for example Walter Arnstein, The Bradlaugh Case--A Study in Late Victorian Opini Politics (Oxford: Clarendon Press, 1965); Hypatia Bradlaugh Bonner, Charles Bradlaugh: A Record of His Life and Work, 2 vols. (London: T. Fisher Unwin, 1894); Le Grugel, George Jacob Holyoake: A Study in the Evolution of a Victorian Radical (Philadelphia: Porcupine Press, 1976); Joseph McCabe, Life and Letters of George Jacob Holyoake, 2 vol (London: Watts & Co., 1908); Charles R. MacKay, Life of Charles Bradlaugh, M. P. (London: D. J. Gunn & Co., 1888); and David Tribe, President Charles Bradlaugh, M. P. (London: Elek Books, 1971).

[8] See for example George Jacob Holyoake, Sixty Years of an Agitator's Life, 2 vols. (London: T. Fisher Unwin, 1892); and George Jacob Holyoake, Bygones Worth Remembering, 2 vols. (New York: E. P. Dutton & Co., 1905).

[9] Bonner's biography of her father is highly emotionally charged for obvious reasons. So also is MacKay's; he was an ardent opponent of Bradlaugh's personality and style. For examples of other "personal" accounts of the freethought movement, see Janet Courtney, Freethinkers of the Nineteenth Century (London: Chapman & Hall, Ltd., 1920); and J. M. Robertson, A History of Free Thought in the Nineteenth Century, 2 vols. (New York: G. P. Putnam's, 1930).

at some systematic scholarly understanding of organized freethought.[10] Largely through the work of the English historian Edward Royle, there now exists a well-documented account of the origins, appeal, membership, geography, organization, and activities of nineteenth-century organized freethought.

If the "facts" of the movement have been articulated, a clear understanding of its meaning has not. One can see the nature of the interpretive problem by juxtaposing the conclusions of several recent Victorian scholars. Edward Royle and, even more pointedly, F. B. Smith, in his essay "The Atheist Mission, 1840-1900,"[11] document the institutional arrangements and proselytizing efforts of the organized freethinkers that attest to their genuine commitment to the de-Christianization of the English working classes. Kenneth Inglis, in his Churches and the Working Classes in Victorian England, argues that there was a nearly universal belief among Victorian religious people of all

---

[10] See for example Susan Budd, Varieties of Unbelief--Atheists and Agnostics in English Society 1850-1960 (London: Heinemann Educational Books, Ltd., 1977); John Eros, "The Rise of Organized Freethought in Mid-Victorian England," Sociological Review, New Series, II (July, 1954): 98-120; Charles Krantz, The British Secularist Movement: A Study in Militant Dissent (Unpublished Ph.D. Dissertation, University of Rochester, 1964); Edward Royle, (ed.), The Infidel Tradition From Paine to Bradlaugh (London: Macmillan Press, Ltd., 1976); Royle, Radical Politics 1790-1900: Religion and Unbelief (London: Longman Group, Ltd., 1971); Royle, Radicals, Secularists, and Republicans: Popular Freethought in Britain, 1866-1915 (Manchester: University of Manchester Press, 1980); Royle, Victorian Infidels: The Origins of the British Secular Movement 1791-1866 (Manchester: University of Manchester Press, 1974); F. B. Smith, "The Atheist Mission, 1840-1900," pp. 205-235 in Robert Robson, (ed.), Ideas and Institutions of Victorian Britain (London: G. Bell & Sons, Ltd., 1967); and David Tribe, One Hundred Years of Free Thought (London: Elek Books, Ltd., 1967).

[11] F. B. Smith, "The Atheist Mission, 1840-1900."

varieties that de-Christianization was not the answer, but the major problem of the working classes.[12] F. B. Smith unwittingly confirms Inglis position when he suggests, in explaining the insignificant results of freethinking proselytizing efforts, that atheism depended on prior Christian experience; since the poor did not have that, they were largely immune to freethought evangelism.[13] The organized freethinkers assumed that the working classes had too much Christian theology and organization, and needed to be freed from it, while the churches assumed that the working classes lacked church contact and wanted it. If Inglis is right, both efforts were equally based on false presuppositions about the religious views of the average working man.

The problem is made even more intriguing when one considers Charles Krantz's dissertation on the British Secular Movement. He is convinced that organized freethought is not nearly so much a true repudiation of Victorian religion and culture, as it is a reaction that depended for its values and practices on the very system it pretended to defy.[14] The organized freethinkers offended their culture because they truthfully highlighted its hypocrisy and inconsistency; their very accusations and standards of measurement betrayed, nevertheless, how very much they too were products and proponents of that system.

To complete the picture of the problem, one should observe Royle's warning that scholars have often begun with wrong assumptions in

---

[12]K. Inglis, Churches and the Working Classes in Victorian England.

[13]F. B. Smith, "The Atheist Mission, 1840-1900," pp. 223-224.

[14]C. Krantz, The British Secularist Movement, esp. pp. 228, 231.

explaining freethought--two of which are that the organized movement had wide appeal and that that appeal was primarily to the working classes.[15] According to Royle, "secularity" was the real power behind the shift in societal presuppositions, not Secularism.[16] Like Krantz and F. B. Smith, Royle sees the Secularists as fitting well in the paradoxical balance of disparities that constituted the Victorian consensus. The Victorian working class Radicals were committed to helping their peers rise within the system, and to removing obstacles they perceived to be hindering that progress; they had little desire to destroy the system.[17] Their fate was inextricably linked to that of the Establishment they decried.

Thus there was the dedicated band of organized freethinkers, laboring diligently to accomplish a mission that had already been accomplished--or that, at best, was being carried out quite apart from their efforts. If the organized freethinkers are to be taken seriously, if the secularity of England's working classes was well underway without the freethinkers, and if the Victorian masses were relatively apathetic about theological matters--all of which seem to be valid premises--how does one account for the zeal and the dogmatism with which the organized freethinkers pursued their mission? Nobody loses his health and expends

---

[15]Royle, Victorian Infidels, p. 233.

[16]Royle, Victorian Infidels, p. 261; Royle, Radicals, Secularists, and Republicans, p. 328.

[17]The extent to which the radical atheists subscribed to the "system" can be seen when it was challenged by the rise of Socialism in the 1880's. See discussion of Secularists and Socialism in Royle, Victorian Radicals, pp. 244-253; and Royle, Radicals, Secularists, pp. 232-241.

his resources convincing people of something they already believe. Given the circumstances, why did theological considerations come to occupy a significant place in the work of certain Victorian working class radicalizers? Such a question cannot be answered solely by a knowledge of what happened, or who was involved in the movement.

This study, which purports to be a response to this question, will be complementary to the extensive work of description and analysis of organized freethought that has already taken place. It is an effort to understand the presence for a time of a phenomenon in the broader framework of the Victorian Reform tradition, a phenomenon that, at first glance, appears neither necessary, nor appropriate, nor useful. The work will be organized thematically, in accordance with several hypotheses that attempt at least partially to account for the evangelistic and theological overtone of much Victorian working class radicalism. It will suggest first, that the theologizing can be understood partly as a function of the personal backgrounds of the freethinkers; second, that it resulted from a genuine belief on the part of the freethinkers that Victorian orthodoxy was morally and epistemologically bankrupt; third, that theological terminology and categories were logical ideological grounds on which personality conflicts among freethinkers could be fought; fourth, that theologizing was a natural and even inevitable by-product of freethought's effort to articulate a position that would allow it to institutionalize; and fifth, that theologizing was a vital component of the religion of freethought that developed in opposition to, though in imitation of, Victorian orthodoxy. The study will conclude with a brief discussion of the eventual decline of organized, self-conscious, secularist propagandizing, and an assessment of the historical significance of organized freethought.

Organized freethought in Victorian England was heir to a variety of traditions, both Continental and English. The freethinkers were akin to the French Deists. As such, they shared the traditional commitment of the **philosophes** to Reason as the only reliable guide to an understanding of the universe, and to belief in Progress if man were to be released from the shackles of priestly and kingly tyranny maintained through fear and superstition. Thomas Paine's birthday was a red-letter day on the freethought "liturgical" calendar.

The English "Radical" tradition, personified in such characters as John Wilkes and Richard Carlile, is reflected in the freethinkers' battle for absolute freedom of speech and press. The Anti-Persecution Union, founded in 1842 at the time of G. J. Holyoake's arrest, for the purpose of supporting victims of government censorship, shared with the freethinkers one of their periodicals--the **Movement**, and one of their leaders--G. J. Holyoake. The freethinkers, like the Radicals, viewed the close alliance of political and ecclesiastical hierarchy in England as detrimental to freedom, and especially to the freedom of the working classes.

Organized freethought grew out of, and continued to be integrally related to Owenite Socialism, the peculiarly English utopian vision of bettering the lot of the working classes by paternalistic planning and organization of their lives. G. J. Holyoake began as a Socialist lecturer and continued to belong to the Rational Society even after he had ceased to be an official Socialist Lecturer. Robert Owen was forever a patron saint of organized freethought because of his efforts to better the plight of the English workers.

Finally, and somewhat paradoxically, organized freethought had roots in radical evangelical Protestantism. It was, as Charles Krantz suggests, the Protestant principle of private judgment carried to its logical conclusion.[18] It will be one of the objects of this paper to explore how very much the freethinkers simply reconstructed a reverse image of the very tradition they repudiated.

For the purposes of description, it is useful to distinguish three phases in the development of this movement: 1839-1854, 1854-1860, and 1860-1870. The first era was marked by G. J. Holyoake's domination, the movement's solid "theological" commitment to atheism, and struggles between the dissenting Socialists and Owen's parent Rational Society over the nature of their organizational relationship. Holyoake assumed the editorship of the *Oracle of Reason* when the government sentenced Charles Southwell to prison for publicly advocating atheism. He edited a succession of short-lived periodicals--*Oracle of Reason* (1841-43); *Movement* (1843-45); and *Herald of Progress* (1845-46)--until the inauguration of the *Reasoner* in 1846. The *Reasoner* survived continually until 1861 when Holyoake resigned as editor. In 1865, and again in 1871-72, Holyoake resurrected the journal as a counterweight in the movement to Bradlaugh's *National Reformer*. Editing the periodicals, and

---

[18]Krantz, *The British Secularist Movement*, p. 3.

lecturing at an exhausting pace in both London and the provinces, gave Holyoake constant exposure throughout English freethought circles, and earned him tacit recognition as the leader of the movement.

During this time, Holyoake clearly espoused atheism, and sought to separate his position from the less theological and dogmatic Owenite Socialists.[19] The tension between the renegades and the Owenites came to a climax over the Harmony Hall project in the mid-1840's. The Central Board of the Rational Society had voted to take a practical step toward realizing the dream of cooperative worker societies, and had established a pilot project of cooperative living known as Queenwood Community, the central feature of which was Harmony Hall. Continuous demands from Queenwood on the Central Board's resources resulted in an inevitable shifting in financial commitment from advancing the Socialist mission to keeping Queenwood solvent. This came to be seen by Holyoake's followers as a selling out of the Rational Society to profit-motivated special interest groups. The Central Board, on the other hand, argued that the Community was the very achievement toward which the proselytizing efforts had been directed. Lectures were nothing until workers were settled on the land in functioning communities.

After several years of argument among the Socialists, Queenwood folded. During the late 1840's, it appeared that the *raison d'être* of Socialism had disappeared as well. It was Holyoake who sought to reunite the Socialist cause along more theoretical and theological lines.

---

[19]See chapter IV for discussion of Holyoake's pilgrimage from atheism to agnosticism.

The distinguishing characteristic of the years 1854-1860 was the growing sectional tension in freethought between Holyoake and his *Reasoner* and Robert Cooper and his *Investigator*. Holyoake's strength was in London; Cooper's in the North. Ironically, Cooper's charge was that the *Reasoner* was not radical enough in battling the political and ecclesiastical Establishment. The radical Holyoake had been outdone at his own game.

The conflict peaked over Holyoake's center for English freethought on Fleet Street in London.[20] To Holyoake, this was the fulfillment of a dream, to have a place where freethinkers could congregate respectably, socialize, purchase literature and publish their pamphlets and periodicals. To Cooper and his friends, Fleet Street House was testimony to Holyoake's egotism and self-serving use of freethought resources. An investigation of the House resulted in accusations that Holyoake had used designated organizational funds for his own profit. The bitter struggle between Holyoake and the *Investigator* centered on whether Fleet Street was really a center for freethought, in which case Holyoake should, according to the *Investigator*, be accountable to the movement as a whole for administrative and financial policy; or whether it was simply a private interest for the profit of the Holyoake brothers, George Jacob and Austin. The issue was not resolved to either party's satisfaction. Holyoake continued to claim to represent freethought. The North continued to view Fleet Street as a monument to

---

[20]For discussion of the Queenwood and Fleet Street controversies, see chapter III.

Holyoake's success at attaining social "respectability," and, in so doing, betraying the cause of working class radicalism.

With 1860 came the beginning of Charles Bradlaugh's **National Reformer**. Two years earlier, Bradlaugh, a Cooper protégé, had made his debut to the London freethought lecture circuit. It is the rivalry between G. J. Holyoake and Charles Bradlaugh that chiefly distinguishes the last decade of "religious" freethought.

The contest took place at several levels. Holyoake and Bradlaugh had very different ideas about the nature of freethought. Bradlaugh had replaced Cooper as defender of militant atheism. Holyoake, by this time, favored an affirmative approach to unorthodoxy, and wrote and spoke prolifically on his formulation of the religion of his life --Secularism. He insisted, very like Owen in 1839, that atheism was not in fact an essential or appropriate dogma of freethought.

More practically, Holyoake sued Bradlaugh in 1862 for refusing to pay him for the entire tenure of his contract after prematurely terminating his services to the **National Reformer**. To say that the two men did not work together well would be an understatement; each suspected the other of seeking to undermine his own credibility and authority. After months of litigation, the court decided in favor of Holyoake. The case was closed. Nevertheless, as far as the freethought movement was concerned, it mattered little who had won and who had lost. The two leaders never quite forgave each other for the ordeal and passed this animosity on to their followers.

By the time Bradlaugh and Holyoake met in 1870 to argue about the relationship of Secularism and Atheism, Bradlaugh had replaced Holyoake as the militant advocate of working class interests. To Bradlaugh, that meant atheism and republicanism. Holyoake, by this time, was too "respectable." He retained a following among some of the older freethinkers in the North, but London had fallen to Bradlaugh.

Personality conflicts, as well as diverging interests among the leadership and changing times, largely account for the fragmentation and eventual decline of proselytizing freethought. Holyoake's Secularism, promulgated in the briefly revived *Reasoner* (1871-2) and in the shortlived *Secular Review* (1875-76), emphasized the positive side of freethought. It sounded more and more like Christian middle class morality without the God-words, or like a revival of utopian socialism, and increasingly less like the anti-Establishment atheism that had been the movement's trademark. Defined as a positive system of thought, freethought was not enough. It could not compete with more clearly articulated and more radical programs, such as trade unionism or Marxism, whose goals seemed immediately pertinent to the daily concerns of the working classes, and among whose adherents the workers could also find fellowship and emotional security.

If Secularism was not "enough," Bradlaugh's tradition of "negative" freethought, carried on by G. W. Foote, Hypatia Bradlaugh Bonner, and the National Secular Society, was too much. Less of the working class had been brought up under the yoke of orthodoxy in 1870 than in 1840. Thus, orthodoxy was less likely to be identified as the villain in the battle for social and political justice. The tendency to view socio-economic and political matters in theological categories would diminish as well.

In short, increasingly after 1870, the "negative" freethinkers were defending a cause that no one was attacking, if one views them as pursuing the legitimacy of challenging the monolithic church-state dominance of English society; or attacking a cause that relatively few were defending, the absolute authoritative rightness of Christian dogma.

Both the Secularists and the Atheists were too preoccupied with old categories and obsolete paradigms to survive the nineteenth century. They were as tied to Victorian England as the dogma and institutions they attacked. Solemn belief and doubt declined together, for they were, in reality, of one piece.

I

Part of a rationalist's creed is that he does what he does because it is the reasonable thing to do. He makes objective choices based purely on the logical merits of the case in question. Thus, according to the militant freethinkers, they argued theologically because one's view of God's existence and character were absolutely fundamental to determining one's behavior in this world. To others, that explanation does not suffice. It seems noteworthy that most significant figures of the militant freethought movement came from Christian, even enthusiastically Christian, backgrounds.

No one among the freethinkers makes more of his Christian upbringing than George Jacob Holyoake himself. Holyoake's childhood experience in the faith haunted him until he died. Holyoake paraded his Christian background as evidence of his credibility as a freethinker. He knew whereof he spoke.[1] In 1850, the Reasoner records Holyoake's discussion of a Methodist service in session during one of his debates.

> Adjoining where we were assembled a Methodist junto were trying some refractory preachers; placards on the wall styled the junto an 'Inquisition.' At the door of the chapel the friends of

---

[1] G. J. Holyoake, The Trial of George Jacob Holyoake on an Indictment for Blasphemy, before Mr. Justice Erskine, and a Common Jury at Gloucester--August the 15, 1842 (London: Printed for Anti-Persecution Union by Thomas Paterson, 1842), pp. 20-21.

the accused were assembled, and in order to drown the voices of the judges they kept up an awful singing. Above my voice and that of Mr. Bowes' rose for about three hours the terrible din of Wesleyan tunes. How they came to the conclusion that God could be gratified by having his praises sung in so offensive a manner, none but a Methodist could tell. All night long these Wesleyan pipers rung in my ears. Melancholy dreams of white neckerchiefs, elongated faces, and turned up eyes, disturbed me all morning, and I felt infinite relief when the bright sun streamed in at the window, dispelling the monotonous humdrum of holy psalms.[2]

In 1901, as an old man, Holyoake recalled his cheerless days in Carr's Lane Chapel, and later, the chapel on Inge Street, both in Birmingham.[3] His Christianity had made him afraid of God, of Hell, and of blaspheming the Holy Spirit.[4] It had made him bored and sad. He echoes this sentiment in reporting on Charles Spurgeon's revival meetings when he notes, in 1855, that "the singing brought back all the indelible and monotonous associations of Carr's Lane. We hope there is no Evangelical singing in Heaven."[5]

Looking back, he remembered going to all the meetings—early and late.[6] Holyoake's memories of punctilious regard for religious matters

---

[2]"The Bradford Debate," Reasoner and Theological Examiner IX (1850): 38-39.

[3]G. J. Holyoake, My Religious Days (n.p., 1901), pp. 2-3.

[4]Ibid., p. 3; G. J. Holyoake, "The Critics of Atheism," Reasoner and London Tribune XX (1856): 17; Holyoake, Bygones Worth Remembering, 2 vols. (New York: E. P. Dutton & Co., 1905), II: 219; Holyoake, "The Terrors of Catholicism," Reasoner and Theological Examiner IX (1850): 37-38.

[5]G. J. Holyoake, Reasoner and London Tribune XIX (April 1855): 28.; See also The Report of the Four Nights Public Discussion at Bradford between George J. Holyoake, of London, ed. of the "Reasoner" and John Bowes of Manchester, ed. of the "Truth" on "The Truth of Christianity and The Folly of Infidelity" (London: E. Ward, W. Horsell, J. Watson, 1850), p. 28.

[6]Holyoake, My Religious Days, p. 5.

would appear to be confirmed by his childhood writings. In his journal of March 30, 1835, one finds two sections headed respectively, "The following 10 articles are those that I consider necessary to believe in Order to Salvation:" and "The Following Articles I consider essential to be believed, observed, and practiced in Order to the Consistent Profession of Christianity."[7] The precepts outlined were as "orthodox" as the Apostles' Creed.

Perhaps most interesting of Holyoake's early religious writings is his poem "The Reign of Time" that appeared in the Baptist Tract Magazine, in October of 1836.

"The Reign of Time"

> The proudest earthly buildings show
>   Time can all things devour;
> E'en youth and beauty's ardent glow,
> And manhood's intellectual brow,
>   Betray the spoiler's power:
> How soon we sink beneath his sway;
> He glances and our heads turn gray.
>
> Though over all this earthly ball
> Time's standard is unfurl'd;
> And ruins loud to ruins call
> Throughout this Time-worn world.
> Yet from this wreck of earthly
>   things,
> See how the Soul exulting springs!
>
> And after the archangel sound,
> Has wav'd o'er earth and sea,
> And time has stopp'd at his command,
> The Soul will flourish and expand,
> Through all eternity.

---

[7]Holyoake's Journal, March 30, 1835, Envelope #1, Holyoake Collection, Bishopsgate Institute, London.

> RELIGION--lovely, fair, and free
> Holds forth this Immortality.
> By all the glories of the sky;
> To mortals yet unknown;
> And by the worm that ne'er shall die,
> The fires that always burn:
> By all that's awful or sublime,
> Ye sons of men,
>   Improve your Time.[8]

The lines are those of a disciple. Nevertheless, though the context and the motivation are supernatural, already one notes Holyoake's concern for behavior over dogma, and for zealous pursuit of duty in this world.

Holyoake lived his life in the shadow of this childhood faith, always seeking to escape. During Holyoake's bout with the law on blasphemy charges, Richard Carlile, thinking to pay Holyoake a compliment, called him a true Christian. Holyoake responded, "I had the misfortune to be born a Christian--it has been my achievement to throw off that degradation--and I protest against its being thrust upon me."[9]

Charles Bradlaugh, no less than Holyoake, began as a solemn believer. He taught Sunday school at St. Peter's--Hackney Road; he even defended the merits of Christianity before freethinkers.[10] Upon questioning the 39 Articles, Bradlaugh was suspended from his teaching post. Rev. John Graham Packer became to Bradlaugh what Rev. John Angell James was to Holyoake--the symbol of anti-intellectual, dogmatic, oppressive, paternalistic Christianity. After Packer's visit to

---

[8]G. J. Holyoake, "The Reign of Time," *Baptist Tract Magazine--Young Christian's Companion and Cottager's Friend* II (October 1836): 341.

[9]G. J. Holyoake, *Oracle of Reason* I (1841-42): 350.

[10]Hypatia Bradlaugh Bonner, *Charles Bradlaugh*, 2 vols. (London: T. Fisher Unwin, 1894), I: 8-9.

Bradlaugh's parents in which he expressed serious concern about Charles' heretical thoughts, and pressed for Charles' recantation, Charles left home rather than compromise his integrity.

At sixteen, Bradlaugh wrote "Examination of the Four Gospels according to Matthew, Mark, Luke & John with Remarks on the Life and Death of the meek and lowly Jesus."[11] The title and introduction suggest the nature of the conclusions. In the Preface, Charles asserts that he can prove there were three Jesus Christs to anyone not blinded by revelation. The Gospels are, according to the young Bradlaugh, "a jumble of nonsense and contradiction."[12] In the work itself, he proceeds to outline systematically the contradictions among the gospel narratives, the points where the gospels disagree with the Old Testament and the similarities between Jesus and other pagan deities.

Bradlaugh does not appear to host the shadow of his early faith as close to the surface as Holyoake. His later writings suggest that he had, however, not forgotten it. In 1864, he outlines for readers of the National Reformer "Reasons for Rejecting Orthodox Christianity." In general, Christianity had proved to be "inadequate to meet the requirements of every day life."[13] He goes on to say:

> Being for years a regular attendant at the 'House of God,' having devoted a great part of my life to attending Sunday Schools, I had

---

[11] Charles Bradlaugh, *Examination of the Four Gospels according to Matthew, Mark, Luke & John with Remarks on the Life and Death of the Meek and Lowly Jesus*, Bradlaugh Papers, #19, Bishopsgate Institute, London.

[12] Ibid., p. 2.

[13] Charles Bradlaugh, "Reasons for Rejecting Orthodox Christianity," *National Reformer* V (November 1864): 531.

> sufficient opportunity of judging of orthodox Christianity. If one
> wished to get the genuine article, he has only to spend a few years
> amongst the Wesleyans. There we can see Christianity in its most
> genuine and demoralising form. I had often heard of the pleasures
> of religion, the happiness it affords, and the joy it imparts. My
> experience, however, was quite the opposite. While under the
> influence of Christianity my life was one of gloom, sadness, and
> despair, perplexed by day and tortured by night. The recollections
> of those days are always a source of regret to me. The horrible
> doctrine instilled into my youthful mind rendered that period of
> life which should be the brightest--the darkest and most miserable.
> If there were no other reason this would be sufficient to justify
> me in rejecting those cruel and gloomy dogmas which threw such a
> cloud over my early life.[14]

He goes on to articulate a more reasoned apologetic for his rejection of the faith, but the reference to its spirit of gloom and despair are sadly reminiscent of Holyoake's childhood experience. For both of them, Christianity was a burden from which they sought relief.

Christian experiences of other major freethought figures sound strikingly similar to those of Holyoake and Bradlaugh. The personal histories of Charles Southwell, William Chilton, James Watson, Annie Besant, John and Charles Watts, and Joseph Barker all included time in which they were under the influence of, and favorably disposed to, the doctrine and community of the "orthodox."[15]

For all the freethinkers, Christianity had been a disappointment. They felt cheated. Though they directed their anger and anguish

---

[14]Ibid.

[15]On Southwell, see Edward Royle, "George Jacob Holyoake and the Secularist Movement in Britain, 1841-1861," (Ph.D. Dissertation, Cambridge University, 1968), pp. 36-37; On Chilton, see Reasoner III (1847): 528; On Watson, see Edward Royle, The Infidel Tradition From Paine to Bradlaugh (London: Macmillan Press, Ltd., 1976), pp. 99-102; On Besant, see Annie Besant, An Autobiography (London: T. Fisher Unwin, 1893), pp. 24-66; On Barker, see Reasoner XXIII (1858): 321-22, 329-30; National Reformer I (1860-61): 4.

differently--some at the dogma, some at the practice, some at the disparity between the two--they appeared to feel that, through Christianity, they had been treated unfairly by the Cosmos.

Holyoake objected to the usual assumption that unbelievers were an immoral lot, seeking to run from known good. To Holyoake, the good and God were not known. That was precisely the problem.

In a letter, presumably to a believer, Holyoake states:

> The case truly stands thus: The Theist says, all things considered--all argument weighed--it is clear to me that God exists. The Atheist says, all things considered--all argument weighed--it appears to me that the infinite secret is beyond our finite powers to grasp it.[16]

To Holyoake, it was heinous to hold people responsible, as the church did, for what those people could not help. Throughout his life, in theory at least, Holyoake clung to the dogma of determinism. Evidence and circumstances conditioned belief. Since man was rational, if he did not believe, it was because he could not. He should not be punished for what he could not help. Holyoake laid the blame for this breach of justice at the feet of the hypothetical deity of the believers.

> The existence of God is a problem to which the mathematics of human intelligence seems to me to furnish no solution. On the threshhold of the theme we stagger under a weight of words. We tread amid a dark quagmire bestrewed with slippery terms. Now the clearest miss their way, now the cautious stumble, now the strongest fall. No treatment of the subject can promise useful results unless the speaker is modest--the auditors patient.
> If there is a Deity to whom I am indebted, anxious for my gratitude or my service, I am ready to render it as any one existent, so soon as I comprehend the nature of my obligation. I,

---

[16] G. J. Holyoake to Elton Andre, *Reasoner and London Tribune* XIX (May 1855): 57.

therefore, protest against being considered, as Christians commonly consider the unbeliever, as one who hates God. Hatred implies knowledge of the objectionable thing, and cannot exist where nothing is understood.[17]

In The Trial of Theism, Holyoake goes on to assert that

Science has shown that we are under the dominion of general laws, that there is no Special Providence, that Prayer is useless, that propitiation is vain; that if Nature be God, it is the God of the iron path that passes on without heeding, without feeling, without resting . . . God is the eternal unanswered "Why?" to which no man has replied.[18]

Frederick Hollick, Holyoake's mentor in the Rational Society and the man who encouraged him to pursue the Socialist lectureship in 1839, expressed similar sentiments in a discussion with Rev. Joseph Baylee at one of London's Social Institutions:

I cannot believe anything which appears to me untrue; and as the Bible does so appear I cannot believe it; and as God has so constituted me, the fault, if there is any, lies with him, and there can be no justice in his punishing me.[19]

The same sort of helplessness in the face of reality appears in one of M. Q. Ryall's invectives on the faith in the Oracle of Reason. Of all the atheistic freethought periodicals, the Oracle, perhaps because it was the first, took least care in infusing a spirit of gentility in

---

[17] G. J. Holyoake, "Relation of Christianity to Morality and to Progress," Reasoner V (1848): 386. See also The Report of the Four Nights Public Discussion between George Jacob Holyoake and John Bowes, pp. 15-17, 18-19, 27; and Holyoake, The Logic of Death (London: J. Watson, 1850), p. 9.

[18] G. J. Holyoake, The Trial of Theism (London: Holyoake & Co., 1858), pp. 43-44.

[19] Substance of the Two Nights' Discussion in the Social Institution, 69 Great Queen Street, London . . . Between Rev. Joseph Baylee, and Frederick Hollick, Social Missionary on The Genuineness, Authenticity, and Inspiration of the Bible (London: B. D. Cousins, 1839), p. 44.

the dialogue with the faithful.

<blockquote>
<u>There is a God</u>, whose earliest recorded act was to create a pair of sentient beings, with a high capacity and relish for enjoyment which they were only suffered to taste, in order, with the greater intensity of bitterness and anguish, to feel the reverse of misery and death, who created a world full of miserable wretches, with wants, feelings emotions, passions, which they were expected to subdue, but which were made too powerful for control: and who finally involved in general and terrible destruction all who failed to regard those mandates which he had made them incapable of obeying.

<u>There is a god</u>, who sent 'strong delusions' and 'lying spirits,' to create and perpetuate fraud and deception, whose delight it was to issue orders to his enemies, which he compelled them to neglect, by 'hardening their hearts,' and then scourged them for disobedience.

<u>There is a god</u>, whose monstrous appetite for blood, required for its gratification, during 4000 years, continual supplies of fresh victims from bands of sacrificial butchers, till the life-blood of 'his only begotten son' trickled down the felon's gibbet, and which to this day, wherever his maleficent influence is felt, compels the sacrifice of the good and just, at the hands of his butcher-priests.

<u>There is a god</u>, whose amusements have consisted in the measurement of dressing-gowns, the stitching of breeches, the counting of buttons, the embroidering of petticoats, the sketching out of candlesticks, &c., for which dignified employment he selected his foremen, journeymen, and apprentices from a particular family or two, set apart from among the fickle, ignorant, and besotted savages, who rejoiced in the title of his 'peculiar people.'

<u>There is a god</u>, whose promises unfulfilled, threats not executed, denunciations without consequences, whose alliance without strengthening, and favoritism without advantage, have stigmatised him as unsurpassed for implacable vengefulness, bitter malignity, horrible atrocity, miserable imbecility, contemptible vanity--in short, an intense concentration of the most detestable passions which have signalised the most notorious of malefactors.
THAT GOD IS THE GOD OF THE CHRISTIANS![20]
</blockquote>

Writing later and with less sarcasm, but the same intensity, William Chilton reiterates the injustice of the expectation of belief:

<blockquote>
. . . if there be a being who knows all hearts or all minds, he knows that I am now writing the truth, and that, had I been
</blockquote>

---

[20] M. Q. Ryall, "A Home Thrust at the Atrocious Trinity," <u>Oracle of Reason</u> I (1841-42): 425-26.

> satisfied of his existence, I would have supplicated him to direct me aright, although I might still think that, in justice, he should have done it without my asking. . . . Mr James speaks of the Bible as the 'map of the road' to Heaven. The road! true, the Bible speaks of but one road, and that strait and narrow; but then there are so many contradictory bearings, and such numerous mystified directions given of how to find the right road, that there are above a hundred opinions upon the questions of which is the correct course men ought to travel to find it; and a chart of the heavenly lines already in existence--to say nothing of those that are yearly projected--would be very like the map of England, given by Punch, as it will appear when all the railways are completed.[21]

Instead of simply lamenting the unfairness of the situation, one of the Reasoner's contributors challenged the orthodox to the same Old Testament test that had authenticated Jehovah's presence to the children of Israel in the days of Elijah. As Barton said, "If we are required to have the same faith as those who lived in the time of miraculous interposition, surely we have a right to require the same evidence."[22] It seemed only fair.

Rather than seeing their rejection of Christianity as a break with their past, the freethinkers could argue that it was simply the logical outcome of that past. The Church had raised hopes that it had not fulfilled. Specifically, its apparent offer of metaphysical certainty had proven to be a fraud. The freethinkers were merely continuing their quest for truth elsewhere.

When reality proves to be a disappointment, the temptation is to blame the reality. In truth, what creates the disappointment is the failure of the reality to be what it was expected to be. The problem--

---

[21] William Chilton, Reasoner III (1847): 528, 532.

[22] F. B. Barton, "The Bible Test of Superstition Applied to the Religion of this Country as--'by Law Established,'" Reasoner XI (1851): 325.

in the sense of the part of the picture that is open to change in
conformity to increased understanding of truth--is the expectation.
Realities are what they are. The freethinkers had high hopes of
Christianity based on their childhood encounters with orthodoxy. The
sermons and the hymns had painted a world in which prayer could solve
real problems, in which sinful humans could come to happiness, in which
the sorrows of this world would eventually melt away in the eternal
bliss of the next. With growing maturity, came the realization that the
pictures were wrong. Prayers did not bring solutions.[23] Holyoake
recalls the moment of truth when he learned from the Rev. Sully Cribbace
that the promise of receiving anything upon request in prayer had
qualifications. That apparently was not what Christ had meant in
Matthew 7:7. In Holyoake's words:

> The answer did not make me disbelieve, but I was never the same
> Christian I had been before . . . Whatever Christianity might be,
> it was no dependence in human need. The hard, material world was
> not touched by prayer.[24]

During this period of his life, he noted in his diary that the
Socialists were the ones who appeared to have the best arrangement.
They did not pray but worked. They had faith, belief in God, hope
amounting to certainty that they were right, and love; they had all that
the Christians had, plus they had committed themselves to action, and to
change in this world, without waiting for someone to act for them.[25]

---

[23] G. J. Holyoake, *Bygones Worth Remembering*, II: 218.

[24] Holyoake, *My Religious Days*, pp. 7-9.

[25] Holyoake Diaries, February 11, 1838, Holyoake Collection,
Bishopsgate Institute, London.

Apart from the question of prayer, it seemed ludicrous for children to be singing of themselves as dissolute sinners, and of a heaven, the whereabouts of which was not to be discovered.[26] When the childhood pictures of orthodoxy did not prove sophisticated enough to contain the freethinkers' increased understanding of reality, they attributed the fault, not to the pictures, but to what the pictures had represented. They confused the pictures and the reality. Furthermore, they had little contact with people who were interested in, and capable of, helping them to make that distinction.

To the freethinkers, the most flagrant misrepresentation of Christianity had been its claim to be true. Increasingly, it became clear that what Christianity offered was not certitude, not truth, but merely faith and hope. Since the freethinkers sought truth first of all, a realization of the apparent dissonance between Christianity and truth necessarily led to abandonment of the former.

Testimonies of this martyrdom to truth are not difficult to find. In F. B. Barton's words:

> But a man who has only a moderate share of mental strength and vigour, and who will inquire far enough, will soon so clearly perceive that religion is a matter in which no certainty or satisfaction can ever be attained, that he will dismiss the inquiry as one not within the proper sphere of the human mind, and direct his attention solely to the probabilities and certainties of sense and experience.[27]

---

[26]"Typo," "Sunday School Hymns," <u>Investigator</u> IV (1857-58): 74-76.

[27]F. B. Barton, "The Eclipse of Faith; or, a Visit to a Religious Skeptic," excerpt from <u>The Eclipse of Faith</u>, 2nd ed. (London: Longman's, n.d.), printed in <u>Reasoner</u> XIV (1853): 407.

Holyoake appears never to have tired of remembering his unflinching loyalty to truth, whatever the cause. In a *Reasoner* editorial "The Spirit of Inquiry," he writes:

> To a mind of high aspiration and refined organisation, the pursuit of Truth is the highest pleasure, its attainment the noblest object of existence. To every mind of any feeling or susceptibility, the importance of some of these 'metaphysical' questions must be of the deepest, the most intense interest. Can minds exist that can fail to be penetrated with the deepest concern when they first hear and comprehend in all its meaning and all its mystery the questions 'Is there a God, a judgment, a life beyond the grave?' To those who would feel inclined, with us, to answer these questions in the negative, we will yet propound another, 'What if we be in error?' Shall we not then, when our error is finally discovered to us, have reason to regret the carelessness and the indifference which prevented us from bestowing our deepest and most earnest consideration upon subjects which at all events <u>may be</u> not only of vital but of eternal moment?
> To those, on the other hand, who would at once reply 'There <u>is</u> a God, a judgment, a heaven for the righteous and a hell for the wicked,' we would put this question, 'How do you know this? Speak; tell us whence comes this your certainty, and believe us you will not find unwilling or inattentive listeners. But if it be, as we feel well assured, from our acquaintance with your creed and many of its professors, that <u>it is</u>--if it be that this confidence is merely the effect of long moral and mental habit and training, without full, fair, and free discussion and inquiry, then, Christian friends, we urge you to look around you--to look well on all sides of you; to feel and examine carefully--by the light which, if there be a God, is <u>certainly</u> God's gift--by the light of Reason to examine carefully and conscientiously the staff on which you lean--on which you would have us lean . . .
> There are two stumbling-blocks which some of our opponents have thrown at the threshold of free inquiry. One is the charge against 'infidelity' of destroying the basis or morals. The other is the threat of damnation against those who do not believe in the orthodox idea of Christianity. Both these outworks of Christianity are open to the same objection of irrelevancy. The question at issue is, Are certain propositions, maintained by certain books and persons, under the appellation of Christianity, true or false? It is no help to a solution, still less is it a solution to say, 'If you don't believe them you will have no reason for being moral:' or, 'If you don't believe them you will be tormented in flames, literal or metaphorical, for ever and ever.' If these propositions are proved to us to be true, by a logical chain of unquestionable reasoning from unquestionable premises, we shall be as certain of their truth as we are that two sides of a triangle are together greater than the third. If it is proved to us that there is

immense balance of probability in their favour, we shall accept that and accept most of them gladly, as truths to be believed and acted upon--subject always to the possibility, greater or less, of error. If it be shown that on the whole it is more probable that they are true, we shall accept them with the requisite amount of doubt. If it be shown that the balance of probability is against them, we shall refuse to believe them. In none of these conclusions, till the conclusion be finally made, after full and sufficient investigation, can the consequences of that conclusion, moral or prudential, be in any way taken into consideration. 'A consequence cannot destroy a truth.'[28]

Reminiscing on his life as an old man, Holyoake again testifies rather self-righteously to his integrity:

I do not disguise that standing by Rightness is an onerous duty. It is as much a merit as it is a distinction to have been, at any time, in the employ of Truth. But Truth, though an illustrious, is an exacting mistress, and that is why so many people who enter her service soon give notice to leave.[29]

This growing perception of a cleavage between Christianity and certainty--between Christianity and truth, is echoed in the works of "Anthony Collins" and William Chilton. According to "Collins":

The Church has taught OPINIONS, where she ought to have insisted on an intellectual moral culture, and instead of holding up the CONDUCT of a man to criticism, she has, in all ages, paid more attention to his 'faith' than his 'acts.' It has not been, What kind of man is he? but 'What does he BELIEVE?' and the matter of belief has been an impassable gulf between those of the Church and the people, which could only be crossed with a golden purse.
What then is this 'belief' and these 'opinions' of the Church, which are necessary to our salvation, or rather, what means the mystic words 'belief' and 'opinions'? The former is a word which records a measured credibility in a statement made respecting the veracity of another: we 'believe,' but we do not KNOW--and knowledge excludes belief. No man can believe the sun shines--he KNOWS it. The evidence of his senses informs him of the fact--and it is to himself the experience is given, and not on the testimony of another. The latter word is but the antithesis to 'judgment.'

---

[28]G. J. Holyoake, "The Spirit of Inquiry," Reasoner XXI (1856): 97.

[29]Holyoake, Bygones Worth Remembering, II: 120.

> The derivation of 'opinion' implies a GUESS. Opinions are but GUESSES. Cloud the word as we like with the meretricious garment of rhetoric, still the fact is the same--that so long as we have 'opinions,' we cannot arrive at a JUDGMENT, without which there is no CERTAINTY.
>   Then the Christian tells us he differs of a matter of OPINION, and accuses us of not 'believing' in what he believes, we reply, that a difference of 'opinion or belief' is insufficient ground for any men to separate or to differ about. The Christian errs in laying too much stress on that which ought only to be considered a whim.[30]

Writing for the Oracle, Chilton asserts:

> The difference between religion and science has, on more than one occasion been insisted upon in the Oracle, namely, that the former is systematized folly, or ignorance, and the latter systematized facts or reason; that religion begins where science ends, and that there can be no legitimate connexion between the two, we hope those persons who may have seen this position clearly, will excuse my again reverting to it; those who do not see it, may have their eyes opened, and my cherished object will be gained. For the general appreciation of this fact, would be a death blow to religious faith. Unless we possess infinite intelligence, we shall always have faith, or a belief in the existences we have not ourselves seen, but then, it will be based upon the analogies of things we have seen; and not like religious faith, which demands the belief in existences which have no type in nature, and cannot be contrasted with anything we know of without palpable contradiction and absurdity, for sure.[31]

G. J. Holyoake idolized the Italian nationalists, and no one more than Mazzini. Mazzini's words capture both the zeal for truth and the conviction that Christianity was not truth that characterized the freethinkers;

> We propose progressive improvement, association, transformation of the corrupted medium in which we are now living, the overthrow of all idolatries, shams, lies and conventionalities. We want man to be not the poor, passive, cowardly, phantasmagoric unreality of the actual time, thinking in one way and acting in

---

[30] "Anthony Collins," "Letters to Our Young Men, No. II," Investigator V (1858-59): 45.

[31] William Chilton, "The Cowardice and Dishonesty of Scientific Men," Oracle of Reason I (1841-42): 193.

another, bending to power which he hates or despises; carrying empty popish or thirty-nine article formularies on his breast, and none within. We would make man a fragment of the living Truth--a real individual being linked to collective humanity, the bold seeker of things to come; the gentle, mild, loving, yet firm, uncompromising, inexorable apostle of all that is just and heroic.[32]

Hidden barely beneath the surface of these testimonials of growing disillusionment with Christianity as conveyer of truth, are, of course, certain presuppositions about the nature of truth. Truth deals in certainties. Faith deals in probabilities. Reason and Science, because they alone deal in certainties, are the legitimate guides to truth. To the extent that Christianity is not subject to Reason and Science, it does not partake of certainty or of truth. One might note further that also involved here is the assumption that what is reasonable in the nineteenth century is reasonable for all time, and the assumption that what is reasonable to the freethinkers is reasonable to all mankind.

To Joseph Barker--Unitarian turned Freethinker--the greatest tragedy of those who persisted in the realm of faith rather than moving on to the realm of certainty was their loss of control over their world. They perceived themselves at the mercy of forces outside of their sovereignty, and spent their lives in pursuit of impossibilities. In an article for the National Reformer, titled sarcastically "The Pleasures of Religion," Barker elaborates on their sorry state.

>The Christian is continually striving after impossibilities, and fearing God's wrath and hell fire as the result of failure.

---

[32]Cited by Holyoake, Reasoner XVIII (1855): 97. For other illustrations of perceived separation of Christian belief and truth, see Charles Bradlaugh, A Few Words on the Christian's Creed (London: Charles Bradlaugh, n.d.), p. 5; George Hammond, "The Misapplication of Speculation," Oracle of Reason II (1842-43): 398.

He strives after impossibilities in faith.

He strives after impossible achievements and attainments in virtue.

He seeks an impossible regeneration, an impossible sanctification, an impossible assurance, and impossible consolations.

He finds it impossible to make his experience agree with the requirements of Scripture.

The Christian is ever trusting, and always betrayed; ever hoping, and always disappointed. God seldom or never keeps his word.

He is also troubled about all who are dear to him. He cannot secure their safety. He cannot compel his children to be pious. He cannot compel his wife or his parents to be pious. He cannot be sure God will make them pious. He prays, but his prayers are not answered. He trains his children piously, but they go astray. Nature is stronger than grace; and the devil than God. He sees it everywhere. Throughout the world the devil reigns, and God is dethroned. And there is no remedy.

He believes the world is cursed,--that the ground,--the hills, the valleys, the plains are cursed,--that birds and beasts, and trees and shrubs, are all under an Almighty blight.

He believes that man is cursed,--cursed in body and cursed in soul,--cursed in intellect and in will,--cursed in instinct and affection,--tainted, vitiated, corrupted throughout.

Even when he has got, as he thinks, all right, he is suddenly startled with the thought that he is only deluded by the devil. If he gets over that trouble, he is horrified by the thought that he may fall away, and sings,

"Ah! Lord, with trembling I confess
A gracious soul may fall from grace,
The salt may lose its seasoning power,
And never, never find it more."

He is a man of sorrows, and acquainted with grief, and even in the hour of death is tortured with the fear that the God he has served has forsaken him.[33]

Having perceived that Christianity did not deal in certainty, being committed to Reason, and assuming that that commitment inherently precluded loyalties outside its accepted realm of operation, the freethinkers sought a truer kingdom for their efforts. Some became

---

[33] Joseph Barker, "The Pleasures of Religion," **National Reformer** I (1860): 1.

sceptics regarding the possibility of religious knowledge.[34] More common was the tendency to transfer the arena of "religious" concern from dogma to morality[35]--morality being more tangible, this-worldly, and therefore, more real. In either case, the freethinkers concluded that limited certainty was much to be preferred over unlimited ambiguity. Better to know nothing at all and to be aware of one's ignorance, than to settle for an explanation of the universe founded in mere faith.[36]

Christianity had seemed to be worthy of one's devotion. It had seemed to be a cause big enough to live--and die--for. When they discovered that their Christian world was too small even to encompass their honest search for intellectual and personal integrity, these freethinkers sought a less confining frame of reference. As has previously been noted, both G. J. Holyoake and Charles Bradlaugh had met with opposition when they first showed signs of questioning the dogmas of Christianity. The sense on their part that Christians feared discussion and openness made them distrustful of orthodoxy. If Christianity really were true, why were its adherents so apparently reluctant to put it to the test of free inquiry? To Holyoake, it

---

[34] F. B. Barton, "The Eclipse of Faith," p. 407.

[35] See for example, "Anthony Collins," "Letters to our Young Men, No. II," p. 45; George Jacob Holyoake, "Secularism: Its Sphere and its Services," Reasoner XIV (1853): 34.

[36] See note added by Holyoake to "Hymn to Death," by "A Student," on the occasion of Holyoake's son's death. Reasoner XIX (1855): 164; Holyoake, "The Critics of Atheism," Part II, Reasoner XX (1856): 33; Holyoake, The Trial of Theism, p. 176; Holyoake, Secularism a Religion Which Gives Heaven No Trouble (London: Watts & Co., 1882), pp. 5-8.

appeared that, to protect orthodoxy, Christians would stop at nothing. In the name of defending truth, they would resort to deception, to hypocrisy, to a sort of stifling "mental despotism," and thus deny the very virtue they sought to affirm.[37]

To avoid the seemingly oppressive intellectual constraints of the faith, in the name of guarding truth, the freethinkers advocated a completely unfettered approach to discussion and free inquiry. It made both good morality and good sense. Since man's first duty was to truth rather than to any particular expression of truth, he must pursue truth, whether or not it was comfortable, or easy, or agreeable with the present status quo.[38] Furthermore, since each man must answer for himself--either in this life, or at some future judgment--it was only logical that he should be encouraged to examine all sides of a question for himself. In Holyoake's words:

> . . . my complaint was that the advocates of revelation did not apprise their hearers, that if they adopted their minister's opinions, their minister would not answer for them at the 'last day' if the views imparted to them proved to be erroneous. My 'complaint' was that they did not therefore instruct them to examine all sides of theological questions; for they who had to

---

[37]See Holyoake, "The Debasing Effects of Religion," Oracle of Reason I (1841-42): 241-42; Holyoake, "Religious Policy," Oracle of Reason I (1841-42): 249; Holyoake, "Modern Freethinking: Its Definition, Sphere, and Defence," Reasoner and Theological Examiner XII (1851-52): 81-82.

[38]Holyoake as quoted in "Teachers of Popular Infidelity," Christian Spectator, and reprinted with Holyoake's blessing in Reasoner XIII (1852): 312.

answer for themselves should think for themselves, and think freely.[39]

Underlying the freethinkers' conviction of the necessity of freethought was an apparent assumption of the self-revealing and self-validating character of reasoned truth. Remove the blinders of tradition and prejudice, and truth would emerge--objective and absolute and self-authenticating. The freer the forum for discussion, the greater the chance for truth to "show itself as it really is" and not "as it was supposed to be."[40] For the benefit of those who equated freethought with "anarchy in thought," Holyoake assured his readers of the power of truth, not only to show itself, but to compel adherence to itself.

> We regard Free Discussion, said Holyoake, as the public policy of free people, who would ascertain the truth and establish it. The theory we accept includes a natural barrier against the contingency of justly dreaded licentiousness, and it creates in us a conviction strong enough to dare the judgment of others, and a conscience large enough to help the development of all sincere opinion, without the apprehension which makes bigots of too many, who cannot see how to do to opponents as they would wish to be done unto, without at the same time helping the propagation of error.[41]

Since the pursuit of truth was man's first moral duty, and since truth flourished best in an atmosphere of freedom, it followed logically that the freethinkers should find, or create, in their "system" of

---

[39] "Reply of Mr. Holyoake to the Rev. Richard Chester," Reasoner and Theological Examiner IX (1850): 158. On the logic of the right of free discussion, see also a later perspective--McCann-Bradlaugh Debate: Secularism--Unphilosophical, Immoral, and Anti-Social (London: Watts & Co., 1881), p. 15.

[40] George Jacob Holyoake, "Utility of Unlimited Inquiry," Oracle of Reason I (1841-42): 137. See also Holyoake, "Expectations of Readers," Reasoner VI (1849): 209.

[41] Holyoake, "Modern Freethinking: Its Definition, Sphere, and Defence," p. 82.

freethought the room to maneuvre that had been lacking in their childhood experience of Christianity.

Even more indicting than its failure to provide room for the freethinkers' search for intellectual truth was Christianity's failure to live up to the moral expectations it had created. It had proclaimed standards of morality, of justice, of fairplay, and then betrayed its own touchstones.

In Holyoake's own mind, three events were decisive in convincing him that the church mouthed one morality and exercised another. First, when he was a small child, his mother had been forced to take money that could have been used to buy medicine for his sick sister, in order to satisfy payment of the church rates.[42] If the church had really cared, that sort of "robbery" would have been unnecessary.

Second, in November, 1841, the government arrested Charles Southwell, editor of the Oracle of Reason, on charges of blasphemy. Specifically objectionable had been the November 27, 1841 issue of the Oracle, in which he had made particularly vituperative allegations against Holy Scripture. Besides including a chart that outlined by historical period the nature and number of crimes committed in the name of the scripture,[43] he had described the Bible as:

> . . . that revoltingly odious Jew production, called Bible, has been for ages the idol of all sorts of blockheads, the glory of knaves, and the disgust of wise men. It is a history of lust, sodomies, wholesale slaughtering, and horrible depravity; that the vilest parts of all other histories, collected into one monstrous

---

[42] Holyoake, Bygones Worth Remembering, II: 219.

[43] Oracle of Reason I (1841-42): 32.

book, could not parallel! Priests tell us that this concentration of abominations was written by a god; all the world believe priests, or they would rather have thought it the outpourings of some devil.[44]

Not being used to thinking of the scriptures in these terms, the Establishment was quite understandably distressed. On January 15, 1842, authorities sentenced Southwell to spend twelve months in the Bristol Gaol and to pay £100 fine. Holyoake, at this time, assumed the editorship of the Oracle.

The third event followed closely upon the second. In May of 1842, Holyoake himself was arrested, not in connection with the Oracle, but for certain blasphemous statements made in a public gathering at Cheltenham on May 24, 1842. According to the official charges, Holyoake had:

> . . . wickedly and profanely uttered made use of and proclaimed in the presence of a public assembly of men women and children then and there assembled certain impious and blasphemous words against God and of and concerning the Christian Religion to wit 'that he was of no religion at all' and 'that he did not believe there was such a thing as a God' and 'that if he could have his way he would place the Deity on half pay as the Government of this Country did the subaltern officers.' against the peace, of our Lady the Queen her crown and dignity.[45]

In August of 1842, the Gloucester Assizes sentenced Holyoake to six months imprisonment at the Gloucester Gaol.

Both in the Oracle and in his autobiographical History of the Last Trial by Jury for Atheism in England, Holyoake credits the circumstances of Southwell's arrest and imprisonment with being a decisive factor in

---

[44]Charles Southwell, "The Jew Book," Oracle of Reason I (1841-42): 25.

[45]Arrest Warrant, July 1842, "Envelopes," Holyoake Collection, Bishopsgate Institute, London.

turning him into an atheist. In the History, he says it was that event that drove him to examine the scripture which inquiry led him to disbelief.[46] Even more strongly in a letter from Cheltenham Gaol to the Oracle in June of 1842, Holyoake asserts, "I never was an Atheist until the imprisonment of Charles Southwell took place."[47] In the same passage, he goes on to write that

> whatever of doubt remained on my mind on the subject, was now removed by the treatment I was receiving; that what of god-belief might have been left in me before, was thoroughly and for ever shaken out of me then.[48]

So, for Holyoake at least, the witnessing and experiencing of "Justice" as meted out in the name of Christian authorities were decisive in sending him to search for an alternative basis on which to construct a "reasonable" social morality.

Equally significant to the impact of these tangles with the Law on the victims was their effect on the freethought community at large. Throughout his imprisonment and long after, Holyoake kept the movement well supplied with detailed information on his treatment in prison as evidence of the depravity of Christian morality. This appeared to have

---

[46] Holyoake, *The History of the Last Trial by Jury for Atheism in England: A Fragment of Autobi Submitted for the perusal of her Majesty's Attorney-General and the British Clergy* (London: James 1851) reprint of "2nd 1000" Arno Press and New York Times, 1972, pp. 11-12.

[47] Holyoake to William Chilton printed as "A Voice from Cheltenham Gaol," *Oracle of Reason* I (1841-42): 214.

[48] *Ibid.* For other examples of his own statements about the impact of his prison experience on his assessment of Christian morality, see "Address from Mr. Holyoake," *Oracle of Reason* II (1842-43): 73; George Jacob Holyoake to the Editor, "Prison Discipline," *Oracle of Reason* II (1842-43): 83-88.

had the desired effect.[49] Holyoake's arrest, whether it created, or merely affirmed, opinions about the lack of Christians' moral integrity, became the occasion for denunciations of Christian morality by several leading freethinkers.[50] Of particular interest is a letter from Richard Carlile, long time friend of Holyoake's, and well known for his own battle with the authorities for the right of free expression. After lamenting the "mock trial" that he had witnessed in which Holyoake had brilliantly defended himself with a "beautiful strain and flow of his noble and ennobling sentiments, through nine hours," Carlile goes on to suggest that it is Holyoake and Carlile, not the Establishment who are the "true" Christians. In his words:

> I have discovered in the understanding of those truths that such men as Holyoake and myself have been the Christians, and our persecutors vile infidels of the most vicious and worst description of character--idolators without reason: Atheists without the true god; politicians without righteous principle; professing moralists without morals.[51]

It should be noted that, though there was agreement between the Oracle "Establishment" and Carlile that Holyoake had been unjustly

---

[49]See, for example Holyoake, "A Voice from Gloucester Gaol, Oracle of Reason I (1841-42): 320; Letter from Holyoake to George Julian Harney, June 8, 1842 printed in Oracle of Reason I (1841-42): 224; Holyoake, "Address from Mr. Holyoake," Oracle of Reason II (1842-43): 73ff; Holyoake, A Short and Easy Method With the Saints (London: Hetherington, 1843).

[50]See M. Q. Ryall, "To the Conductor of the Oracle of Reason," Oracle of Reason I (1841-42): 214; Thomas Paterson to the Editor of the Oracle of Reason," Oracle of Reason I (1841-42): 215; Thomas Paterson, "A Note From the Third Priest," Oracle of Reason I (1841-42): 325-326; William Chilton, "Notes Upon the Gloucester Prosecutions," Oracle of Reason I (1841-42): 307-9.

[51]Carlile to Editor of the Oracle of Reason printed as "Trial for Blasphemy," Oracle of Reason I (1841-42): 290.

treated at the hands of Christians, they disagreed on whether the problem was with Christian morality itself, or with Christians' failure to practice their morality. In his later years, Carlile came more and more to believe that the "failure" of Christianity in England was a result of a failure of so-called Christians to understand their faith.[52] Carlile's "reclamation" of the faith, albeit under new guises, had resulted in a rift between himself and Holyoake's *Oracle*. This explains the almost grudging acceptance of Carlile's support for the cause that is so evident in both William Chilton and Charles Southwell.[53] In one sense, the matters at issue between Carlile and the *Oracle* were related to a larger question which was to plague the freethought movement through its existence, and which the Holyoake trial brought into focus: To what extent was the intellectual basis of the freethought movement derived from denunciation, not of Christian dogma as falsehood, but from Christian practice as hypocrisy?[54]

Apart from the emotional ardor and intellectual speculation precipitated by Holyoake's and Southwell's imprisonments were the more down-to-earth organizational and financial responses of the freethought world. Thomas Paterson agreed to carry on the work of editing the

---

[52]For a sampling of Carlile's ideas about the true nature of Christianity, see Richard Carlile, "What is God?" *Oracle of Reason* I (1841-42): 312.

[53]See response to Carlile's letter in *Oracle* I (1841-42): 291 and extract of letter from Southwell to friend printed in *Oracle* I (1841-42): 327.

[54]See "Why Are We Atheists?" in *Oracle of Reason* I (1841-42): 318 and William Chilton's response, also entitled "Why Are We Atheists?" *Oracle of Reason* I (1841-42): 329-332.

Oracle. A nation-wide subscription campaign was organized to collect funds for the imprisoned martyrs and their families.[55] The Oracle recorded the donors and their contributors each week as an inspiration to the endeavor. Finally, Holyoake's arrest was the occasion of the organization of the Anti-Prosecution Union, whose sole aim was to "uphold the Right of Private Judgment and Free Discussion for all, whether Christian, Jew, Turk, Theist, or Atheist."[56] Though Holyoake eventually became secretary of the organization, it continued to seek to draw from a broader base of support than that of freethought. This move of the freethinkers into single-issue political and social activism was only the first of many such ventures in which freethinkers cooperated freely for the achievement of specific goals with those who did not share their world view. This phenomenon accounts for much disagreement among the freethinkers. It explains some of the difficulty of isolating the movement of freethought. Finally, it suggests a vision of the freethinkers that measures their contribution to Victorian society in other than simple figures of membership and "conversions" to freethought.

It is evident then, that both in the life of G. J. Holyoake, and in the life of the freethought movement, the specific historical events of

---

[55] J. C. Farn, "Report of Progress," Oracle of Reason I (1841-42): 221.

[56] M. Q. Ryall, "Circular of the 'Anti-Prosecution Union,'" Oracle of Reason I (1842): 225; For a more complete discussion of the background, aims, and goals of the Anti-Persecution Union, see special Oracle supplement in No. 31 of the Oracle, July 23, 1842.

Southwell's and Holyoake's arrests and imprisonments contributed significantly to their persuasion to reject Christianity--or at least current Christian moral practice--as a suitable pattern around which to establish social justice and stability.

On a different level, but nonetheless significant in considering freethought's moral impressions of Christianity, is the word of Joseph Barker. His struggle was in the abstract, rather than in the experiential, realm, but it resulted equally powerfully in a personal revulsion at Christian morality. According to Barker:

> My unbelief came upon me while I was diligently striving in all things to do God's will. My virtue outlived my faith. The only reason why I do not believe in God and immorality is, that I can nowhere see any signs or proofs of them, but everywhere see proofs to the contrary. At the same time, I acknowledge that I should now be very sorry that there *should* be such a God as the God of the Jews or the Christians, or that there should be such as eternal future as orthodox Christianity portrays. I did not *begin* by wishing there was no God and no future life; but I have ended by thinking it is infinitely better that there should not be any, than that there should be such monster masses of cruelty and horror as the God and future life of orthodox Christianity . . .[57]

He is offended especially by the Christian doctrine of the Fatherhood of God, and suggests that it is actually a savage picture of fatherhood, understood only in terms of power and authoritarianism. For Barker, "I had rather be an orphan in the universe than the child of such a Being."[58]

It seems clear that the issue of Christianity's moral credentials was in the forefront of concern for both individual freethinkers and the

---

[57] Joseph Barker to Mr. Holyoake, printed as "Religious Confessions," *Reasoner* XXIII (1858): 322.

[58] Ibid.

movement as a whole at critical times in the formation of their decision to pursue alternative moral foundations to Christianity. After a certain point, continued denunciation of Christian moral practice loses its force as convincing argument, for one can argue that the freethinkers--like everyone else--saw what they chose to see. Nevertheless, it would be safe to say that there were sufficient encounters between the freethinkers and "Christian" society, especially "Christian" authority, to keep reinforcing the assessment that the freethinkers had made of Christian morality. Furthermore, occasional noting of such encounters would suggest that freethinkers continued to see the moral inadequacies of Christianity as reason to pursue other presuppositional options on which to construct their ethics.[59]

The background of the freethinkers helps to explain much of what they were reacting against. But it is important, not only for accounting for the discontinuity in their lives, but for understanding what stayed the same. That the freethinkers wanted to be committed to something is without question. They were pious and zealous, whether or not on behalf of Christianity.

Few of the freethinkers' traits are more compellingly attractive than their sincerity. Their seemingly self-righteous dogmatism about the results to which their sincerity led them is, of course, another matter, and opens them to the same charges of which they accused the orthodox. That in no way detracts, however, from the fact that they believed they desired to serve truth more than anything. They wanted to

---

[59]See, for example, Holyoake, "Religious Visits," Reasoner XVII (1854): 81-84.

know, no matter what the cost. They wanted to know so that they could do. They wanted to be people of integrity, whose knowledge and action were one--people who were true to reality and therefore, true to themselves. Annie Besant speaks of her desire to "sacrifice to something felt as greater than the self."[60] Holyoake, whose ardent search for a cause led from Wesleyanism, to Unitarianism, to Owenism, to Atheism, and finally, to Secularism, marvelled at the apparent apathy of the Unitarians.

> The Unitarian is a mystery to me; with his faith, I never could live with his apathy. With the orthodox, God is an image of terror--with the Unitarian, an object of trust. When I first saw this distinction, it had all the force of magic on my mind; it was the first deep thought of unchequered consolation I derived from theology, and I never can understand how it is, that the Unitarian does not burn with a noble passion to impart to the orthodox this inspiring and refining idea, and to take in public affairs the lead that freedom gives him. Whereas (with some noble exceptions on the part of persons scarcely counted orthodox by their brethren) we find Unitarian preaching a sonorous pastime, and the body, a school of conservative doctrinaires, carefully guarding themselves against an identification with others, which others do not desire.[61]

Holyoake's intensity is even more pronounced in the following excerpt from an 1852 *Reasoner*.

> Life is a very serious thing: every gleam of truth reveals to us more of the laws of absolute fact, inexorable and eternal, which make up the inscrutable Future and Invisible, as they do the visible and mysterious Present. Shall we raise our puny hands or voices and fight against those laws? Shall we lie against eternal truth or shut our eyes and ears against it? I dare do none of these things deliberately. My share in the work of the world is doubtless of the minutest consequence, but to *me* it is of infinite consequence. To me it is of infinite consequence whether I live a

---

[60] Annie Besant, *An Autobiography*, p. 57.

[61] Holyoake, "Secularism Distinguished From Unitarianism," *Reasoner* XIX (1855): 97.

traitor and a coward, or a true man. Good or bad, this is my work, I found I had it to do, and I have done it.[62]

This sincere desire to be people, not only of pure thinking, but also of right doing, makes it difficult to tell at times which of the two desires--for right thinking and for right doing--was cause and which was effect of the other; or which was end and which was means. They remained inextricably linked throughout the movement, but it seems that, increasingly, concern for right ideas was subordinated to concern for right action and truth was more and more measured by its apparent moral results. The freethinkers were above all, people of this world. They wanted tangible improvement and material progress, and so sought the ideas that would bring them about.[63]

Whatever criticisms they levelled at Christian dogma as a whole, there remained room among the freethinkers for admiration of individual traits and individual Christians. Ironically, in light of frequent and scathing attacks on Catholicism,[64] Holyoake greatly admired Ignatius Loyola. In a *Reasoner* series, Holyoake notes, among other qualities, Loyola's sense of purpose, desire for excellence, self-discipline and,

---

[62]Holyoake, "The Task for Today," *Reasoner* XII (1851-52): 69. For other examples of his self-confessed sincerity in seeking truth, see Holyoake, The Logic of Death, p. 13; and "George Jacob Holyoake to Dr. Robert Kalley," *Movement* I (1843-44): 87.

[63]See, for example "George Jacob Holyoake to Central Board of Utilitarian Society," June 3, 1841 in Letters of George Jacob Holyoake, Holyoake Collection, Bishopsgate Institute, London; Diary Entry-September 2, 1849, Holyoake Diaries, Holyoake Collection, Bishopsgate Institute, London; J. Jaggar to the Sheffield Secular Society, reported in "Meetings, &c." *Investigator* V (1859): 160. (It should be noted that the Utilitarian Society is the same institution as the Rational Society.)

[64]See especially editorial series in *Reasoner* IX (1850).

passion for learning.[65] So, though he may have despised the cause, Holyoake was drawn, even as an adult, to the quality of devotion to a cause.

Finally, the freethinkers shared with those in their religious background a reverence for the Ultimate. Whatever or Whoever it was who was responsible for the Cosmos deserved respect and devotion. Holyoake had no patience with the charge that atheists were irreverent.[66] Ironically, on a number of occasions one even finds freethinkers denouncing Christians for their flippant manner in dealing with the Almighty.[67] Nowhere is the continuity of reverence for truth more self-consciously evident than in the writings of Joseph Barker. He goes so far as to say of his progress from Methodist preacher to Secularist lecturer that,

> As to my religious views, I am not aware of any essential change in them . . . What was the object and drift of my favourite sermons, is the object and drift of my lectures now.[68]

In the **National Reformer**, Barker presents a detailed listing of what factors were, and what factors were not, significant in his departure from the faith. The overarching reason that "made him an infidel" was

---

[65]Holyoake, "Loyola an Exemplar to Modern Reformers," Part II **Reasoner** III (1847): 625-29.

[66]Holyoake, **Reasoner** XIX (1855): 90.

[67]R. L. B., "The Mawworms in High Places--or the Day of Humiliation," **Reasoner** XVIII (1855): 146-47; Holyoake, "The Rev. Hugh M'Neile and the Rev. Mr. Spurgeon," **Reasoner** XIX (1855): 28.

[68]Joseph Barker, "Letters from Mr. Barker," **Reasoner** XXV (1860): 52.

"a love of truth and virtue; a hatred of falsehood and vice."[69] What had driven many of the freethinkers into the Church would appear to be often the very things that later would take them out.

One cannot systematically prove a causal connection between the freethinkers' background in Christianity and their later concern for theology in working class radicalism. At the very least, one might safely say that the qualities that made one an enthusiastic Christian are the same ones that make one a committed freethinker--zeal for truth, desire for commitment to a cause, scrupulous conscience, concern for the "lost."

The connection seems to go even beyond this. One might argue that their Christian upbringing helped to determine the shape of their ultimate questions, but left a vacuum where the answers should have been. It provided the categories of their thought, which remained after the content had been replaced. It created the touchstones by which the freethinkers judged truth, goodness, and justice long after they had rejected Christianity for not living up to those standards. In short, their Christian roots left the freethinkers with the old questions and without an intellectual home. That they could not accept the old answers cut them off from their past. That they were still asking the old questions kept them from feeling comfortable in the emerging a-theological, a-dogmatic culture of the future.

The freethinkers still sought answers to metaphysical questions, though they limited drastically the confines in which the search was to

---

[69]Barker, "What was it That Made You an Infidel?" *National Reformer* I (1860-61): 4.

be conducted, and narrowed considerably the realm in which certainty of the answer might be assured. Few passages depict this juxtaposition of the old and the new quite so well as George Holyoake's line to brother Austin:

> The Poor man, harassed by cares, worn by excessive toil, fettered by poverty, and pursued by death, by what light shall he walk--how shall he best solve the problem of existence? This, you know, is the practical question; and it is this question that Secularism tries to answer.[70]

---

[70]Holyoake, "Notes on the Debate in Glasgow," *Reasoner* XVII (1854): 275.

II

Looking on the freethinkers from outside, one cannot ignore the factors inside the freethinkers that colored their perception of the world. The historian might easily overemphasize the subjective element in their theologizing of explanations and remedies for the world's ills. To the freethinkers themselves, the reasons for their positions were convincingly grounded in objective data external to themselves--data that were available to be examined by all men and that would yield the same interpretation to all men whose reason was free of the corrupting influence of tyranny and superstition. Their literature is replete with all manner of indictments against existing orthodox Christianity and its established position in the political, social, and economic structure of Victorian England. Not only did the freethinkers sincerely believe in the vileness of established religion; they held that the institution of organized Christianity was the disease of which the social, political, and economic ills of human society were merely symptoms. The source of infection must be dealt with if efforts to treat the symptoms were to be anything but band-aid measures. So, in looking for explanations of the religious element in freethought, one cannot ignore the freethinkers' own view of the situation. The church merited destruction. It was an enemy to be defeated. What quicker way to engage and foil the opponent than by taking the offensive on his territory?

Though the variations on charges against the church are legion, they can be grouped under two broad headings--intellectual and moral. In the former, orthodoxy is not living up to truth, or is proving too strait to contain reality. In the latter, the church is not living up to "right." It is holding truth dishonestly. It goes without saying that such accusations imply that the freethinkers believed themselves privy to some standard of "Truth" and "Right" higher than established Christianity--in their case, Reason. Curiously and perhaps less consciously, though just as frequently, the freethinkers actually appear to be using ostensibly Christian standards of truth and right by which to measure Christian dogma and practice. They appear to be holding the faithful up to their own light--as if the freethinkers thought themselves better interpreters, evaluators, and even practitioners of Christian truth and morality than those who claimed to be its adherents.

At the intellectual level, the freethinkers criticized first, orthodoxy's failure to accommodate reality, and second, its epistemology. There were numerous areas, according to the freethinkers, in which Christian dogma simply did not deal with vast realms of human knowledge and experience, especially as they impinged on matters perceived fundamental to orthodoxy. Further, orthodoxy was far too dependent on faith and not nearly dependent enough on reason.

To be a Christian meant to the freethinkers to choose to wear blinders while traveling through the world, to choose to ignore truth, and to choose to refuse to exercise power to do what was humanly possible to improve the world for the good of all mankind.

Christianity, as practiced by the Victorian Establishment, was removed from the real world, that is, from this world. Christians were naive, and according to the maxim, "so heavenly minded as to be no earthly good." Belief in the afterlife, with its notion of possible deferred reward and eventual recompense for suffering in this world, was particularly obnoxious to freethinkers. It discouraged active participation in the affairs of this world, even more so than other religions that also shared a belief in immortality.[1] It clouded existence with guilt and uncertainty.[2] Furthermore, because of its preoccupation with spiritual matters, it tended in its ministry to apply spiritual remedies to physical need--even to ignore physical need altogether. Though his line of argument might be challenged logically, Holyoake seizes almost eagerly on a study lamenting the number of prison inmates who had spent time in Sunday School. Holyoake concludes his commentary by saying, "The way to Heaven seems to be the way to gaol, unless spiritual instruction be accompanied by practical knowledge of this life."[3] Freethinkers never tired of pointing to absurdities in Christian practice, including calling a national fast day to pray for

---

[1] G. J. Holyoake, "Methodism in the Provinces," Reasoner VII (1849- 50): 65; Charles Watts, "The Christian and Secular View of a Future Life," National Reformer VI (1865): 321-22; William Maccall, "The Immortal Life," National Reformer IX (1867): 246-47.

[2] Joseph Barker, "The Hope of Immortality," National Reformer I (1960-61): 3; F. B. Barton, "The Doctrine of the Resurrection," Reasoner XII (1851-52): 439.

[3] G. J. Holyoake, "Sunday Scholar Convicts," Reasoner XXII (1857): 33.

relief from an outbreak of cholera,[4] sending flannel and Watts' hymns to the Africans,[5] and leaving Bibles when soap would have been more appropriate.[6] In part of a satire on the good intentions but ludicrous outcomes of so much Christian charity, one character, a "Cynical, Elderly Gentleman," suggests to three pious ladies:

> This unwashed specimen of humanity illustrates the suggestion I was about to render to you. Suppose that instead of giving the poor, tracts which they will not read, you were to give them soap which they could use?
>
> Young Lady: (with a simper.) Soap, Sir!
>
> Elderly Lady: (with severe incredulity.) Soap, Sir?
>
> Gentleman: Soap, ladies. Instead of a tract, give them a cake or slice of soap. Let the Established Church give yellow soap, and the Dissenters stick to mottled, for the sake of distinction. Charitable ladies, who give from their own resources, and wish to convey an allegorical expression of the sweetness of their faith, could bestow honey soap on the recipients of their bounty, while the aristocratic lady-dowagers might come down with old brown Windsor.[7]

Freethinkers asserted that Christians were not only missing the point practically by allowing spiritual concerns to dominate physical life, they were engaging in sloppy thinking as well. The natural and theological worlds are totally separate, with separate systems of cause and effect. Man, existing as he does in the natural realm, can know nothing of, and therefore can have nothing to do with, the spiritual

---

[4]Holyoake, "Secularism in the Cabinet," Reasoner XV (1853): 355.

[5]Report from Little Bethel in "Examination of the Press," Reasoner IX (1850): 233.

[6]Holyoake, "Methodism in the Provinces," p. 65.

[7]Henry Tyrrell, "The Tract Distributors," Investigator V (1858-59): 151.

realm. He must not, then, be continually acting as if it were relevant to this life.[8]

In clinging to orthodoxy, Christians failed to give adequate consideration to new discoveries in the realm of science. Assuming that frequency of treatment of a subject is some indication of importance attached to a subject, it is safe to say that the Oracle of Reason, especially, among the freethought periodicals, placed great importance on the findings of natural science. Their serialized edition of William Chilton's "Theory of Regular Gradation"[9] attempted to acquaint readers with the latest theories of biological classification and development. It is clear that Chilton espouses belief in a material origin to life, and a random development of botanical and zoological forms.[10] Introducing a non-material agent in the discussion of origins merely complicated the question of causes unnecessarily. To Chilton, evidence of the development of superior forms from inferior rendered the doctrine of a creator, not only unnecessary, but even nonsensical, for "we do not find a coachmaker when he has to build a nobleman's carriage, begin by making a mud cart or pair of trucks."[11] Charles Southwell, though not a

---

[8]Frank Grant, "Bishop Butler on Rewards and Punishments in a Future Life," Reasoner VI (1849): 114-15; M. Q. Ryall, "Anatomy of Heterodoxies," Oracle of Reason II (1842-43): 62-64.

[9]William Chilton, "Theory of Regular Gradation," Oracle of Reason, begins in I (February 19, 1842) and continues in weekly segments. See also William Chilton, "Vestiges of the Natural History of Creation," Movement II (1845): 9-12.

[10]See, for example, Parts I, XII, XIII, XIV, XVI of "Theory of Regular Gradation."

[11]William Chilton, "Theory of Regular Gradation," Part XVI, Oracle of Reason I (1841-42): 206.

scientist himself, delighted in science's ability to explain the world materially. In his mind, science put religion on the defensive. In his words:

> If cocks by instinct distinctly crowed, 'there is a god,' the thing would be strange and tolerably convincing, but no such thing, it is not written anywhere, but only in books, and crowed by the cocks of humanity, the teachers of unknown knowledge, who find it very convenient to make us familiar with their god, that our eyes may be blinded to their duplicity. Finally, upon what principle, I ask, are we justified in wasting our energies, and corrupting our intellects by the vain pursuit of a phantom, an *ignis fatuus*, an 'unreal mockery' to the neglect of that accurate knowledge, of those virtuous delights, those unspeakable joys that lie within our reach . . .[12]

Southwell goes on to address clerics and several prominent politicians of the day, "Bring forth your 'strong reasons,' and show by argument that self-existent matter is an impossibility."[13]

Besides the question of origins, freethinkers examined other issues of potential conflict between science and religion, including phrenology and geology.[14] Whatever the issue, the consensus among the freethinkers suggests that they overwhelmingly considered religion to be the inhibitor of science,[15] and thereby the inhibitor of truth. Occasionally, a freethinker would be content to rest with the conclusion

---

[12]C. Southwell, "Is There A God?" Part XV, Oracle of Reason I (1841-42): 172.

[13]Ibid., p. 173.

[14]Thomas Paterson, "Phrenology and Materialism," Oracle of Reason I (1841-42): 312-13; T. Paterson's Report on W. C. Engledue's address on "Cerebral Physiology and Materialism," Oracle of Reason I (1841-42): 345-46; "P. G.," "Geology and the Bible," Movement I (1843-44): 451-53; Letter from William Chilton to Editor, "Modern Geologists and the Mosaic Creation," Reasoner XIII (1852): 91-92.

[15]"The Saint and the Secularist--Which Has the Best of It?" National Reformer I (February 2, 1861): 1.

that religion and science were not contrary; they were merely separate.[16] More often they were treated as mortal enemies, with mutually exclusive claims. Religion was the dark villain oppressing science, the helpless victim. Primarily because of its *a priori* claims to infallibility, religion discounted itself in the face of scientific evidence. According to Malthus Q. Ryall, "Science and religion, then, in whatever close or distant relationship they may have appeared to subsist, are, when brought to the test of analysis, essentially irreconcilable."[17] In typical "Oracular" style of overly graphic imagery, Thomas Paterson describes the stage at which a young science encounters the Church:

> Then comes the time of tribulation--then has the infant science most to fear from the embraces of its new foster-mother--the church, whose boa-constrictor like gripe [sic] nearly proves fatal to the tender nurseling, who is often long in recovering from the spasm.[18]

If the church did attempt to endorse the discoveries of science, freethinkers were equally critical of what appeared to be merely accommodation of expedience. Joseph Barker states, in his article on "Geology and Christianity," that the church did in the field of geology only what they had done in other sciences. They waited until they had lost the fight, then "invented new and unnatural meanings for Scripture

---

[16]William Maccall, "Pantheism and Secularism: A Lecture," **Reasoner** XVI (1854): 233-35.

[17]M. Q. Ryall, "Science and Religion," **Movement** I (1843-44): 196- 97.

[18]T. Paterson, Engledue lecture, p. 345.

words, to make Scripture and geology agree."[19]

Besides its emphasis on the imaginary spiritual world to the neglect of the real temporal world, and its resistance to science, the Church betrayed reality, according to the freethinkers, in its promulgation of the doctrine of free will and the closely related explanation of the "problem of evil." By holding men responsible and blameworthy for their choices, the church ignored the laws of cause and effect. Men are what they are because of circumstances. They are not accountable and should therefore neither be blamed nor praised for being what they cannot help being. By placing such weight on man's power of choice, the church loads him with a burden too heavy to bear, and drives him to despair and hopelessness.[20]

The Church's efforts to explain evil present an even grosser problem to the freethinkers. Either the Church lays the responsibility on man, which as already mentioned, means ignoring man's contingency on circumstances, or it must lay it at the feet of God which calls in question either God's power--His ability to eradicate evil, or His goodness--His desire to eradicate evil. Either way, it works against

---

[19] Joseph Barker, "Geology and Christianity," *National Reformer* I (June 2, 1860): 3.

[20] See for example G. J. Holyoake, "Relation of Christianity to Morality and Progress," *Reasoner* V (1848): 385; J. Barker, "Free-Will," *National Reformer* I (September 1, 1860): 4; See also sample lecture titles from Holyoake Diaries, Holyoake Collection, Bishopsgate Institute, London--November 9, 1856--"Christian Morality Undefined, Contradictory, and Inoperative"; November 12, 1856--"The Christian Doctrine of Responsibility False, Obstructive and Disastrous"; G. J. Holyoake, *New Ideas of the Day* (London: Freethought Publishing Co., 1887), pp. 12, 13, 15.

remedying of present evil, for, in the first case, it refuses to come to terms with man's dependence on circumstances, and to work for creating good conditions that will result in good men; in the second case, it accepts evil passively as somehow in the very order of things.[21]

Perhaps the most flagrant of the Church's failures to accommodate known truth is in its dogma regarding the scriptures. In attacking the aspiration of Holy Writ, the freethinkers saw themselves destroying the very heart of the Christian claim to authority, and hence its power over the faithful.[22] In 1854, the Reasoner printed an article by unitarian-turned-freethinker Joseph Barker entitled, "What Harm Have the Scriptures Ever Done You?" Barker answers the title question:

> I answer, I do not exactly consider that the Scriptures have done me harm; but the erroneous notions respecting the divine authority of the Scriptures.[23]

blames orthodoxy's view of Scripture for causing him "to spend a considerable portion of [his life] in preaching and teaching error," for prejudicing him against science, for preventing his participation in social and political life, and for giving him false advice on the

---

[21] See G. J. Holyoake, "Relation of Christianity to Morality and To progress," p. 385; G. J. Holyoake, "Is There a God?" Oracle of Reason I (1841-): 140-141; Two Nights Public Discussion Between Thomas Cooper and Charles Bradlaugh--On the Being of a God the Maker and Moral Governor of the Universe (London: Austin & Co., 1864), pp. 42-60; iconoclast," "A Plea for Atheism," National Reformer V (1864): 10-12; undecimus," "Omnipotence," Reasoner IX (1850): 267-69; C. Bradlaugh, "Is There a God?" Investigator V (1858-59): 167 taken from Bradlaugh, The Bible; What Is!

[22] See, for example, Investigator I (1854-55): 136; and Investigator III (1856-57): 55.

[23] J. Barker, "What Harm Have the Scriptures Ever Done You?" Reasoner II (1854): 177.

importance of accumulating property.[24] In the early 1850's, the Reasoner prepared several Reasoner tracts specifically on the theme of scriptural authority. Though these four-page statements appeared in the Reasoner itself, they were intended for wider public distribution. The number of tracts on this particular subject suggests the freethinkers' estimate of its centrality to their cause.[25]

At the intellectual level,[26] the freethinkers attacked the scriptures on the grounds of its lack of historical veracity,[27] its failure to be consistent with the findings of science,[28] its

---

[24] Ibid.

[25] Tract titles included "The Old Testament," "The New Testament," and "The Age, Authorship, and Authenticity, of the Old Testament," Part 1, 2. All appear in Reasoner X (1850-51).

[26] Criticism of the Bible on moral grounds, of which there was a great deal, will be treated as part of the general moral attack of freethinkers on orthodoxy.

[27] G. J. Holyoake, "Mr. Holyoake's Provincial Reports," Reasoner V (1848): 321; "W. J. B.," "The Age, Authorship, and Authenticity, of the Old Testament," Reasoner X (1850-51): between 390 and 391; "Who Were the Writers of the New Testament?" National Reformer II (February 22, 1862): 5; Charles Bradlaugh, "Genesis: Its Authorship and Authenticity," National Reformer VI (1865): 114ff. For summary statement of freethought objections to the scripture, see C. Bradlaugh, "To the Rev. W. Cooke, D.D.," National Reformer XIV (1869): 193-94.

[28] Extract from "The Bible Not Reliable" in London Secular Society's Propagandist Tracts cited in Investigator V (1858-59): 126; William Chilton, "God's Words vs. God's Works," Part III, Movement II (1845): 89-92; Chilton, "The Noachian Deluge," Reasoner XIII (1852): 99-102; Three-part series printed in Reasoner as "Conversations on Bible Difficulties Between Brown and Robinson," XVII (1854): 217ff., 232ff., 249ff.

presuppositional foundation in the supernatural,[29] and its failure to be internally congruent.[30] On this side of the controversy over Higher Criticism and Biblical Inerrancy, the specifics of these various charges hardly need be delineated. They included the now familiar questions over the Genesis Creation and Flood accounts, the problems of prophecy and miracles, discrepancies in genealogies, and the synoptic problem of the Gospels. What is significant for this discussion is the prominence given to the question of Biblical authority, and the perception that if they succeeded in discrediting scripture, the freethinkers would have destroyed the foundation of orthodoxy. With the foundation gone, the edifice would fall quite naturally.

Apart from its Procrustean approach to fitting reality into orthodoxy, the Church was, according to the freethinkers, at least epistemologically backward, if not outrightly dishonest. Its appeal to faith in addition, and even in opposition, to reason was at best unnecessary, and at worst, manipulative and evil. A material world governed by the unrelenting operation of cause and effect had no room

---

[29]Extract from "The Bible Not Reliable," Investigator V (1858-59): 126; "Undecimus," "The Gospel Narrative," Reasoner IX (1850): 127. A variation of this is Christian acceptance of the possibility of prophecy. To the freethinker, such an occurrence was inherently impossible. Where scripture discussed such matters, it was thus presuppositionally viewed as unreliable. See for example, "Undecimus," "The Evidences of Prophecy," Reasoner IX (1850): 140-43.

[30]"Iconoclast," "The Bible--History of Joseph," Investigator V (1858-59): 132; See series of articles by W. J. B., "Prophecies," Oracle of Reason beginning II (April 8, 1843): 129; M. Q. Ryall, "Anti- Clerical Artillery," Movement I (1843-44): 426-27; See also series by William Chilton, "God's Words vs. God's Works," Movement II beginning (February 26, 1845): 68-69 and continuing in March 5, 1845 and subsequent issues.

for revelation. Thus, all religious statements couched in language of the supranatural had to be re-interpreted to fit the presuppositional framework of freethought. "Procrusteanism" worked on both sides.

Orthodoxy had violated the principle of Occam's razor. The Church, not the unbelievers, had been false to reality by multiplying causes and complicating explanations. Freethinkers could explain the world as rationally and convincingly in material terms as the believers could in supranatural terms. It was the Christian who had gone beyond the evidence.[31] In the words of William Chilton:

> Men can only believe in this god by a process of abstract reasoning, which reasoning the writer states would lead men to virtue without a god; where then is the utility of the addition?[32]

Some of the criticism of this matter took the form of serious philosophical discussion. In challenging a Mr. MacKintosh's argument for Theism, the Oracle states that since it is the theist who is asserting the existence of something, the burden of proof is on him, for "negative" truths are by their nature more difficult, if not impossible, to prove. In its words:

> To allow all sorts of assertions to pass unchallenged, because it may be impossible logically to demonstrate their falsehood, would

---

[31]"Undecimus," "Plurality of Causes," Reasoner X (1850-51): 267; C. Bradlaugh, The Freethinkers' Textbook, Part II (London: Freethought Publishing Co., 1876), pp. 137ff; H. Townley (ed.), Report of a Public Discussion carried on by Henry Townley and G. J. Holyoake in Scientific Institution, John Street; on the Question "Is There Sufficient Proo Existence of a God?" (London: Ward & Co., 1852).

[32]W. Chilton, "A 'Vulgar Atheist's' Opinion of Mr. Mackintosh's 'Pure' Humbug," Oracle of Reason I (1841-42): 197.

be to give free and undisputed passage to every wild conceit, every crude and undigested notion of vagrant imaginations.[33]

Occasionally, the freethinkers stooped to the level of sheer ridicule. In his article "Celestio-Inferno-Super-Humano-Mundanities," Malthus Ryall writes:

> Soul! God!! Devil!!! Hell!!!!!--what complicated perplexities, what sublimated immaterialities, what monstrous phantasies, and what abhorrent enormities have not these speculations called forth when taught and accepted as realities? Should we then dismiss these subjects with contempt or disgust? Not while they are sincerely and conscientiously entertained by the few or the many. Who shall presume to decide in what particular instances, under what peculiarities, or apparent absurdities of belief, sincerity and conscientiousness abide? None . . . When personal interference is a result, resistance is a duty. When active oppression is practiced, self-preservation may warrant a defensive or aggressive course in return, the right measure of which would be appropriately determined by our comparative strength and judgment.[34]

About the only achievement of these outbursts was to confirm to the orthodox that freethinkers were indeed irreverent and troublesome rabblerousers who were to be squelched at all costs.

Even more serious to the freethinkers than the charge of multiplying explanations was their conviction that the entire superstructure of orthodoxy rested on a belief that was intellectually absurd--that is, belief in a personal, all-powerful, all-good deity. According to the Oracle:

> Belief in a god is the fallacy of fallacies, the most preposterous, the most impudent, and the most mischievous of all fallacies. That fallacy once fully exposed, religion's death-warrant is signed and sealed.

---

[33]"M.," "Is There a God?" Part XX, Oracle of Reason I (1841-42): 285.

[34]M. Q. Ryall, "Celestio-Inferno-Super-Humano-Mundanities," Movement I (1843-44): 58.

> To strike at the fallacy the *Oracle of Reason* was first set on foot. To show it a lie has been the great aim of those who write for this paper.[35]

The evidence was intellectually compelling. Furthermore, given their system in which rational man is of necessity convinced when presented with sufficiently rational evidence, failure to be convincing is all a lack in the evidence--never in the receiver of the evidence. To be deficient in instilling conviction of truth is to be false. Or, more accurately, to the freethinker, to be deficient in instilling rational conviction of truth is to be false. Reason alone carried truth.

The freethinkers liked nothing better than to turn the traditional arguments for God against their proponents. If the victim incriminates himself, what more need be said? In concluding an article on just this point, M. Q. Ryall seems almost to gloat:

> The other god-believers pitted against each other are Mr. Gillespie and the Rev. J. Smith, and if like the Kilkenny cats, they have fairly devoured one another body and bones, why the less trouble is left to us the ungodly--we have nothing to do but to pitch the tails after them.[36]

Contemporary arguments for God included variations of the traditional bases for a natural theology--argument from first cause, argument from motion, argument from design, and argument from god-consciousness. The argument from adaptation--that change in aid of survival implied a changer--was simply the design argument updated and modified to accommodate observation of development in species over time.

---

[35] "Is There a God?" Part XXII, *Oracle of Reason* I (1841-42): 321.

[36] M. Q. Ryall, "Armour for Atheists," *Movement* I (1843-44): 290.

To the argument from the need for a First Cause or a Primer Mover, the freethinkers responded that the orthodox violated their own first premise, that all effects must have a cause. Why should the premise be invalid when applied to the Uncaused Cause or Unmoved Mover? Who was responsible for them? The believers then merely pushed the problem farther back. Why not simply assume the eternality of the material Cosmos? Such a belief explained the evidence equally as well in rational terms.[37]

Attacking the design argument was particularly enjoyable because its soundness had been a central theme of that nineteenth-century cornerstone of Natural Theology, William Paley's **Natural Theology, or evidences of the existence and attributes of the Deity**. To the freethinkers, it was absurd to argue that seeing "design" proved a designer unless one had the idea of a designer in mind already. The most one might deduce, according to one freethinker, "is a fashioner of that which was previously existing." He goes on to state that

> if we understood the fashioning of worlds as well as we do the fashioning of watches, we might then perhaps be justified in pretending to talk seriously about world fashioners--not **makers**, be it again observed.

Orthodox theologians were clearly arguing out of their element.[38]

---

[37] G. J. Holyoake, "Is There a God?" Part XXI, Oracle of Reason I (1841-42): 291-94; Robert Cooper, "The Logic of Atheism," Investigator IV (1857-58): 113; "Anthony Collins," "Letters to Our Young Men" Part II, Investigator V (1858-59): 46; G. J. Holyoake, "Is There A God?" Part XIV, Oracle of Reason I (1841-42): 163; Holyoake, "Is There a God?" XV (1841-42): 170-71; W. Chilton, "Twenty-Five Reasons for Being an Atheist," Reasoner X (1850-51): 380.

[38] "G. A.," "The Watch Argument," Oracle of Reason I (1841-42): 160.

Furthermore, as Thomas Paterson pointed out, Paley's watch-finder could deduce a watch maker from a watch because he had had previous experience with watches and watchmakers. No such experience had prepared men for confronting universes.[39]

If one were to move from the existence of apparent "order" in the world to that of an "orderer," he also had to explain the existence of "disorder." Did the disorder exist with the Orderer's permission--in which case one must question his morality? Or did it exist in opposition to the Orderer--in which case one must question his power? Why not simply accept what is and forego the need to explain?[40]

Charles Southwell noted that the argument from design is as equally capable of proving multiple designers as one designer. The orthodox again undercut their own position, for, without the aid of revelation, which the natural theologian wants to leave out of the picture as long as possible, there is nothing in the realm of reason to necessitate the Christians' dogmatic acceptance of one designer over many.[41]

---

[39] T. Paterson, "Harmony of the Godlies," Part II, Oracle of Reason II (1842-43): 237.

[40] "Mr. Thomas Cooper's Lectures in Blackburn," Investigator V (1858-59): 224; G. J. Holyoake, Paley Refuted in His Own Words (London: Hetherington, 1843); C. Southwell, "Is There a God?" Part VIII, Oracle of Reason I (1841-42): 111; G. J. Holyoake, "Is There a God?" Part X, Oracle of Reason I (1841-42): 130-131; "'R. M.' to the Editor of the Oracle of Reason," Oracle of Reason I (1841-42): 184; T. Paterson, "Harmony of the Godlies," Part I, Oracle of Reason II (1842-43): 218; "Sentimental Theists and Natural Theology," Part III Movement I (1843-44): 52-53.

[41] C. Southwell, "Is There a God?" Part XII, Oracle of Reason I (1841-42): 149.

As far as seeing in adaptation reason for belief in God, freethinkers argued that, again, the orthodox are guilty of begging the question. They assume that which they seek to prove. That which exists can be as rationally explained in terms of having survived because of its adaptation as in terms of its having been adapted in order to survive. There is no need for an adaptor.[42]

To argue from man's conscience or consciousness to the existence of a Supreme Being seemed especially presumptuous. For one thing, it was a non-rational source of knowledge. Second, it was a sort of aggregate response of a person to his world and could not contain other than that to which it had been exposed. Therefore, it would be inherently impossible for an Atheist to have an intuitive sense of God. If his consciousness spoke to him of a God, he would not be an Atheist.[43] This position could, of course, be attacked on the ground that here the freethinkers are assuming what they set out to prove. Nothing is in the consciousness that has not first been in experience; God has not been in the experience. Therefore, he cannot be in the consciousness.

All of the orthodox arguments were, at bottom, the result of circular reasoning in which the conclusions were presupposed in some way at the outset. Equally as fallacious as the various supposed arguments for a Supreme Being was the ascription to this Being of such properties

---

[42]"Mr. Thomas Cooper's Lectures in Blackburn," p. 223; G. J. Holyoake, "Is There a God?" Part XIII, Oracle of Reason I (1841-42): 156.

[43]"Mr. Thomas Cooper's Lectures in Blackburn," p. 224; "W. J. B.," "Descartes," Oracle of Reason II (1842-43): 218.

as intelligence, independence, personality, goodness, and so on. These qualities could in no way be logically derived from existing evidence.[44] The Christian God was clearly the product of faith in revelation, not of sound reason. As such, He was, at best, unknowable, and therefore irrelevant to daily existence, and, at worst, a figment of the imagination capable of all sorts of abuse in the hands of power, and of much foolishness in the hands of ignorance.

If the freethinkers were impatient with the orthodox defense of deity, neither did they have time for half-way efforts to accommodate reason and the supernatural.[45] Reason and revelation had no common ground. Honesty, in the sense of loyalty to things as we know them, demanded a forsaking of any explanation that went beyond the demands of tangible evidence. Man was on his own in the world, for all practical purposes; the sooner he came to terms with that truth, the better for everyone.

What was true of the central dogma of Christianity was true of the whole. It was irrational. If its tenets could not be "known" through rational means, they were not worthy to be called "knowledge" at all.

---

[44]"Aliquis," "New Argument on Theology," Reasoner XIX (1855): 58; "Sentimental Theists, and Natural Theology," Part III, p. 53; C. Southwell, "The God of Nature and of the Bible Identical," Movement I (1843-44): 235-36.

[45]See refutations of William Gillespie's philosophical argument for God. G. J. Holyoake, "The A Priori God," Movement I (1843-44): 120; C. Southwell, "Fallacy of 'The Argument A Priori,' for the being and attributes of God, as that Argument is stated by William Gillespie," Movement I (1843-44): 105-6; "Aliquis," "Mr. Gillespie's Argument A Priori," Movement II (1845): 110-113; "Deists," Oracle of Reason I (1841-42): 393-94.

Continuing to pursue this road to "truth" was futile, and an affront to the human quest for progress and improvement.

Apart from the belief in God, several other doctrines of the Church received particular attention as manifestations of Christianity's essentially irrational character. Among these were, first, the doctrine of the Atonement--which, apart from its moral repulsiveness, made no sense at all. How was it reasonable to punish innocence instead of guilt? How could the punishment of the innocent have any bearing on the state of the guilty?[46] Second was the belief in resurrection. Even if it were sensible to think that eternal life was desirable, and even if it were plausible that Jesus did rise from the dead, there is no rational basis for extrapolating from his experience to that of mankind.[47] Third was the doctrine of the Trinity. The Christians themselves, much to the delight of the freethinkers, had furnished the language for this discussion. It was they, not the unbelievers, who had, in their attempt to articulate their belief, first applied the term "incomprehensible" to the three-person God.[48] On that point of orthodoxy, the freethinkers could only agree.

---

[46] "The Atonement," Investigator I (1854-55): 113.

[47] F. B. Barton, "The Doctrine of the Resurrection," Reasoner XII (1851-52): 407-410; "The Early Christians and Their Opponents," Conclusion, Oracle of Reason II (1842-43): 20-1.

[48] Reference to Athanasian Creed. For further discussion of the "problem" of the Trinity, see "The Conversion of the Rev. Joseph Barker," Movement II (1845): 27; J. B. Lear, "What is God?" Oracle of Reason I (1841-42): 379; G. J. Holyoake, "The Jew Book," Part II, Oracle of Reason I (1841-42): 289.

Clearly, the Christian claim to be rational could be discounted. Moreover, its other bases for making truth statements were in no way adequate to shore up a dogma that could not be defended on rational grounds. The freethinkers took a dim view of Christian arguments from history or miracles or personal experience.[49]

Finally, unbelievers deplored what appeared to be Christians' efforts to switch the ground of the conflict when their own position was in danger. Christians were forever using the very abstruseness of their doctrine as proof of its veracity or minimizing the seriousness of their leap of faith by seeing precedents for such behavior in daily life. If all else failed, they fell back on arguing from majority opinion.[50]

To the freethinkers, reason and faith were enemies, not allies, and reason was the way of truth and the way of life in this world. In Holyoake's words:

> If practical measures are to be our aim, . . . we ought only to talk of practical things. The gods we should leave to those who can afford to be crazy. . . . I think that the most careful believer in a barren god is influenced for the worse by his belief. The idea is unphilosophical. A single error is pernicious. The belief in a deity is an error of cardinal magnitude. For this reason I could not advocate the belief of the abstractest conception of deity. It would be, in my opinion, advocating a lie.

---

[49]Austin Holyoake, "A Catholic Organ Reasoning on a Miracle," Reasoner X (1850-51): 319-320; "Miracles," Oracle of Reason I (1841- 42): 417; "E. L. T.," "A Few Words on the Historical Evidence of Christianity," Reasoner VI (1849): 50-53; "L. H. Holdreth," "Apology for the Secularists," Reasoner XXII (1857): 21; "Holdreth," "Theism of the Heart," Reasoner XXII (1857): 82.

[50]"W. J. B.," "Oxford Theology," Part IV, Oracle of Reason II (1842-43): 221-13; "W. J. B.," "Oxford Theology," Part III, Oracle of Reason II (1842-43): 166-67; "W.," "The New Argument 'A Posteriori' For the Existence of God," Part III, Oracle of Reason I (1841-42): 430-31; Edward H. Guillaume, "Christian Reasoning," National Reformer V (1864): 145.

Besides, that which is not to influence human conduct is useless. If a man is uninfluenced by the belief in a deity, he does not want one--and if he is influenced by such belief, he is no longer a practical atheist--he is no longer strictly moral. Lastly, the christian world are influenced for the worse by their belief in deities. I know no shorter way of effecting their conversion, than by showing that such belief is unfounded in reason.[51]

Closely related to--at times even inseparable from--the intellectual objections to orthodoxy, were the moral objections. If Christianity as established in Victorian England was not true, neither was it right. Ordinarily, one might assume the first of these charges to be the more serious. With the freethinkers, one cannot be sure. To traffic in truth dishonestly was as heinous as, and certainly **more** destructive practically than, not to deal in truth at all. If pressed on the point, a freethinker would no doubt deny placing morality over orthodoxy. In fact, he would assert precisely the opposite--that right thinking must precede right doing. Why else would he be so concerned about the theology of the average Englishman? Nevertheless, increasingly, at the practical level, moral criteria came to judge issues of orthodoxy. And perhaps the two positions are not, after all, opposites, but affirmation in a sense of what both the freethinkers and the orthodox firmly believed--that ultimately, Truth and Right are one.

The moral charges against orthodoxy far outnumbered the intellectual. Whether this says more about the state of established religion or about the concerns of the freethinkers is a matter of perspective. At least it suggests that, given the practical objectives

---

[51]G. J. Holyoake, "The Socialist God," Oracle of Reason II (1842- 43): 212.

of the freethinkers, they perceived the long arm of organized religion more onerous on questions of behavior than on questions of thinking. No aspect of church behavior escaped the freethinkers' notice. They criticized its behavior in the political, socio-economic, moral, intellectual, and emotional realms.

Politics is the game of power. To say that the freethinkers criticized the Church's political behavior is to say that they objected to its way of dealing in power, especially its dealings in power with truth.

The freethinkers viewed the Church's hold on truth as a violation of traditional English liberty. An Englishman's right to think and speak as he pleased included the right to think and speak as he pleased about religion. This common ground of belief in the inviolability of the right of free expression united freethinkers with the fight for the unstamped press.[52] Further, it brought together several varieties of theological persuasion in the work of the Anti-Persecution Union that was founded after G. J. Holyoake's imprisonment in 1842.[53]

To the freethinkers, freedom of thought on religion and freedom to

---

[52] G. J. Holyoake, "The Government and the Working Man's Press," Reasoner XIV (1853): 209.

[53] See M. Q. Ryall, "Circular of the Anti-Prosecution Union," Oracle of Reason I (1841-42): 225; See note under "Subscriptions," Oracle of Reason I (1841-42): 224; At one point, the Anti-Prosecution Union even worked on behalf of an avowed Christian believer Robert Kalley. (See Kalley-Holyoake correspondence in Movement I.) Note that the terms "Anti-Prosecution Union" and "Anti-Persecution Union" are used interchangeably by the freethinkers.

express that thought were logical extensions of traditional rights.[54] It was inconsistent that they, as English freethinkers, should be denied rights accorded to Englishmen of other ideological persuasions.[55] As the following passage illustrates, the freethinkers plainly saw English justice operating on a double standard.

> Sceptics may be deluged with vituperative epithets, by the champions of 'the truth as it is in Jesus,' their characters may be assailed, they may be accused of the vilest motives, and the whole force of wit be expended to bring them and their most hallowed principles into contempt; and yet, if a sceptic let fall a strong expression, or with raillery, would shame men from the folly of their creeds, he is to be thrust into gaol. We have heard from the lips of persons, and read in works, purporting to be apologies for Christianity, language as abusive as the English vocabulary will supply and sarcasm as withering as they could make it. <u>Our</u> feelings are not to be respected. It is not supposed that the sentiments we entertain and which we consider essential to the happiness of our fellow-creatures, principles for which we would make sacrifices of station and prosperity, are as dear to us as are the doctrines of a religionist to him. The opponents of sceptical philosophy may let fly the arrows of ridicule, but the same weapons we may not use in return. We are to be treated as though we had a hide like a hippopotamus, while they are to be handled as tenderly as lambs.[56]

In fact, according to current statutory law, the freethinkers, if he had once been a believer, was less free to express disparaging views of orthodoxy than the Jew or Moslem who had never come under the influence

---

[54]"W. J. B.," "The Right of Private Judgment," <u>Oracle of Reason</u> II (1842-43): 177; G. J. Holyoake, "On the Connection Between Style and Thought," <u>Oracle of Reason</u> I (1841-42): 178; Holyoake, <u>Last Trial By Jury For Atheism</u>, p. 66.

[55]G. J. Holyoake, "Letter to Lord John Russell," <u>Reasoner</u> XVIII (1855): 1; "H. J.," "Shallowness of Persecutors' Pleadings," <u>Oracle of Reason</u> I (1841-42): 125-127.

[56]<u>Ibid.</u>, p. 126.

of Christian teaching.[57]

The logic of the freethought position was not as clear to everyone else in England as it was to the freethinkers. Blasphemy laws had protected deity since time immemorial. Whether the original lawmakers had thought that God needed the defense, or whether they had had some interest in seeing that He be defended is debatable. What is clear is that the status quo stood in opposition to unlimited freedom of expression in areas that affected the freethinkers. That they made repeal of blasphemy laws a primary agenda item is quite understandable.[58]

The unbelievers despised Christianity's use of force to propagate and defend its position. Apart from the moral question involved, using force to defend orthodoxy suggested, at the very least, doubt about one's position. More important, it was an offense against truth, for truth is its own power of conviction. It needs no help. In Bradlaugh's words:

> If Christianity be from God, it needs no Act of Parliament to defend it; if it be not from God, it should not have its falsehood guarded from attack by a Parliament-created shield.[59]

Resorting to force to defend one's position was, to the freethinkers, a sign of weakness, not of strength. It confirmed in their mind the

---

[57]C. Bradlaugh, "Freedom of Opinion," **National Reformer** IV (January 10, 1963): 5.

[58]G. J. Holyoake, "The Abrogation of Blasphemy Laws," **Movement** I (1843-44): 225.

[59]Bradlaugh, "Freedom of Opinion," p. 5.

impoverishment of the orthodox case, for who would defend with force what would be obvious to reason.[60]

In one of his travel reports, Holyoake seems to delight in comparing his own calm, even-handed manner with those of his opponents whose "intellect lay in their fists." He notes that the police at the scene of the debate only too obviously sided with the faithful while the freethinkers "managed their own affairs."[61] It was a matter of honor, with a hint of self-righteousness, to the freethinkers that they did not respond to Christian provocation in kind.[62]

Its perceived violation of English liberty and its use of force are manifestations of what, to the freethinkers, was the heart of the problem of orthodoxy and power. That is--secular and sacred authority spoke with one voice in Victorian England. Together they formed an unbreachable line of defense of the status quo. Existing institutions

---

[60]See, for example, "Dissenters," Oracle of Reason II (1842-43): 41; G. J. Holyoake, "The Evidences of Christianity Displayed," Part II, Oracle of Reason I (1841-42): 95; W. Chilton, "Another Prosecution for Blasphemy," Oracle of Reason I (1841-42): 203; "Manifesto of Matilda Roalfe, Bookseller," Printed in Oracle of Reason II (1842-43): 404; For a sarcastic treatment of the implications of the use of force, see M. Q. Ryall, "God's Instruments," Movement I (1843-44): 186-87; G. J. Holyoake, "The Police of Religion," Reasoner XIII (1852): 70; Karl Heinzen to Archbishop Hughes," Reasoner XXI (1856): 105-6.

[61]G. J. Holyoake, "Adventures in Whitehaven," Reasoner XI (1851): 254-55.

[62]G. J. Holyoake, "Rationalism, the Legitimate Opponent of Catholicism," Reasoner X (1850-51): 277-80.

could claim divine sanction.[63] Existing orthodoxy could muster the secular powers-that-be in its aid.[64]

The freethinkers viewed the monopolistic wielding of Truth and Power represented by the Political-Ecclesiastical Establishment as the source of much evil in Victorian society. That conglomerate was the chief perpetrator of working class oppression and stood in the way of any aspirations of remedying the sorry state of the masses. Above all, it militated against the free reign of Reason, which alone would bring ordered reform and justice for the individual and society alike.[65] As it was, those with the most power to change the situation had everything to gain by keeping things the same.

The State and Church each brought its particular weapons to the defense of their collective authority against the light of Reason and Knowledge. The State used force. The Church used fear.[66] Both

---

[63] Wm. Chilton, "Notes Upon the Gloucester Prosecutions," Oracle of Reason I (1841-42): 308; G. J. Holyoake, "O'Connell and Jesus Christ," Movement I (1843-44): 114; T. Paterson, "Little Faith Much Gain," Oracle of Reason II (1842-43): 81; M. Q. Ryall, "A Scourge for the Godmongers," Oracle of Reason I (1841-42): 346; "Iconoclast," "Last Words," Investigator V (1858-59): 258; "Politics of the Apostles," Oracle of Reason II (1842-43): 49.

[64] "English Justice," Oracle of Reason II (1842-43): 208; G. J. Holyoake, "Dogmatism and God," Oracle of Reason I (1841-42): 258-59.

[65] John Scott, "Reform," Investigator V (1858-59): 200; Preface to Reasoner XVIII (1855): iii; Oracle of Reason I (1841-42): 18.

[66] See especially series in Reasoner IX on "Catholicism, The Religion of Fear," published later as a single volume by the same title (London: James Watson, 1850). With the aid of illustrations, Holyoake seeks to portray the irrational and manipulative nature of all reli- gion-- Catholicism simply serving as a particularly hideous variety. Chapter titles include "The Case Stated between Catholicism and Rationalism," "The Terrors of Catholicism, as exemplified by its expounders," and "Father Pinamonti Measureth the Thickness of the Walls of Hell."

exploited ignorance and superstition to maintain traditional faith in hierarchy, authority, and revelation that buttressed their seemingly unassailable position.[67]

The Church's socio-economic stances grew logically out of its privileged position in England's power structure. This being the case, the freethinkers' "social" and "economic" criticisms of orthodoxy are hardly surprising. First, to the freethinkers, the establishment betrayed a decided class bias. Second, an established Church was an indulgence that England could ill afford. Third, as in the political realm, the church was, in the socio-economic realm, a hindrance to necessary reform for England's working classes.

Both the application and enforcement of orthodox dogma worked against the poor. England did not get nearly so worked up over the excruciating poverty of the masses as over a slight misfortune to someone of the wealthy classes.[68] Some suggested that the very fact that the poor existed at all was proof of the bias of God, and hence his followers, in favor of the wealthy.[69]

The Victorian Sabbath was particularly noxious to the freethinkers and specific evidence that the religious law of the land weighed more

---

[67]"The 'Reasoner' Among the Red Coats," Reasoner XV (1853): 261-62; "Hints of Politics," Oracle of Reason II (1842-43): 22-23; J. Griggin H., "Christian Charity and Forbearance," Oracle of Reason I (1841-42): 398.

[68]"W. J. B.," "The Right of Private Judgment," Oracle of Reason II (1842-43): 178.

[69]T. Paterson, "Religion," Oracle of Reason I (1841-42): 353; W. Chilton, "Can Sceptics Be Philanthropists?" Reasoner XI (1851): 295-96.

heavily on the poor than on the rich. The wealthy had perpetual leisure. They were free six days a week to enjoy nature and to take advantage of opportunities for cultural enrichment. Furthermore, they had their own means of transportation. Closed galleries and curtailed train service one day in seven created no hardship for them. It was the poor, those who most needed the rest and recreation of the day, who bore the brunt of Sabbatarian Blue Laws.[70]

Freethinkers suspected the Establishment of using religion to keep the poor in their place. The Church was not as interested in the salvation and wellbeing of the poor as ends in themselves, but as means to keeping them servile.[71]

Further evidence of this conviction was the apparent variation in degree of alarm expressed toward unorthodoxy, depending upon the social status of the professed unbeliever.[72] Freethinkers had no patience with a government which permitted "blasphemy in guinea volumes" while

---

[70]"The Moral of the Sunday Agitation," Reasoner XXI (1856): 1; G. J. Holyoake, "The Rich Man's Six, and the Poor Man's One Day: A Letter to Lord Palmerston," Reasoner XXI (1856): 1-2; Arthur Trevelyan, "The Insanity of Mankind," Reasoner Tract 27, p. 3., printed in Reasoner X (1850-51); H. L. Harrison, "A Sunday in London," Reasoner Tract 10, p. 4., printed in Reasoner IX, (1850); "Priestcraft," Movement I (1843-44): 304; Holyoake, "The Religious Side of the Sunday Bill," Reasoner XIX (1855): 113; G. J. Holyoake, Bygones Worth Remembering, II: 271; "Notable Things," Movement I (1843-44): 229.

[71]G. J. Holyoake on Southwell's Trial. Oracle of Reason I (1841-42): 88; Holyoake, "The Bishop of Down and Connor and Dromore," Movement I (1843-44): 362.

[72]Bradlaugh, cited in Bonner, I: 139; G. J. Holyoake, "Lewes's 'Comte' and Leigh Hunt's 'Religion of the Heart,'" Reasoner XV (1853): 273; M. Q. Ryall, "Atheophobia," Oracle of Reason II (1842-43): 155.

displaying "the holiest horror" when it appeared in penny pamphlets.[73]

In the Holywell Street Case,[74] the charges of a double standard of justice for rich and poor were mixed with charges of a different justice for Christian and Atheist. The seizure of an apparently blasphemous poster from the window of a freethinker's shop had resulted in a broken window. On hearing the case, a judge decided against the shopkeeper and refused to award him compensation for damages on the grounds that he should not have been displaying the poster in the first place. In the words of the Oracle:

> The aristocrat, acting upon the principles of feudality, considering all plebians as his serfs, **commands** the removal of the offensive paper, and obedience not following, breaks the windows, steals and destroys the property, and threatens the owner with death. On the other hand, the man of traffic and fraud, goes to his den, takes counsel with his cub--a whelp after his own heart, and whom he is evidently bringing up in the way he should go-- sneaks back, when there are no men present, jumps upon the counter, and, like his proto-type, steals a placard, which he hands, in the language of the Old Bailey, to his 'juvenile associate.' Had a similar robbery been committed upon a christian, by a fellow-Christian, the penny-a-liner reporting it would have commenced, with 'HOARY VILLANY AND YOUTHFUL DEPRAVITY,' but
>   When an Atheist's in the case,
>   All villany, _of course_, gives place,
> and it will be found recorded in the journals of the lord, as 'praiseworthy zeal,' and 'pious enthusiasm.'[75]

It was the second socio-economic issue, the cost of an Established Church, that first brought the ire of the authorities against G. J. Holyoake. In the presence of the men, women, and children of

---

[73] G. J. Holyoake, Last Trial by Jury for Atheism, p. 55.

[74] For a description of this case, see the following issues of Oracle of Reason: December 31, 1842, January 7, 1843, and January 21, 1843.

[75] W. Chilton, "More Robbers of 'Our Shop,' and more Christian Justice," Oracle of Reason II (1842-43): 11.

Cheltenham, Holyoake had been so bold as to suggest that, given the present amount of suffering in England, it might be more sensible if the Deity were to be placed on half pay.[76] The audience was not amused. To the freethinkers, however, the burden of rates and compulsory tithing, like the Sabbath laws, hit hardest on the poor who could least afford to pay, and who least availed themselves of the services of the Church.[77]

Finally, the Church was a roadblock to lasting significant social and economic change. It worked against the best interests of the working classes. Most detrimental was the notion that poverty was somehow in the very order of things, even perhaps God-ordained.[78] It was not to be fought, but to be accepted. This, to the freethinkers, was a lie of unforgivable proportions. The doctrine of original sin merely encouraged this attitude of resignation and passivity. If man is flawed, he is incapable of significant improvement. Even were he to produce a better state of affairs for himself, he could not pass it on to the next generation.[79] Thus, there would be no permanent progress.

---

[76]Arrest Warrant for Holyoake at Gloucester Assizes, 1842. Holyoake Collection, Bishopsgate Institute, London. For Holyoake's own account of the situation given at his trial, see The Trial of George Jacob Holyoake, p. 22.

[77]Walney Wilverhurst, "The Injustice of Tithes," National Reformer VI (1865): 701-2.

[78]"A Parable for the Poor," National Reformer III (May 10, 1862): 5; E. Guillame, "The Christian Church and the Working Classes," National Reformer V (1864): 307; F. B. Barton, "The Doctrine of the Resurrection," p. 426; "Discussion at Northampton," Investigator V (1858-59): 232; T. Paterson, "Signs of the Times," Oracle of Reason I (1841-42): 385-86; M. Q. Ryall, "Call to the Unconverted," Movement I (1843-44): 37-38.

[79]"J. C. F.," "Christian Ignorance of the Contents of the Bible," Oracle of Reason I (1841-42): 279.

Even apart from its doctrines, the Church's actions showed a marked bias against social improvement. The Church was always the last to adopt change of any sort.[80] It favored capital punishment, which served only to satisfy the masses' baser instinct for revenge.[81] The Church persisted in sending vast quantities of money to convert the heathen while people starved in England.[82] It ignored bodies in an effort to save souls.[83]

The Victorian faithful would, no doubt, have had much to say in defense of their social efforts. There are always two sides. But a balanced account of the "facts" is really beside the point here. The freethinkers believed that Christianity and social reform were antithetical. That is the truth upon which they acted. Thus, in one sense, that is the truth that matters in seeking to understand their position.

To the freethinkers, the Church fell painfully short of being "right" in matters of moral teaching. The Church, according to the unbelievers, was thoroughly deficient in moral character. First, God himself and his revelation in the scriptures established poor examples

---

[80] G. J. Holyoake, "Civilization in Scotland," Movement I (1843-44): 34; Holyoake, "What Have the Priesthood Done for Progress?" Reasoner VI (1849): 13.

[81] "W. A.," "The Influence of the Religious Teachings of the Age on Questions of Social and Political Progress," Reasoner VI (1849): 306-7.

[82] "The Statistics of Demoralization," Movement I (1843-44): 68.

[83] "Eugene," "The Church and the Poor," Reasoner IX (1850): 89; "Interesting State of Sheffield," Reasoner XI (1851): 249; "C. H. M.," "Christian Influence on Physical Development," Reasoner XVI (1854): 285; "Iconoclast," "Cleanliness," National Reformer I (April 14, 1860): 5; J. Barker, "The Obstructives," National Reformer I (September 22, 1860): 2.

for upright living. Second, Biblical teaching on the nature of man degraded human nature to the point that man did not have a right view of himself and his capabilities of pursuing the good. Third, Biblical morality, because it emphasized and appealed to what was worst in man rather than to what was best, was unworthy of being the basis of morality in a civilized society. Fourth, the Bible very unfairly held man accountable in the end for what he was incapable of accomplishing on two counts--both because he is the product of necessary patterns of cause and effect beyond his control, and because he is divinely predestined to eternal salvation or eternal destruction with absolutely no say in the matter.

Not only was its moral teaching corrupt. The Church, both past and present, had a hideous record of failure to live up to its own moral standards. The freethinkers never tired of reminding the Church of the Inquisition, the Crusades, various forced conversions, and other violent chapters in its history. Churchmen were hypocrites, and encouraged hypocrisy in others. They were arrogant and self-righteous. When it was to their advantage to do so, freethinkers even referred to themselves as the "true" Christians or at least as the ones better embodying Christian morality than the Christians themselves.

Freethought literature abounded in illustrations of the depravity of Biblical characters, including the person of God Himself.[84]

---

[84]See, for example, "W. B.," "Abuse and Ridicule," Oracle of Reason I (1841-42): 334-35; W. Chilton, "The Lewdness, Impurity, Grossness, and Obscenity of the Scotch God," Oracle of Reason II (1842-43): 297- 99; Chilton, "Second Arrest of Paterson and Robbery of His Shop," Oracle

According to the Oracle:

> . . . Its [the Old Testament] unphilosophical description of the earth's creation, its accounts of the chosen people fuddling, whoring, robbing, cheating, lying, and commission of incest--its cities and towns, like Sodom and Gomorrah, . . . its minute details of most detestable cruelties and horrid murders, all presided over by an immoral monster!--must necessarily drive the finest sensations out of the human heart, and make it the receptacle for everything corrupt, vitiated, and depraved. . . .
> Come we now to glance at the Christian theology, or new-testament doctrine, which its admirers have not failed to puff off to the best advantage. Here too, their god who professes to white-wash others, has not whitewashed himself, but comes in his bloodstained garments to be clothed with other specimens of cruelty and injustice, in the death and suffering of his own son![85]

Christian morality, as represented by the Bible, was unjust. It demanded, in many cases, what was contrary to nature.[86] It punished innocence and forgave guilt.[87] The concept of atonement, especially, was plainly unfair. If Christ were innocent, his death could be nothing

---

of Reason II (1842-43): 306; T. Paterson, "Godology," Oracle of Reason II (1842-43): 327-28; "W. A.," "The Influence of the Religious Teachings of the Age on Questions of Social and Political Progress," p. 309; W. Chilton, "The Immoralities of Christianity," Reasoner XII (1851- 52): 315; Speech by J. Barker, "Work for the Christian To Do," printed in Reasoner XVI (1854): 247; J. Watts, "A Secularist's Estimate of Jesus Christ," National Reformer I (June 23, 1860): 6; Francis Neale, "The Obscenity of the Bible," National Reformer XVIII (1871): 172; Charles Watts, "Thoughts on the Character of the Bible God," Part II, National Reformer XIX (1872): 406-7; See "Iconoclast's" various "Lives of Bible Heroes" in Investigator, e.g. Vol. IV (1857-58): 101, 115.

[85] T. Paterson, "The Christian Religion," Oracle of Reason I (1841- 42): 335.

[86] "Radical Opponency of Religion to Humanity," Reasoner VI (1849): 60; J. Barker, Investigator I (1854-55): 15-16; T. Paterson, "Religion Destructive of Morality," Oracle of Reason II (1842-43): 138.

[87] "The Faith and Facts of Christianity," Reasoner XXI (1856): 18.

but cruel, and his Father who allowed it, nothing but sadistic.[88] If God were as loving as scripture claimed, how could he condemn people to hell anyway? Why could He not forgive without payment?[89] Christian morality belittled man's good works.[90] What particularly irked the freethinkers was the phenomenon of death-bed conversions.[91] The worst sinner could escape with apparent impunity simply by uttering a few words prior to departing this world.

Holyoake was deeply troubled by the corrupting influence of scriptural narratives on the minds of impressionable readers. In revealing and combatting the immorality of the Bible, unbelievers themselves, according to Holyoake, only exacerbated the situation by focusing on the lurid passages they wished to discount.[92] Holyoake

---

[88]A. Besant, An Autobiography, p. 99; G. J. Holyoake, "Defence of Opinion Against the Clergy of Lancaster," Reasoner XI (1851): 61; "Progress of Dissenting Theology," Reasoner XII (1851-52): 321-22.

[89]"Report of Meeting at Nottingham," Investigator V (1858-59): 182; "The Recent Prosecutions for Blasphemy," Circular of the Anti-Persecution Union published as a Supplement to the Oracle of Reason, p. 4.-- Found in July 23, 1842 Oracle; "The Faith and Facts of Christianity," Part II, Reasoner XXI (1856): 25; "The Faith and Facts of Christianity," Part III, Reasoner XXI (1856): 33; "Hell," National Reformer II (August 10, 1861): 1-2; "Hell," cont., National Reformer II (August 17, 1861): 1-2; H. V. Mayer, "The Doctrine of Hell and Eternal Punishment Scripturally and Morally Considered," National Reformer XX (1872): 113-14 and continued in three subsequent issues.

[90]"Newcastle Debate on the Moral Aspects of Christianity," Reasoner XV (1853): esp. 56.

[91]See, for example, G. J. Holyoake, "Don't Tell us How He Died, Tell Us How He Lived," Reasoner XVIII (1855): 49-50.

[92]This issue later became a point of issue between Holyoake and Bradlaugh. Holyoake broke a publishing contract with Bradlaugh after the first chapter of The Bible, What It Is on the grounds that it glorified Christian immorality inadvertently by magnification.

argued that a more edifying strategy would be to eliminate all of the scriptures that were unsuitable for human consumption and then publish an abridged edition "rendered on the neutral ground of morality."[93] If the Bible must be read--and Holyoake thought it would be, by the young, from necessity, because thoughtless parents compel; by the old, because interest commands; by many, from peculiarity of taste[94]--let it at least be a rendition "that guardians may recommend without compromise of their scruples, and children may read certainly without injury to their morals."[95] The edition featured annotated paraphrases of Bible stories with predominant emphasis on especially moral and especially immoral aspects of the narrative.[96] The "Ten Commandments" became Five.

> 'Honour thy father and mother. Neither kill, nor steal, nor bear false witness, nor covet the property of others.' Exodus, chap 20. These are all of the ten commandments which are repeatable now. The others are wanting in justice or truth, in utility or decency.[97]

To the freethinkers, what was "true" in Biblical morality could be known as well without special revelation. So, for the reasoner, even the "good" of scripture was rendered superflous in the search for

---

[93]G. J. Holyoake, "The Moral Remains of the Bible: A Version of the Scriptures not 'Authorised' but Suitable to be Read in 'Churches' and 'Sunday Schools,'" Reasoner V (1948): 17.

[94]Ibid.

[95]Ibid. For a more complete discussion of this abridged Bible, see the series on "The Moral Remains of the Bible," Reasoner V (1848): June 7, June 14, June 21, June 28, July 5, July 12 and so on.

[96]For examples, see Holyoake, "Magnanimity of Esau," Reasoner V (1848): 81-83; Holyoake, "The Adventure of Moses in Midian," Reasoner V (1848): 97-98.

[97]Holyoake, "The Moral Remains of the Bible," Reasoner V (1848): 113.

truth.[98] The rest was downright pernicious and fit only for elimination.

Apart from providing such poor examples for a person to follow, Christianity left a man with a distorted view of himself that militated against his striving for moral justice and improvement in this world. The Church degraded human beings so that they lost sight of their value and potential.[99] The introduction to Volume I of the Reasoner illustrates this notion when it laments the existence of 23,000 clergymen in Great Britain who "cripple the moral energies of men, humiliate their native spirit, and divert them from independence and social amelioration."[100]

Specific targets of this criticism were the Christian doctrine of original sin, and, following from that, man's need for a salvation which he is inherently incapable of procuring.[101] Such beliefs make man

---

[98] Holyoake, "Relation of Christianity to Morality and To Progress," Reasoner V (1848): 357; T. Paterson, "The Christian Religion," Oracle of Reason I (1841-42): 335-36.

[99] "Mr. Holyoake's Reply to the Rev. Dr. Kerns, of St. James Church," Reasoner X (1850-51): 459; Holyoake, "The Sting of Conscience," Reasoner IX (1850): 73.

[100] "Editorialities," Reasoner I (1846): 1.

[101] "Reviews," Investigator IV (1857-58): 77-78; Charles Dent, "The Worth of Man," Oracle of Reason I (1841-42): 350-51; Joseph B. Lear, "What Is God?" Oracle of Reason I (1841-42): 411; M. Q. Ryall, "Scheme of Universal Progression," Movement I (1843-44): 4-5; Ryall, "Scheme of Universal Progression," Part II, Movement I (1843-44): 10-11; Charles Watts, "Secularism and Christianity," National Reformer IX (1867): 258-59; "Firmian," "Rationalism in the Church," Reasoner XII (1851-52): 103; John Watts, "The Christian Fallacy of Human Depravity," National Reformer VII (1866): 9; "The Fall of Man," National Reformer IV (December 12, 1963): 5; "The Christian Doctrine of Man's Depravity Refuted," National Reformer VI (1865): 835-36.

dependent, and lead, either to a false sense of security, or to apathy and despair. Either way, it takes away his sense of control and dignity, and as such, places him in a false and unjust position.

Equally devastating to human potential is the Christian notion of prayer. By placing man in the helpless role of supplicator, it too decreased his sense of self-reliance and independence. It encouraged him to hope instead of to work. To the freethinker, any hope that was not grounded on one's own work was no hope at all. Thus, dogma about prayer simply provided man with a counterfeit panacea that fostered laziness and ended in hopelessness.

From a number of angles, petitionary prayer was ludicrous. For one thing, according to the freethinkers, there was no listener to hear prayers. The laws of the universe worked, irrespective of prayer. Rain falls on the just and on the unjust. So does sunshine.[102] Attributing these occurrences to a Person provides comfort for the ignorant, but has nothing, in reality, to do with explanation.[103] Second, even supposing there was a God, it would be counterproductive to ask him to change the very laws of the universe as a way of counteracting man's irresponsibility that failed to take those laws into account. Such notions grew out of, and continued to perpetuate ignorance, irrationality, and irresponsibility.[104] Third, again supposing there were an all-wise, all-powerful God, would it not be foolish to tell Him what He already knows? The man of prayer:

> . . . tells the Lord his wishes, his wants, and desires, as if he did not know these things--as if infinite wisdom and goodness did not know what is best for him. Now, if God knows all these things better than man; and will perform that for his creatures which he

in his wisdom knows best, what is the use of prayer? where is its utility?[105]

If God is moved in response to prayer, He is changeable, and therefore not to be relied upon. He is at the mercy of His creatures, and hardly therefore the omniscient, omnipotent Being that He is purported by the faithful to be.[106] Furthermore, what if an equal number of petitioners asked God for opposite things? Would the prayers cancel out? A favorite scenario of this criticism was the case of war. As the *National Reformer* described the situation:

> In the late war between France and Germany, the armies and people of either side undoubtedly prayed for success. It was an impossibility for the prayers of both to be granted. If success in arms is to be regarded as the answer given to prayer--and Jewish history seems to have been written with the express purpose of showing that it is--then the German prayers were heard, and the French prayers were rejected. To regard any person or nation as humbled and cast down by God, is to administer a powerful stimulant to one's own pharisaism and spiritual pride. But the result was just what would have happened if both the French and German nations had been Infidel; that side won which had the greater numbers, superior discipline, better generalship, and exacter information. And the Germans won equally when they believed they were resisting invasion and annexation, and when they were practising invasion and

---

[102]"The Christian Theory of Prayer," *National Reformer* III (April 26, 1962): 1-2; "G.," "On the Doctrine of Special Providence," *National Reformer* XX (November 3, 1872): 1; "W. B.," "The Efficacy of Prayer," *National Reformer* I (June 23, 1860): 6; Holyoake, *The Uselessness of Prayer*, Secular Tract, No. 5, 1860.

[103]"Vorley," "An Inquiry into the Efficacy of Prayer," *National Reformer* XX (1872): 177.

[104]"The Christian Theory of Prayer," p. 1.

[105]Ibid.

[106]Ibid.

intending annexation. The goodness of a cause has nothing to do with victory in arms.[107]

Prayer is, all told, simply irrelevant.

Even more than it is ludicrous, petitionary prayer is dangerous to the human race. It wastes human energy that could best be put into the pursuit of practical matters. Knowledge, not prayer, is the answer to human need. Prayer is a "badge of slavery, a sure sign of barbarism and superstition."[108] Prayer fosters a "spirituality" in man that is characterized by "self-distrust and self-abasement, and a tendency to morbid fear."[109] It discourages him from doing what he could do himself. Men overlook the sensible and obvious because of reliance on the irrational and obscure.[110]

Christianity, because of the fact that it degraded men, and appealed to what was basest in them, rather than to what was best, was unworthy of being the basis or morality in a civilized society. The morality built on Christianity was constructed of fear, anger, ignorance, and superstition. It was a negative morality, cajoling people to do the right to avoid the consequences of doing wrong, rather

---

[107] "Vorley," "An Inquiry into the Efficacy of Prayer," Part II, National Reformer XX (1872): 197-98.

[108] "The Christian Theory of Prayer," p. 2.

[109] "Vorley," "An Inquiry into the Efficacy of Prayer," Part II, p. 197. See also Reasoner Tract 57, Sylvian Marechal. (trans. by J. B. Lear) "What is An Atheist?--Being the Preliminary Essay to the Dictionary of Atheists," printed in Reasoner X (1850-51): immediately following 462.

[110] For examples, see "The Christian Theory of Prayer," p. 1; "Report from Hanley," Reasoner XV (1853): 166; "Discussion at Northampton," Investigator V (1858-59): 221.

than from love of right doing as an end in itself.[111] To the freethinker, goodness needed no foundation apart from itself, and it was its own reward.

It was an insult to moral law to make it dependent on personal relationships. That was to make it capricious. Morality was a science whose laws were as inexorable and discoverable as the laws of physics or biology. Knowledge of its operation and power was public property, to be harnessed for the common good.[112] One freethinker suggested that Christ's moral teaching made each individual his own judge of morality in telling people to do as they would have others do to them. (Matthew 7:12) It was subjective and therefore unworthy of a scientific age.[113] Charles Watts, too, denied the universal applicability, and therefore, the adequacy of Christian morality, but for a slightly different reason. Christian morality was not, in fact, available to all men. Furthermore, it was not consistent with itself. The same actions were sometimes right, sometimes wrong, and most contradictory, Christian morality

---

[111] T. Paterson, "Fruits of the God-Idea," Oracle of Reason II (1842-43): 10; Frank Grant, "Bishop Butler on Rewards and Punishments in a Future Life," Reasoner VI (1849): 116; "W. J. B.," "Jesus and the Moral Aspects of Christianity," Reasoner XI (1851): 243-46; F. B. Barton, "The Doctrine of the Resurrection," p. 410.

[112] George J. Holyoake, Reasoner I (1846): 147; "Supernaturalism, Considered As a Question of Moral Influence," Part III, Oracle of Reason II (1842-43): 50-52; T. Paterson, "Religion Destructive of Morality," p. 138.

[113] "W. J. B.," "The Law of Jesus," Oracle of Reason II (1842-43): 355.

demanded perfection while teaching man's incapacity to attain that perfection.[114]

Freethinkers argued that Christianity, in some cases, actually worked against good. It made "faith," an abstraction, more crucial than "works," a reality. Biblical passages about the need to "hate" father and mother, wife, children and one's own self (Luke 14:26) only confirmed suspicions that Christianity and morality were not on the same side.[115]

Christian morality, too often, fostered deferred goodness. It encouraged postponing the good things of this life, which seem to be equivalent to those things that make for happiness, for the life hereafter. The Christian finds himself in constant turmoil between the pull of the things that make for joy in this world and the things that make for joy in the world to come.[116] He is, of all men, most to be pitied.

Perhaps the most indicting moral charge leveled at Christianity is the problem related to the Biblical doctrines of accountability and predestination. Man is a depraved creature, whose best efforts are no better than "filthy rags." (Isaiah 64:6) He is ordered to be perfect, (Matthew 5:48) only to be told that it really does not matter what he does or does not do since all matters of eternal destiny have been

---

[114]C. Watts, "Christian and Secular Morals," **National Reformer** VI (1865): 113-114.

[115]**Investigator** V (1858-59): 91.

[116]"Religion," **Investigator** V (1858-59): 154; Holyoake, "To Dr. Kalley," **Movement** I (1843-44): 345.

decided irrespective of action on his part. (Romans 9) Thus, Christian morality assumes man has choices--demands rewards, and punishes as if he does--when he does not. It presupposes a freedom which it does not give him. Christian morality is an unforgivable mockery, unworthy to be called a morality at all.[117]

Apart from the injustice inherent inside Christian theology itself is the injustice that is created when Christian morality encounters the "real world." Man **must** not be held accountable for his actions because he is a creature of cause and effect. Especially, it would be grossly unfair to punish him eternally for what he cannot help.[118]

The freethinkers argued that, by recognizing the necessitarianism in the universe, man is free to rise above it and become master of his fate. The Christian thinks he is free when he is not; the freethinker, in accepting that he is not free, is the truly liberated one. To G. J. Holyoake, the concept of freewill in the universe was not, as it apparently was to the believer, a good thing. Rather, "freewill seems the synonym of chaos in nature, of disorder in ethics, of confusion in life."[119] It leaves man uncomfortable, insecure, with no sure logical foundation on which to stand.

---

[117]"The Saint's Consolation," Oracle of Reason II (1842-43): 224; "W. A.," "A Word About the Jews," Reasoner VI (1849): 184; "Undecimus," "Omnipotence," Reasoner IX (1850): 267-68.

[118]See, for example, C. Southwell, "The Free Inquirer's Why and Because," Oracle of Reason I (1841-42): 395; "The Responsibility of Christians Examined," Reasoner XX (1856): 145; "Theological Responsibility False and Obstructive," Reasoner XX (1856): 137-38.

[119]Holyoake, "The Philosophic Type of Religion--Developed by Professor Newman: Stated and Examined," Reasoner XI (1851): 99.

Christianity was morally objectionable on practical as well as theoretical grounds. Not only did Christianity not have a morally-sound morality; Christians did not even practice the morality they had.

Freethinkers were not reluctant to remind Christians of their past and present record of intolerance and persecution, both at home and overseas. The very present arrests and trials of the freethinkers kept the practical moral question alive. When there were no martyrs for truth on the English scene, examples from far off places and other times provided ample illustration of Christians' failure to live up to the moral light available to them.[120] Difficulty of documentation seemed no hindrance to compilation of the following table--purported to be a record of the Church's efforts to burn the "branches" that failed to abide in the "vine." (John 15)

---

[120]Charles Watts, "Secularism and Christianity," National Reformer IX (1867): 243-44; Holyoake, "Prison Discipline," Oracle of Reason II (1843): 86-88; W. Chilton, "Second Arrest of Paterson and Robbery of His Shop," p. 305; "The Scotch God War: The Trials of Robinson and Paterson," Oracle of Reason II (1842-43): 391; Holyoake, "Trial of Miss Roalfe," Movement I (1843-44): 61-2; Arthur Trevelyan, "To the Right Honorable Sir James Graham, Bart., & Her Majesty's Ministers," Movement I (1843-44): 269-70; "On the Materialism of Philosophers and Poets," Reasoner III (1847): 406-7; Holyoake, The Spirit of Bonner in the Disciples of Jesus (London: Cleave & Hetherington, 1842); Lectures by Mr. Holyoake on "Missionaryism in India," Reported in Sheffield and Rotterham Independent March 27, 1858; "God and Anti-God in India," Oracle of Reason I (1841-42): 406; W. Chilton, "The Wonders of Missionary Meetings," Reasoner X (1850-51): between pp. 98 and 99; C. Bradlaugh, "To the Rev. C. H. Kelly, Wesleyan Home Mission Society," National Reformer XVIII (1871): 177.

Epochs.	Grand Inquisitors and Sovereigns	1st Class, burnt alive	2d Class, burnt in effigy	3d Class, imp. with confisca. of property
1481 - 1498	Torquemada	10220	6860	97321
1498 - 1507	Archbishop Disa	2592	896	34952
1507 - 1517	Cardinal Ximenes	3564	1232	48059
1517 - 1522	Car.Adrian aft.Pope	1520	560	21845
1522 - 1523	Interregnum	324	112	4369
1523 - 1538	Cardinal Manrique	250	1125	11250
1538 - 1545	Cardinal Tavera	840	420	5460
1546	Cardinal Loaisa	120	66	600
1556	Charles V	1200	600	6000
1556 - 1597	Philip II	3690	1845	18450
1597 - 1621	Philip III	1840	920	13848
1621 - 1665	Philip IV	2816	1408	10386
1665 - 1700	Charles II	1728	864	6912
1700 - 1746	Philip V	1584	782	11730
1746 - 1754	Ferdinand VI	10	5	179
1759 - 1788	Charles III	4	-	56
1788 - 1808	Charles IV	-	1	42
	Totals	32382	17690	291450 [121]

In general, Christians were hypocrites and encouraged hypocrisy in others. They said one thing and did another. To uphold accusations on this count, freethinkers used examples from Christian behavior in workhouses,[122] Christian behavior in speaking and debating,[123] and Christian behavior toward the poor.[124]

Freethinkers resented the equation of "respectability" and piety that seemed rife in actual Victorian Christianity. "Respectability" was

---

[121]"Holy Use of the Bible," Oracle of Reason I (1841-42): 32.

[122]"Chaplains for Workhouses," Herald of Progress I (1845-46): 61.

[123]Holyoake, Reasoner IX (1850): 157-58; Holyoake, Reasoner IX (1850): 229; Holyoake, "Religious Policy," Oracle of Reason I (1841- 42): 250.

[124]W. Chilton, "Christian Consistency," Oracle of Reason I (1841- 42): 211.

not exactly Biblical,[125] yet the Church seemed remarkably amenable to change in that direction when it proved to her advantage to do so.[126]

Christians were so ready to lower the heavy hand of law and order on freethinkers. Yet, if they were truly interested in instituting Christianity as "part and parcel of the law of the land," they themselves would be as guilty of offenses as the worst heretic in the country. Nothing was more universally accepted as representative of Christianity than the Sermon on the Mount; on its terms, all Christians stood indicted.[127]

The Christian hypocrisy closest to the heart of the freethinkers was the insistence that an Englishman, regardless of religious belief, swear an oath in order to be considered a credible witness in a court of law. To refuse to swear was to be a non-person. To swear by that in which one does not believe was at best, foolish; at worst, it was a blatant lie. If a man's word was not enough on its own merit, how was its credibility to be improved by being accompanied by an oath when, in the process of taking the oath, the man perjured himself?[128]

Christians were hypocrites. They were also arrogant to the point of "blasphemy." The freethinkers who claimed not to believe in a God, accused Christians of presumption and nerve in speaking so confidently

---

[125] T. Paterson, "A Shot At a Shutter," Oracle of Reason I (1841- 42): 332-33.

[126] C. Southwell, "Common Sense," Oracle of Reason II (1842-43): 183.

[127] "Christians in Danger," Oracle of Reason I (1841-42): 377-379.

[128] See, for example, Holyoake, Bygones Worth Remembering, II: 80.

of His existence, of His actions, and of His attributes.[129] Ironically, the freethinkers, at a number of points, actually put themselves in the position of defending God against His own followers.

Holyoake, especially, charged the Christians with being the true party of irreverence. No one offended him more on this count than Baptist evangelist Charles Spurgeon. After one service, Holyoake accused him of an "irreverence of insensibility and presumption" that was far less pardonable than the "irreverence of passion." In Holyoake's words:

> For the space of an hour, he spoke of the Son of God with a gross familiarity that he would not dared to have employed in the case of the Prince of Wales, nor would the audience of Exeter Hall have permitted the same liberties to be taken with the Court of St. James's they thought rather good when taken with the Court of Heaven. Such is the Evangelical Mind.[130]

The National "Thanksgiving" given in 1849, in honor of the retreat of the cholera epidemic, also drew Holyoake's "righteous indignation." He argued that "To thank heaven that it has spared us, is to assume that after all it *did* inflict the late epidemic upon us. Can that gratitude be pleasing to Deity which carries with it so offensive an imputation?"[131] If "straight" is best understood by being next to

---

[129]Holyoake, "Lessons in Blasphemy by an Evangelical Minister," Reasoner XVIII (1855): 97-101; Holyoake, "Letter to Mr. Elton Andre," Reasoner XIX (1855): 57; Holyoake, "Review," Oracle of Reason I (1841-42): 263; "W.," "The New Argument 'A Posteriori' for the Existence of God," Part I, Oracle of Reason I (1841-42): 317- 318; Holyoake, "The Principles of Naturalism," Part III, Movement I (1843-44): 20; "God-Belief and God-Believers," Movement I (1843-44): 437.

[130]Holyoake, Reasoner XIX (1855): 28; Holyoake, Reasoner XIX (1855): 90.

[131]Holyoake, "The Inconsistency of the late 'Thanksgiving,'" Reasoner VII (1849): 321.

"crooked," the theological arrogance that so offended Holyoake is perhaps best seen in Holyoake's "Secular Prayer." Prepared to begin a second night of debate, Holyoake outlined a hypothetical reverse image of the Christian prayer of the previous evening.

> O Lord, who art so loudly said to exist, and to answer the call of thy creatures: if such be the case, we may without irreverence ask Thee to answer ours also.
>
> Thou whose secret every priest professes to have penetrated--Thou upon whose Name the most illiterate are encouraged to call, and whose powers even the vulgar are taught to invoke--we pray Thee to pardon the familiarity which approaches Thy great Presence, and dares to trouble the God of a Million Worlds with our petty strifes and our insignificant claims.
>
> Conscious that if any seek the Truth the ample Book of Nature lies open to all, and the only fee demanded of the poorest is Attention--we therefore will not prefer requests which presuppose that the Great Author of all Knowledge requires continually to amend His lessons--or which pretends that He has given to his creatures such imperfect powers, that ever so honestly exercised they are inadequate to the duties of the sphere in which he has seen fit to place them.
>
> Nor will we be guilty of the irreverence of supposing the Unchangeable--who is no respecter of persons--will stoop from High Heaven in order to give one obscure disputant a victory over another! Did a petition seem to us becoming, all we would ask would be good taste and goodwill, that we might clothe the truth in grace and keep our hearts in love--good taste, that if having the truth we might so present it that others might come to see it, clearly and undeformed--goodwill, that we might so speak of the truth that others might learn to love it. But good taste is an incommunicable talent. It can come only of cultivation, and is ever the inherent result and reward of study--and goodwill is the highest triumph of the noblest creed. It is that discipline which a pure and true life should give. It is not what men should ask. It is the true, the silent, the unpresumptuous homage, they should offer to God. Men therefore ought, once for all, to ask Thy pardon for ever praying, and learn that self-reliance is the reverential duty, discipline the chastest worship, and good feeling the purest praise. Amen.[132]

The prayer suggests that perhaps arrogance was not the monopoly of the Christians. Affected humility does as well as indecent presumption.

---

[132]Holyoake, "A Secular Prayer," Reasoner XVII (1854): 370.

Thus, to the freethinkers, apart from the question of "truth," Christianity was to be discounted for its failure, both on grounds of belief and grounds of behavior, to live up to the "right." That it also was not true in the minds of freethinkers is a belief of which the reader has already been apprised. The final moral indictment of Christianity that involves both the freethinkers' standards of truth and right is the charge that the Church deliberately discouraged the pursuit of accommodation to Reality. It, in effect, handled truth dishonestly.[133] That it taught falsehood was incriminating enough. That it hindered the unbridled pursuit of truth--therein suggesting its preference for falsehood--sealed the case.

The right of private judgment was a Protestant and an English legacy. The right to be rationally convicted of truth was a human legacy. Christians violated both in their dogmatic, emotionally-laden[134] efforts to maintain their own articulation of truth as the established expression of orthodoxy. By telling men what to think, the Church discouraged the exercise of man's best gift, his reason. It took away his right and duty to think for himself.[135] Furthermore, such

---

[133]For example, see Holyoake, "Is There a God?" Part X, Oracle of Reason I (1841-42): 129.

[134]For examples of freethought's objection to emotional manipulation, see: T. Paterson, "Harmony of the Godlies," Part II, Oracle of Reason II (1842-43): 235; J. Griffin H., "Christian Charity and Forbearance," Oracle of Reason I (1841-42): 397; "Sermon Card," Reasoner VI (1849): 102; "The Showman and the Gospel," Reasoner X (1850-51): 23; "Decomposition in the Churches; Revivalism the Sign," Reasoner XXIV (1859): 369.

[135]"Christianity Tried by Cases for Half an Hour," Reasoner XVII (1854): 337; Passage from Wigan Debate cited in Bonner I: 168; See Martineau quote in leader of Reasoner XVIII (1855): "Among the

behavior suggested that the Church had something to fear or something to hide from truth. Only the guilty run from light.[136]

To the freethinkers, any restraint of total freedom to pursue truth was, of necessity, detrimental to the triumph of reason and progress for the human race. Truth would show itself and the honest had nothing to fear.[137] Moreover, truth showed itself best in the forum of free discussion where it was least likely to be shackled by the biases of an individual perspective.[138] To put limits on the discussion was to violate, not only human nature, but truth itself. It was evil of the lowest order.

As if it were not enough to charge Christianity with immorality in politics, in ethics, in handling truth, the freethinkers added a further

---

few things of which we can pronounce ourselves certain, is the obligation of inquirers after truth to communicate what they obtain."; J. Maughan, "Freethinking, Its Sphere, Power, Necessity and Results," Investigator V (1858-59): 50; M. Q. Ryall, "Godlies and Ungodlies," Oracle of Reason I (1841-42): 363; "Address from Mr. Holyoake," Oracle of Reason II (1842-43): 75; Holyoake, "Modern Freethinking: Its Definition, Sphere, and Defence," Reasoner XII (1851-52): 81-2; F. B. Barton, "Free Inquiry Has No Limits But Truth," Reasoner XV (1853): 177-79.

[136] T. Paterson to the Editor of the Oracle of Reason, Oracle of Reason I (1841-42): 215; Holyoake, "The Better to be Safe System," Oracle of Reason I (1841-42): 281; C. Southwell, "The Free Inquirer's Why and Because," Part V, Oracle of Reason I (1841-42): 297-98; T. Paterson, "To Our Readers," Oracle of Reason II (1842-43): 1-3; "Freedom of Expression," Movement I (1843-44): 218.

[137] Holyoake, "Utility of Unlimited Inquiry," Oracle of Reason I (1841-42): 137; Holyoake, "Why?" Reasoner XVIII (1855): 97-98; Joh Scott, "The Investigation of Truth Requires the Exposure of Religious Contradictions," Reasoner XXII (1857): 42.

[138] "Speech of Mr. Holyoake Immediately Preceding His Arrest," from Circular of the Anti-Persecution Union--Supplement to Oracle of Reason I (July 23, 1842).

count of injustice. Christianity was immoral in the emotional realm. It failed to provide man with the basic human right of joy.[139] From Sunday school on, Christianity burdened man with unnatural rules, and clouded his mind with fear and dread of the consequences if he failed to meet the demands. "What a melancholy and unnatural state of things does it disclose in this school where not so much as a smile is permitted under pain of severe chastisement?"[140]

Thus, for the freethinkers, Christianity as established in Victorian England was bankrupt in either intellectual or moral terms. It embodied neither truth nor goodness. As interesting as the charges themselves is the fact that freethinkers, at one point, argued rather vehemently whether it was truer to be an atheist on moral or intellectual grounds.[141] Is it sounder to be a freethinker because Christians are hypocrites? or because Christianity is not true? The

---

[139]"Summary of the Debate Between Mr. D. King and Mr. G. J. Holyoake," Reasoner IX (1850): 301; Holyoake, "A Visit to Dr. Cumming's Church," Reasoner X (1850-51): 241; Holyoake, "The Preachers and People in Newcastle-on-Tyne," Reasoner X (1850-51): 422; "The Saint and the Secularist--Which Has the Best of It?" National Reformer I (January 26, 1961): 1-2; "Reasons for Rejecting Orthodox Christianity," National Reformer V (1864): 531; "Pious People," National Reformer VIII (1866): 146.

[140]"Sunday School Vices," National Reformer, III (December 21, 1861): 1.

[141]"The Late Malthus Questell Ryall," Herald Of Progress (1845- 46): 82; Letter to the Editor, "Why Are We Atheists?" Oracle of Reason I (1841-42): 318-320; Wm. Chilton, "Why Are We Atheists?" Oracle of Reason I (1841-42): 329-32; Chilton, "Why Are We Atheists?" Oracle of Reason I (1841-42): 341-43; Holyoake, "Three Causes of Scepticism," Reasoner XXII (1857): 65; Holyoake, "The Rev. Thomas Pearson's Prize Essay on Infidelity," Reasoner XV (1853): 8; Holyoake, "The Religious Views of the 'Leader,'" Reasoner X (1851): 386.

former implied a problem with adherence to a standard, the latter with the standard itself. The party line came down clearly on the side of fighting the standard: "We war not with the church, but the altar; not with the forms of worship, but with worship itself; not with the attributes, but the existence of Deity."[142] In refuting Robert Cooper, Holyoake argued that "The Universal Cause of Scepticism, and reason of its permanence, is the discovery of the insufficient evidence offered on the side of Theism."[143] Christianity, no matter how consistent, is still false.

In studying the nature of the freethinkers' conscious evaluation of Christianity, one cannot but be struck by several interesting elements implicit in the evaluation, though no doubt less obvious to the freethinkers themselves. For one thing, the freethinkers, despite their protestations of intellectual humility, proceed with a remarkable sense of confidence that their own standards of right and truth are accurate. They, of course, claimed to be relying on the sure foundation of reason. In doing that, they retained the almost naive Enlightenment idea that reliance on reason was of a fundamentally different nature than reliance on revelation. One led to knowledge and certainty; the other only to belief and faith. What they failed to see, or at least to acknowledge, was the assumptions that they themselves had accepted _a priori_.

Second, is the curious and paradoxical inter-relationship of the two sorts of charges against Christianity. The moral accusations in

---

[142]Attributed to M. Q. Ryall in "The Late Malthus Questell Ryall."

[143]Holyoake, "Three Causes of Scepticism," p. 65.

many cases appear to be presupposing the inappropriateness and even
falsehood, of the intellectual indictments. If Christianity is not
true, what does it matter if its adherents are hypocrites about their
own faith? It would then be purely an in-house affair. That the
freethinkers thought it significant to measure the practice of orthodoxy
against itself suggests at least that they found something of truth in
the existing structure, something more than they were consciously
willing to admit.

Though the freethinkers persisted in vowing to destroy established
religion, there is in their writing the slightest hint of "protesting
too much." One has the i pression that Holyoake, at least, wanted, not
"no religion," but rather a religion that he could be party to with
integrity. That is, in fact, precisely what he eventually got.

In judging the establishment by the very standards of which it
claimed to be the source and arbiter, the freethinkers had, in a sense,
allowed the Church to set the terms of the struggle between them. In
holding a mirror to orthodoxy, the freethinkers brought upon their heads
the wrath of all respectable Victorian Churchmen. If the reflection had
not been so painfully true to life, and the criticism so fraught with
frightening implications, the Church might have seen the freethinkers,
not only as enemies who threatened the foundations, but as allies who
saw and valued the same truth. In reality, they were both. That the
establishment chose to treat them as infidels simply confirmed to the
freethinkers the righteousness of their own cause, and lost for the
Church a class of men who could have been among its best critics.

III

Explaining the freethinkers' concern for theology in terms of their backgroun and perceptions of the Church is convincing, but hardly complete. It reflects merely the view from inside. From outside, it appears that "theologizing" tainted working class radicalism partly because it served a useful function. A Christian editor, reporting on one of the many debates between Christians and freethinkers in Sheffield, commented:

> Religious controversy on the platform has seldom yielded any beneficial results . . . It falls to but few to be able so to deal with these questions as, if not to convince the sceptic, at all events to inspire him with a feeling of respect for its advocate.[1]

The very element that discouraged this believer brought joy to the heart of the freethinker. People liked a good fight. They understood theological language. The Christians ended up on the defensive, and, characteristically, responded unbecomingly to being put in that position. Freethinkers accepted this as vindication of their own stand.

Thus, apart from the freethinkers' own background and convictions, theology was a popular subject for public discussion.[2] The clergy and

---

[1]Editor, **Sheffield Daily Telegraph**, Mon., May 17, 1858. From newspaper clippings in 1858 folder in Holyoake Collection, Bishopsgate Institute.

[2]The preponderance of theological topics in public discussions is

Christianity provided convenient whipping boys for a class of Victorian England that was essentially anti-clerical. It was easy to mistake enthusiasm for a good argument, and relish for the "exposure" of "respectability," for agreement with freethought dogma. The two were not to be equated. Nevertheless, the apparent response might well justify continuing a strategy focused in content and format around theological issues.

Even more compelling than the popular response as a functional explanation of theologizing in working class radicalism, is the way in which theological controversy served to cloak personality conflicts in intellectual legitimacy. This is not to suggest that freethinkers deliberately set out to cover up their interpersonal antagonisms with theological language. Rather, it is to acknowledge the tendency for human conflict to become de-personalized and abstract. People become symbols for causes. The more ultimate and righteous the cause, the more vicious and significant the fight, and the more heroic and innocent the participants. Regardless of the beliefs of participants or observers, the language of abstraction and principle in Victorian England was the language of theology. It is not strange then, that Victorian conflicts

---

evident in lecture advertisements of the various Institutes. In 1853, out of Holyoake's twelve standard lectures, 5 titles suggested strong anti-Christian sentiment--(e.g. "Moral Objections to Christianity," "Christian Secularism, Limited, Subordinate, and Contradictory"); 4 more had what one might safely call theological themes--(e.g. "Science the Providence of Life," "The Progress of Reason in Religion.") See Lectures by George Jacob Holyoake, for the year 1853, Holyoakes Envelopes, Holyoake Collection, Bishopsgate Institute, London. See also programs in Holyoake folders for John Street Literary Institution, Manchester Hall of Science, Finsbury Square Hall of Science, and in Bradlaugh Papers, 1865 Slate of Lectures at Hall of Science. National Secular Society Collection, Bishopsgate Institute, London.

would be argued in theological terms with theological categories.

The freethought movement was a tangle of interpersonal antagonism. The very qualities that made one a free spirit in the first place militated against the cooperation and submission necessary to constitute and perpetuate a "movement." In a logical sense, the very idea of a "Freethought Movement" was impossible. The freethinkers themselves were not blind to the threat of anarchy inherently present in the ranks. Though committed dogmatically to absolute liberty of individual thought and expression, they were quick to reprimand their own who appeared to be engaging in personal power plays, and persistently affirmed the existence of some transcendental truth that would eventually triumph amidst the vicissitudes of any particular person or project.[3] The natural element in such a conglomerate as freethought would be disparity. That there was at least the appearance of a measure of coherence is the surprise. And it is to the focus on theological matters that we, in part at least, owe this coincidence of the "Freethought Movement."

At times, the rivalry among freethought leaders did stoop to the level of blatant attacks on persons. More often it took on the categories and the self-righteous dogmatism of the power against which all the freethinkers had declared war. As individual freethinkers

---

[3]T. Paterson, **Letters to Infidels on Charles Southwell's Manifestations of Friendship and Pangs of Gratitude for the Late Deeply Lamented MQR of the 'Movement'** (London: T. Paterson, 1846), pp. 6-8, 16; Holyoake, **Rationalism: A Treatise for the Times** (London: J. Watson, 1845), examines freethought movement after the failure of Owen's Harmony Hall; W. Turley, **Mr. Holyoake and His Detractors--An Address to the Friends of Progress** (London: W. Goddard, 1858).

staked out their own claims, they found enemy weapons and enemy territory, not only useful, but essential, for they did not yet have their own.

There was a conflict to match every meeting of two freethinkers. To say that, is, in one sense to say nothing more than one might say about the meeting of any two persons. In another sense, however, it is to highlight the emotionally-charged atmosphere inevitable in a movement that espoused both the ideals of tolerance for individual thought and commitment to finding and articulating ultimate truth. One might very appropriately choose to summarize the history of freethought in terms of personal rivalry. Between 1840 and 1870, four inter-personal conflicts embody the major points of tension over dogma, proselytization strategy, and allocation of resources that characterized the freethought movement. These rivalries include Holyoake and Southwell versus Owen; Holyoake versus Southwell; Holyoake versus Robert Cooper; and Holyoake versus Charles Bradlaugh.

The leading freethinkers of the 1840's had been groomed in Robert Owen's Rational Society. Charles Southwell and G. J. Holyoake were both, at one point, commissioned Socialist missionaries. Holyoake continued to serve on the Rational Society Central Board even after resigning as a stationed missionary. During the 1840's, it is not always easy to determine where Socialism ends and freethought begins, for both were heirs of the Rationalist Enlightenment tradition. In terms of an immediate cause, it was in combatting the monolithic organization and autocratic leadership of the Rational Society that the freethought movement began to take shape. Southwell and Holyoake were such devoted followers that they became, in their own minds, more truly Socialist than the Socialists--more Owenite than Owen.

Two issues became the center of the controversy between Owen and his disciples, Southwell and Holyoake: first, the degree to which atheism was essential to Socialism; and second, whether a new rational world order could be built before the old supernatural world order had been dismantled. In other words, should socialist efforts be primarily constructive or destructive? Southwell's Oracle of Reason became the platform and focal point of the Atheistic Socialists. Owen continued to publish the New Moral World. Harmony Hall, an experiment in community living, gave form to Owen's constructive vision of Socialism and proved to be the financial and emotional undoing of the Old Socialists.

In 1839, at the 8th Rationalist Congress, the Central Board of the Rational Society had ordered its missionaries to refrain from theological discussions. Socialists had, during meetings, traditionally been anti-supernaturalist. Since that image was thought to have offended many potential Socialists, atheism was no longer to be part of the official Socialist credo. Such a pronouncement proved easier to make than to enforce. In 1841, Charles Southwell founded the Oracle of Reason with the declared purpose of upholding the atheist tradition. The editor viewed the Oracle as the "only exclusively Atheistical print that has appeared in any age or country."[4] In his words:

> Atheists reject supernaturalism in toto, as a principle and a thing--holding deism to be just as much a rank superstition as any other form of supernaturalism . . . Now, atheism, or anti-

---

[4]Preface. Oracle of Reason I (1841-42): i.

> supernaturalism (for both terms mean precisely the same thing,) is in our view, the only consistent, the only useful, and the only justifiable conclusion, to which those who take reason for their guide can arrive at--and we are of the opinion, that in the volume of the Oracle of Reason, now submitted to the investigation of all, who dare to read and think, there are arguments against the existence of supernatural being or agency, that may safely defy, and will ultimately bear down, all opposition.[5]

The Oracle, and its successor, the Movement, provided the forum for a lively discussion of the proper relationship between atheism and socialism that carried over into the Rational Society's local branches.[6]

Part of what offended the Anti-Owenites was, not the directive against theological discussion itself, but the fact that the directive had been given. The very idea that one segment of freethought could declare a position that rendered another part of the movement "unorthodox" was inimical to the spirit of freethought. In one of nine objections to the policy, a "Coventry Socialist Lecturer" argued that:

> . . . the resolution is an infraction of the principles of the society as laid down in the Outline of the rational system, more especially as laid down in the chapter on 'liberty of conscience,' the Outline having answered the purposes of the society, hitherto, when 'strictly' observed.[7]

When criticizing, Holyoake praised the virtues of criticism, particularly socialist self-criticism, by which he apparently meant rank-and-file comments on the leadership. In words that he would have done well to remember when he later found himself the "Owen" of

---

[5] Ibid., pp. v, vi.

[6] T. E. "To the Editor of the Oracle of Reason," Oracle of Reason II (1842-43): 365; "A Coventry Socialist Lecturer," "The Burnley God-The Coventry God-and G. J. H.," Oracle of Reason II (1842-43): 248.

[7] "A Coventry Socialist Lecturer," Oracle of Reason II (1842-43): 262.

freethought, Holyoake denounced the socialist dogmatic stance that, in effect, limited the freedom of thought for which the society stood.

> And why in another word should Socialists always be criticised by others and never by themselves? Why should we assume on our parts the possession of all virtue? I never could see why, and this is the reason I have more freely than any other member of the social body criticised the sayings, doings, professions, and pretensions of my friends. Not as some have erroneously thought, because I wished to quarrel with them, but because of anxiety to render them as perfect as possible.[8]

Holyoake, in a report on two of Owen's talks to his disciples, went so far as to suggest that Socialism had fallen into the theists' trap of relying on authority instead of on reason. Tactfully, he suggested that:

> Truth owns no man's name, but stands like a tower upon a hill, and the arrows of criticism fall harmlessly at her feet. Error, like Jonah, requires a gourd, flies to covers, deprecates searching, and fears attack because of mortality. The observation, which is more trite than newly born, is not without its application. Men, even the most rational, are too apt to grow in love with their opinions, and tremble to see them questioned . . . This may not be true of Mr. Owen, but probably somewhat correct of many of his friends.[9]

Southwell echoes similar sentiments in response to the reorganization of the Socialist movement in 1842. It would, in his mind, place too much power in the hands of the leaders, and like the Jesuits, share the advantages and disadvantages of an organization suffocated by unity.[10]

In opposing the "no theology" policy itself, atheists argued, in a sense, on grounds that were mutually contradictory. On the one hand,

---

[8]Holyoake, "Socialism and Social Policy," Oracle of Reason I (1841-42): 273.

[9]Holyoake, "Mr. Owen's Thirteenth and Fifteenth Addresses," Oracle of Reason I (1841-42): 97.

[10]C. Southwell, "Policy versus Principle--To the Socialists of England--Letter XII," Oracle of Reason I (1841-42): 179.

they objected to the policy as an artificial hindrance to the free pursuit of truth. Dogma is inherently limiting. On the other hand, they proceeded to defend dogmatically as a <u>sine qua non</u> of freethought, absolute disbelief in the supernatural. True, it was a negative limitation, but a limitation no less restrictive than that which Owen had proposed.

Any effort to put a fence around truth was inconsistent with Socialist principle. It placed Socialists in the position of compromising their integrity. In August 1842, while suffering in Gloucester gaol on blasphemy charges, Holyoake played the martyr to the hilt on this matter of Socialist consistency. He had not abandoned Socialism; in fact, he suggested that, in the minds of his persecutors, it is precisely because he is a Socialist--an Owenite--that he is suffering. At this very point when he is being held for the "cause," his own party is questioning his loyalty and maligning him as an atheist.[11] Later, after a public confrontation, in which Holyoake's position is challenged by one of the local Socialist branches, he announced that he would no longer be defending Socialism in public as he had done for two hours during his trial. Because his integrity had been questioned by his own party, he was, for the first time, "ashamed of being a socialist." In his words, "I shall still continue a member, and wait better times and the dominion of better principles before I can own, without blushing, that I am a Socialist."[12]

---

[11]Holyoake, "Socialism and Social Policy," p. 274.

[12]Holyoake, "Socialism According to Branch A1," **Movement** II (1845): 14.

Charles Southwell resigned as a Socialist missionary in protest over the prohibition against theological discussion. To him, the new policy smacked of expediency. To ask Socialist missionaries to swear to an oath to lend them the appearance of respectability in a hypocritical society was to ask them to be less than themselves. The issue for Southwell was clear-cut.

> The real question between those who take the oath, and those who will not, is simply this, are we justified in speaking falsely; when an inconvenience attaches to the promulgation of truth, can Socialists, on the ground of universal expedience, defend a course that is only to be commended because it is safe, and guarantees them for the present, at least, from the attacks of their enemies; I take the question on this broad ground, and distinctively say, no, they are not justified in the eye of reason, unless they are content to occupy a lower position than heretofore, as it is monstrous, and imbecility itself to prate about honesty and truth . . . while we dabble in falsehood upon occasion.[13]

While objecting to any dictated doctrinal policy from the top, Holyoake was absolutely convinced of the centrality of anti-supernaturalism to the Socialist position. The difference, of course, was that he was advocating truth based on reason. Owen was resting on the shaky foundation of personal expedience. It was inconceivable to Holyoake that anything could be more important than exposing the falsehood of religion. In a piece on "The Utility of Unlimited Inquiry," Holyoake asserted that:

> It probably is not exceeding likelihood to say that metaphysical errors have produced more suffering, done more to strengthen priestcraft and retard the progress of the human mind than all other mistakes put together.[14]

---

[13]"Aristides" (C. Southwell), "Policy versus Principle--To the Socialists of England--Letter IX," Oracle of Reason I (1841-42): 133.

[14]Holyoake, "Utility of Unlimited Inquiry," Oracle of Reason I (1841-42): 137.

This being the case, how could the destruction of this evil be given, not second place, but **no** place on the agenda of Socialist priorities?

In an early *Movement* editorial, Holyoake did pay at least lip service to the ideal of cooperation between the *New Moral World* and the *Movement*. What he appears to concede at the beginning of a paragraph, he quickly retracts by the end--in spirit, if not in letter. In Holyoake's words:

> Some have supposed that there will exist an antagonism between the *Movement* and the *New* [sic] *Moral World*. Nothing of the kind. Both papers labour to attain the same great objects--liberty and happiness; but the *Movement* takes a different field of exertion. I think the *New Moral World* should have embraced the *Movement* and wish that it would. *We* add theology to political economy. The errors of the priests are not less dangerous than the mistakes of capitalists. Socialism will be criticised in the *Movement*, but not in the spirit of antagonism. The present policy of Socialists I think not sound--the interpretation of Socialism not correct--the measures neither so vigorous nor practical as they might be; but they *may be* right. I arrogate no infallibility; I only venture to explain differences. I question not the Central Board's integrity--assume no dishonesty; I only impugn their judgment, and desire, if, indeed, I am able, to improve, not condemn.[15]

Somewhat paradoxically, Holyoake and Southwell and friends[16] found Owen's brand of Socialism objectionable both because it was too religious, and not religious enough. To Holyoake, religion was either the pillar of human conduct, government, education, employment and family life or it was nothing. If it is true, it "ought to occupy our

---

[15]Holyoake, "Editorialities," *Movement* I (1843-44): 17. Note Holyoake's use of word "theology." (line 6)

[16]The *Oracle of Reason* and the *Movement* housed supporters of the atheistic socialists who included M. Q. Ryall, W. Chilton, "A Social Missionary" with initials J. C. F., and a correspondent with initials R. R. See especially the two-part series "Principles of Socialism and the Policy of the Socialists" by a "Social Missionary," *Oracle of Reason* I (1841-42): 137-39, 161-63.

first attention." If it is false, it is a danger of the highest order and must not be toyed with for the sake of convenience. Either way, it was for Holyoake in 1843 the central issue. He could not abide Owen's apparent dismissal of religion as unworthy of serious discussion. In Holyoake's mind:

> He who cannot give sound reasons against religion should embrace religion; and he who would cavalierly denounce the faith of his fellow men, and refuse to justify his scepticism by argument, deserves not attention, be he Robert Owen, or G. J. H.[17]

Holyoake announced his intention to persist in making the question of atheism central to socialist thought whether or not Owen considered his opponent worthy to be taken into account. The issue was not merely a matter of semantics or quibbling for its own sake, as Owen had apparently suggested. Holyoake preferred to be hated honourably than to endure the shame of being despised.[18]

Nevertheless, in the very act of refusing to deal with theology, Socialism, under Owen, had, according to Owen's antagonists, taken on a religious character of its own. It had become a belief system, complete with a god, a doctrine, and an ethic. According to Southwell, Owen had mistaken his own vision of truth for an exhaustive vision of truth, and set himself up as a demi-god.[19] In addition to elevating himself as an infallible authority, Owen had committed the error of believing that two

---

[17]Holyoake, "Is Socialism a Religious System?" Movement I (1843-44): 51.

[18]Holyoake, "A Lesson to Atheists," Movement I (1843-44): 90.

[19]See Southwell, "Policy versus Principle--To the Socialists of England--Letter IX," Oracle of Reason I (1841-42): 116-18; Holyoake, Oracle of Reason I (1841-42): 90.

mutually incompatible elements--faith and reason, religion and philosophy--could co-exist.[20] To Southwell, reason and faith had no common ground. Reason was the province of truth, faith of belief and delusion. Philosophy belonged to the first, and religion to the second. The very suggestion of a Socialist doctrine, especially one that suggested Socialism's compatibility with orthodoxy, was anathema. Socialism was science, and therefore, must not resort to the weaker foundation of dogma.[21] Southwell concluded one of his "Letters to the Socialists of England" with the warning:

> Now I do not say that Mr. Owen, or those who have <u>urged him on</u> to stultify men's intellects by a 'modern antique' religion 'in accordance with the doctrine of the old and new testaments' commenced with downright roguery, but this I do say, that if they continue their doctrinaire tricks, they will end with downright folly. Who can bring a clean thing out of an unclean--<u>not one</u>.[22]

Holyoake's thoughts on the matter of Owen's "Rational Religion" are summarized in an editorial "Another New Religion." He also objects to the notion that religion has anything to do with truth, the former being a function of faith, the latter of fact. Unlike Southwell, Holyoake expresses concern over the detrimental practical effects of Owen's accommodation of Socialism to religion. The religious people will still distrust socialism because it is socialism and true socialists will despise it because it has stooped to clothe itself in "borrowed

---

[20]Southwell, "Policy versus Principle--Letter VII," Oracle of Reason I (1841-42): 108.

[21]Southwell, "Policy versus Principle--Letter X," Oracle of Reason I (1841-42): 147-49; See also Southwell, "Policy versus Principle--Letter XI," I (1842): 153; and Southwell, "Policy versus Principle--Letter XII," I (1842): 178-80.

[22]Southwell, "Policy versus Principle--Letter X," p. 149.

feathers."[23] There was nothing to gain by accommodation.

Owen's efforts to gain respectability for Socialism by disassociating it from atheism proceeded simultaneously with his efforts to give concrete form to Socialist dreams of an economic system in which the English working class could prosper.[24] In 1842, the Socialist Congress had authorized the beginning of a cooperative community project at Queenwood in Hampshire. This Home Colonization project symbolized for Owen and the "Old Socialist" the beginning of the New Moral World. To his opponents, it was a diversion that was sapping vital resources from the real mission of destroying tyranny and superstition. Holyoake criticized the project for its shaky financial foundation, for its obscure site, for its vague and ill-conceived goals, and finally, for its paternalistic treatment of the English working class.[25] His description of the difficulties encountered in trying to reach Harmony Hall appears deceptively in good fun. In reality, Holyoake saw no redeeming qualities in the project that he termed "squanderization" rather than "colonization."[26] He was particularly critical of the contempt in which the "rulers" at Harmony Hall held the ruled, given the

---

[23]Holyoake, "Another New Religion," Oracle of Reason I (1841-42): 169-70.

[24]For a brief history of the Rational Society's aims from its founding in 1835, see "The Duty of the Next Congress deduced from the history of Socialism, by a missionary of seven years' standing." Movement I (1843-44): 146-49.

[25]See the three-part series by Holyoake, "A Visit to Harmony Hall," Movement I (1843-44): 401-3, 409-13, 417-21; and Holyoake, "What Ought Congress to Do?" Movement I (1843-44): 137-38.

[26]Holyoake, "A Visit to Harmony Hall," Part II, p. 409.

society's supposed commitment to democracy.[27] Holyoake suggested that it would be wrong to blame the workers themselves for the failure of Harmony Hall. The fault was in the planning and the organization for which the Central Board should be held responsible. That the capital sources reneged on their commitments following Harmony's inauspicious beginning merely confirmed to Holyoake the folly of building working class prosperity on a middle class foundation. Clearly, the Central Board had abandoned its true raison d'être in too hastily diverting energy from anti-theological agitation to Harmony Hall. It had lost sight of its proper priorities and was bound to suffer the consequences.[28]

The acquisition of Queenwood for the Socialists proved to have been easier than its disposal. Occasional references to its failure and its financial implication for the society suggest that it remained a topic of controversy throughout the first half of the 1840's.[29] The Socialist/Freethought cause suffered a setback with the outcome of the Harmony Hall experience. Nevertheless, those, including Holyoake, who insisted that the cause of truth and freethought was bigger than any one project continued undaunted. Holyoake's new periodical, the Herald of Progress, begun in 1845, represented a deliberate effort to keep alive non-Owenite freethought.[30] For those who thought Queenwood's demise

---

[27] Ibid., p. 412.

[28] Holyoake, "A Visit to Harmony Hall," Part III, pp. 418-19.

[29] See, for example, "Communist Plans," Reasoner I (1846): 255.

[30] Introduction, Herald of Progress I (1845-46): 1.

signalled the end of freethought, the alarm--or hope--proved to be premature.

The fact that Holyoake and Southwell found themselves allies against Robert Owen did not prevent their fighting each other in the process. Holyoake was the junior member of this pair. He had joined the Oracle as editor after Southwell's imprisonment, and carried on the tradition of atheistic freethought for which the Oracle had been noted.[31]

Much of the rivalry between Holyoake and Southwell stemmed from their interaction while working on the Oracle. Holyoake charged Southwell with leaving the Oracle in such a way as to escape the impact of the notoriety which the Oracle had attained, due largely to Southwell's irresponsible accusations and dogmatic intolerance of Christianity.[32] Southwell replied that he, not Holyoake, was the one who had been betrayed. Holyoake had broken faith with Southwell in editing some of the material sent from Southwell's prison to be published in the Oracle "as is."[33] The two remained rather free in their character attacks on one another. Southwell, writing in the Investigator, accused Holyoake of the very crime with which they had

---

[31] Interestingly, William Chilton, regular columnist for the Oracle, asserted that the Oracle was not, in fact, proposing that all Socialists be atheists. Rather, it was simply supporting the right of freethought within Socialism. See Chilton, "You Will Injure Our Cause," Oracle of Reason I (1841-42): 262.

[32] Holyoake, "A Vindicatory Chapter," Reasoner III (1847): 613-14.

[33] "Mr. Southwell's Reply to the 'Vindicatory Chapter,'" reprinted from Daily News, Reasoner IV (1847-48): 19-20.

charged Owen--"Secular Popery."[34] He thought Holyoake rather presumptuous in claiming credit for the originality of ideas in his new work on secularism. In Southwell's words:

> Without a shadow of claim to originality, without even the semblance of a veritable 'system,' he has no right to assume, or attempt to make others think, Secularism something new, and something infinitely better than Freethinkers have, up to the coming of Geo. Jacob Holyoake, offered to the world.[35]

According to Southwell, Holyoake objected to stooping to personal recrimination in anyone but himself. Finally, he suggested that Holyoake could be bought, that flattery and financial contributions had diverted him from honest pursuit of truth.[36]

Not to be outdone, Holyoake charged Southwell with courting martyrdom, and with seeking to shock for its own sake. He then turned Southwell's own praise of the *Investigator*'s milder style against the *Oracle*, as further proof that Holyoake's positive approach to freethought was, in fact, the right one.[37]

Amidst the *ad hominem* darts flying through the air between Southwell and Holyoake were at least two matters of principle. (The protagonists, of course, would have us believe that it was all of principle. Southwell closed his lengthy letter to Holyoake protesting that "not a sentence of this letter has been written in a carping,

---

[34]Southwell, *Investigator* I (1854-55): 56.

[35]*Ibid.*, See also p. 55; and Southwell, *Investigator* I (1854-55): 27.

[36]Southwell, "Mr. Southwell's Reply . . . ," p. 26.

[37]Holyoake, "A Vindicatory Chapter," pp. 613-17.

petulant, or vengeful mood."[38]) First was their disagreement over the right reason for not being an atheist; second, their disagreement on proselytizing strategies. It need hardly be mentioned that these are variations of the very issues that had drawn Southwell and Holyoake from the Owenite camp in the first place.

Both Southwell and Holyoake had come, in the mid-1840's, to reject their dogmatic stance on atheism. Neither seemed terribly troubled by his own volte-face. Southwell outlined his apology in a series entitled "Impossibilities of Atheism Demonstrated." Holyoake, though never indulging in a full-fledged explanation for his change of heart, did acknowledge a reversal in Reasoner policy on the matter.[39] Holyoake's position during the late 1840's and 1850's might be termed classical agnosticism. He no longer denied the possibility of a God, but asserted the impossibility of knowing whether or not such a being existed.[40]

In responding to Southwell's arguments against theism, Holyoake suggested, first, that Southwell had made no argument at all. He had merely asserted its illogic and inexpedience--scarcely worthy service to truth.[41] The second of Holyoake's commentaries on Southwell's denunciation of atheism attacks Southwell's reasoning as word trifling. Holyoake argues that, just because "theism" is a logically absurd word

---

[38]Southwell, "Mr. Southwell's Reply," p. 28.

[39]Holyoake, "Mr. Southwell's New Pamphlet Examined," Reasoner XIII (1852): 115.

[40]For an understanding of Holyoake's views during this period, see Holyoake, The Trial of Theism (London: Holyoake and Co., 1858); and Holyoake, Principles of Secularism (London: Holyoake and Co., 1859).

[41]Holyoake, "Mr. Southwell's New Pamphlet . . . ," p. 115.

in that it does not correspond to a tangible object in human experience, does not, in itself, prove its negation meaningless.[42] Furthermore, in disputing the assumption that "Atheism" presupposed "Theism," Southwell was, in effect, putting truth at the mercy of error.[43]

Holyoake proposed an epistemological foundation of empiricism rather than logic. To Holyoake, the non-theist "affirms that natural reason has not yet attained to evidence of Supernatural Being." He does not deny that it may be so, because the capacity of natural reason in the pursuit of evidence of Supernatural Being is not, so far as he is aware, fixed. The capacity of reason, is not, as Southwell supposes, a matter of logic, but of experience.[44] In Holyoake's mind, Southwell's atheism is a pure negation, a belief in nothing. Holyoake's "non-theism," in the other hand, asserted a position that allowed for the possibility, at least, of truth outside of human comprehension.[45]

Apart from the question over proper atheological presuppositions, Southwell and Holyoake argued over the problem of "accommodation"-- easing the barriers between religion and freethought. Southwell thought Holyoake inconsistent and too ready to cater to the wishes of influential contributors.[46] Holyoake saw his actions as no different from what Southwell had done in moving from the Oracle to the

---

[42] Holyoake, "Mr. Southwell's New Pamphlet Examined," Part II, **Reasoner** XIII (1852): 129.

[43] Ibid., p. 130.

[44] Ibid., p. 130.

[45] Ibid., p. 131.

[46] "Mr. Southwell's Reply to 'A Vindicatory Chapter,'" pp. 24, 26.

Investigator.[47] Given the degree to which both Southwell and Holyoake would eventually espouse the language and faith of religion,[48] their suspicions of one another were no doubt justified. Holyoake's apparent confidence in the self-authenticating power of truth is reminiscent of the very stance he denounced in Owen's thought. Truth, if proclaimed to men of "disciplined intelligence," will produce obedience. Disseminating truth, then, clearly had become more important than tearing down religion. Bring in the new. Let the old care for itself.[49]

Reconciliation among the self-righteous is, on the scale of impossibilities, very close to camels walking through needles' eyes. Holyoake and Southwell were sparring partners to the end. Holyoake declined the invitation to the public tea in honor of Southwell's last lecture in 1848. Polite to punctiliousness, Holyoake sent a note regretting that the "habits I have been obliged to impose upon myself" prevented him forming "one of your company." He protested a friendship with Southwell that went beyond differences of opinion, and wished him the very best.[50] The uninitiated might have thought him genuinely cordial. More characteristically, he was simply exhibiting for all to see the virtue with which he dealt with his persecutors, after they had ceased to be a threat.

---

[47]Holyoake, "A Vindicatory Chapter," p. 616.

[48]Southwell eventually returned to the Christian faith, while Holyoake established a belief system that he called "Secularism."

[49]Holyoake, "Loyola An Exemplar to Modern Reformers," Part II, *Reasoner* III (1847): 628.

[50]Holyoake to Walter Cooper, *Reasoner* IV (1847-48): 237.

Nobody likes a winner for long. G. J. Holyoake was the public face of freethought in the early 1850's. As a writer, lecturer, outdoor Parliamentary agitator, Holyoake represented "respectable" working class radicalism. The challenge to his authority came, first, from Robert Cooper, editor of the London Investigator. Between Cooper and Holyoake stood the questions of freethought strategy and authority. Cooper fought the strategy question in the pages of the Investigator. The authority controversy took the form of an attack on the integrity and utility of Holyoake's darling center for British freethought, Fleet Street House.

In 1854, Robert Cooper began publishing the London Investigator with the declared commitment to precision in thought and purity in position. He denounced two errors that were supposedly creeping into the freethought movement--"trimming" and "accommodation."[51] The "trimmer":

> . . . only follows reason as far as it is fashionable, or, as it is now the fashion to designate it, 'useful,' is only a hanger-on of progress. If truth is only to be spoken so far as it is 'useful,' or, in other words, convenient, we are necessarily led to the conclusion it is sometimes 'useful' to allow error to remain unchallenged. This is only the old doctrine of the Christian Fathers recast--the end justifies the means . . . Popular advocacy, to be honourable or healthy, must be based on principle--not 'art.' The warmth of honesty, rather than the coolness of expediency, can alone give life and vigour to a great movement. Temporizing till error seems in the humour to give way will always keep truth in the rear and enable oppression and superstition to ride in pomp and pride through the world.[52]

The Investigator stood for uncompromising avowal of truth, by which it

---

[51] See outline of policy, Investigator I (1854-55): 1-2.

[52] Ibid.

meant atheism and materialism, no matter what the social consequences. Uncertainty and ambiguity about ultimate questions was not enough. Freethinkers must take as strong a position as their opponents if there is to be a contest.

Trimming led naturally to the second of the current heresies, accommodation. The trimmer, by declaring himself an agnostic about God, left room for the possibility that there might be one, and hence, room for cooperation with the Theist. The accommodator minimized, rather than maximized, the ground that, according to the Investigator, ought irrevocably to separate the naturalist and the supernaturalist.[53] Robert Cooper argued that hedging on the doctrine of atheism simply weakened policy and objected to any efforts to arrive at a doctrine of God that satisfied both the materialist and the spiritualist.[54] Cooper's refutation of Holyoake's compromising position sounds very like Holyoake's own position of ten years earlier when Owen was the leader to topple. This life is all there is. To allow even for possible future existence is to betray Secularism, and to make it no longer a science, but a creed. According to Cooper:

> Inasmuch as their [Secularism and Religion] principles are different, their policy different, their influence different, their object different, such an alliance would be an absurdity, a hypocrisy, and a fraud. . . . What is the Secular profession but a war against the superstition of the age. If it is not, what is it? The Freethinkers of this country are in a false position if such is

---

[53] Ibid.

[54] R. Cooper, Discussion of John St. Institution, Investigator I (1854-55): 3-4.

not the character of the incipient organisation recently formed in their name and by their funds.[55]

Like the younger Holyoake, Cooper insisted on the priority of destroying the old world view if a new world were ever to appear.[56]

The Cooper-Holyoake rivalry embodied in their competing periodicals was essentially a conflict over G. J. Holyoake's leadership in the freethought movement. It represented an alliance of the Old Guard freethinkers and the new militantly atheistic radicals. Both Charles Southwell and Robert Owen heartily endorsed the Investigator--at least according to the Investigator. The second issue carried letters from the two leading freethinkers of the old school. Both letters voiced praise for the straightforward, honest approach of the new journal.[57] Southwell's enumeration of the Investigator's potential merits only slightly veiled his attack on Holyoake and the Reasoner. According to Southwell:

> Whatever else may be doubtful, it is quite certain that the want of an unsectarian, unsnobbish, and unegotistic periodical has long been bitterly felt by first-class freethinkers. On what principles The London Investigator is to be conducted, as yet I know not, but take for granted that its pages will be open to friend and foe alike; that you will not, with a modesty equal to that of Anarchsis Clootz, set yourself up as editor for the entire human race; . . . that no attempt will be made to form alliances, offensive or defensive, direct or indirect, with clerical incorrigibles; . . . and that with your editorial hammer you will knock, not the brains, but the life, out of that new creation--that most hybridish of all hybrids, part pro- part anti- Christianity,

---

[55]R. Cooper, "Substance of a Lecture to London Secular Society, July 15, 1855, 'Secularism, and Its Aims,'" Investigator II (1855-56): 97-98. See also rejoinder to Holyoake's response to Cooper's speech on Secularism, Investigator II (1855-56): 145-47.

[56]R. Cooper, "The Social Congress of 1850," Reasoner IX (1850): 103-5.

[57]Investigator, I (1854): 27.

to believe in the Divine nature of which is the whole duty of secularists.[58]

The Investigator, throughout its five years of existence, persisted in advocating materialism, atheism, and the absolute incompatibility of freethought--secularism--and Theism.[59] Claiming disinterest except where truth is concerned, the Investigator responded to a Sheffield correspondent:

> Neither vanity nor personality have anything to do with the present controversy with G. J. H. The question in dispute is not between the editors of the Investigator and Reasoner, but one involving high principle.[60]

The Investigator saw itself as the true organ for principled freethought, in contrast to the Reasoner, which had been co-opted in the interest of personality--that of G. J. Holyoake, to be specific.

Holyoake, not strangely, remained noticeably quiet about the Investigator's allegations. Being on the defensive, the Reasoner could only lose by responding in kind. To defend itself would open it to charges of "protesting too much." To attack would only be to acknowledge that it considered the Investigator an opponent worthy of serious consideration.[61] In quiet ways, the Reasoner affirmed its

---

[58]Ibid.

[59]See especially "Preface to Volume IV (April 1857) and Editor's Address in Vol. IV; also letters by R. Cooper and "Anthony Collins" on old and new policy of Investigator; J. P. Adams, "A Survey of Secularism," Investigator IV (1857-58): 4; "Anthony Collins," "Party Criticisms," Investigator V (1858-59): 12-13.

[60]To H. T. Sheffield--"Letters to Correspondents," Investigator V (1858): 20.

[61]Letters from G. J. Holyoake and "Lionel H. Holdreth" did appear in both the Reasoner and at the Investigator offices in response to the Investigator's charges. Nevertheless, the Reasoner, judging from amount

innocence and good will toward its opponent. To read its columns, one would gather that it sought only truth and understanding, and was the victim of unfair harassment at the hands of a jealous challenger. According to Editor Holyoake, the Reasoner is "willing to cooperate" with the Investigator "so far as this paper devotes itself to the exposition and advocacy of freethought views."[62] He goes on to express a desire that:

> When personal differences arise, let them be ventilated. We have no objection to any criticism of ourselves. We would not pursue a course which would not bear criticism of the freest kind. We could wish it to be conducted in terms which should give the enemy no handle by degrading the party--in terms which should exclude no truth and include no personal quarreling. . . . We shall adhere to the rule of acting, when principle is in question, in concert with all who seek the triumph of principles opposed to superstition. . . . We shall be glad to see the Investigator writers winning independent distinction in Freethought literature.[63]

When Cooper wrote to Holyoake, lamenting the absence of enthusiasm in the Reasoner, Holyoake printed the letter in the Reasoner, but noted that enthusiasm is no guarantee of success or effectiveness. After reminding readers of the good that the Reasoner had done, Holyoake conceded that "We . . . shall be glad of Mr. Cooper's help to augment the enthusiasm he desires, and of which we are as much friends as himself."[64]

---

of copy devoted to the matter, was either far less concerned with the Investigator than vice versa, or so concerned that it wished to avoid drawing attention to the growing rift among freethinkers. See, for example: "Notices to Correspondents," Investigator IV (1857-58): 140; and V (1858-59): 20.

[62]Holyoake, "'The Investigator' and Its Writers," Reasoner XXIII (1858): 322-23.

[63]Ibid.

[64]Report from Robert Cooper, Reasoner, XII (1851-52): 331.

Each editor saw his own journal to be the disinterested one--the one best serving the intentions of the freethought movement and the long term welfare of the working class. The opponent's journal, in each case, appeared to be the "sectarian"--the Investigator because of its dogmatic adherance to affirming negatives, the Reasoner because of its compromising of principle in the interest of personality. They agreed only that the "cause" was hurting. On the source of the pain, there was no consensus.

Not all the interaction over policy and strategy between Cooper and Holyoake took place at such a highly principled level. In the summer of 1858, the Investigator printed a series of letters, in which Cooper defended himself against Holyoake's insinuation that he, Cooper, had appropriated a gift to the "work" for his own purposes.[65] Cooper referred sarcastically to Holyoake as the "great leader"[66] and accuses him of making "more hypocrites than any orthodox journal in Europe."[67] In exonerating himself, Cooper charged Holyoake with refusing to follow up on Cooper's offer of an open investigation of the gift in question. In Cooper's words:

> . . . it was your duty to accept my proposition, or to announce to the accusers that you did not believe it true. But you have not the manliness to do either. You skulk from the responsibility . . . The future history . . . of Freethinking will have to record that no 'publicist' had more quarrels with co-adjutors, all of whom left him with contempt.[68]

---

[65]Cooper Correspondence, Investigator V (1858-59): 77-79.

[66]Ibid., p. 77.

[67]Ibid., p. 79.

[68]Ibid., p. 78.

To the new generation of freethinkers, Holyoake appeared as unbending, as autocratic, and as dogmatic as Owen had been for Holyoake. The response in both generations was strikingly similar. The *Investigator*[69] accused Holyoake of secular popery and warned Secularists that if they "sink discussion in Sectarianism"--if they follow the lead of men who object to every thought, or form of thought, but their own-- they will deserve more than all the opprobrium now so lavishly heaped on them.[70]

Queenwood's Harmony Hall had symbolized the folly of Owen's reign. Its failure had been his personal discreditation in the minds of the younger generation of his day. What Queenwood had been for Owen, Fleet Street House was to Holyoake.

The establishment at 147 Fleet Street in London began in 1853 with a gift to Holyoake from the Friends of Freethought. The building was to be a "Central Publishing House" and "Propagandist Institution"--in short, an organizational and administrative center for British freethought.[71] What eventually made Fleet Street House suspect was that it prospered at a point when freethought as a whole was languishing with

---

[69]There was apparently some question as to whether Cooper was responsible for initiating the controversy over Fleet Street. Whether or not he initiated the crisis, it *is* clear that he was the one to whom the anti-Holyoakites looked for leadership. See C. Bradlaugh, "Mr. G. J. Holyoake and Mr. Robert Cooper," *Investigator* V (1858-59): 30.

[70]*Investigator* I (1854-55): 56. See also "G. J. Holyoake," *Investigator* IV (1857-58): 100-101.

[71]*The History of the Fleet Street House* (London: The Promoters of Free-thought, 1856), p. 8.

little direction or motivation.[72] Without in any way absolving Holyoake of all responsibility for his public image of arrogance and self-importance, it seems safe to suggest that Fleet Street and Holyoake were convenient scapegoats to account for the depressed state of freethought enthusiasm in the mid-1850's. It was easy and plausible to blame Fleet Street for draining the movement of funds, and for diverting its vitality from the real mission of proselytizing to petty business and bureaucracy.[73]

The question of Fleet Street was whether, in fact, "147" was a public institution in the service of freethought, or a private business venture for the personal benefit of G. J. Holyoake and friends.[74] Holyoake could hardly have been pinned in a more helpless position, for he clearly wanted it both ways. When he wanted freedom to make unilateral decisions over finances, policy, and personnel, he pointed to the extensive personal funds he had committed to the institution. When he wanted financial backing from the movement, he pushed Fleet Street's role as the center of British freethought activity.[75]

---

[72] See, for example, J. P. Adams, "Suggestions to Secularists," Investigator IV (1857-58): 36-37; "Secularism--What Are We Doing?" Investigator IV (1857-58): 108-9; R. Cooper to Editor of Investigator, Investigator V (1858-59): 31-32.

[73] "The Fleet Street House," Investigator IV (1857-58): 117.

[74] John Maughan, "Report of the Committee of Inquiry on '147,'" Investigator IV (1857-58): 123; "Mr. Holyoake's Equivocations," Investigator IV (1857-58): 140-41; C. Bradlaugh, "Holyoake versus Wilkes," Investigator IV (1857-58): 141-43.

[75] Maughan, "Report of the Committee on Inquiry on '147,'"; "Report on the Fleet Street House," Investigator IV (1857-58): 124-25; See The History of the Fleet Street House; Secular Institute Report 1858-59; British Secular Institute of Communication and Propagandism, Report of

At a special meeting of "Fleet Street House Promoters" in November 1857, called specifically to discuss Holyoake's lack of accountability for funds,[76] Holyoake, to protect his autonomy, agreed that the House was truly his own venture.[77] The assembly passed a resolution of approval following Holyoake's defense, though no one seemed quite certain of what was being approved.[78] Some interpreted it as an assent to the acknowledgement that freethought and Fleet Street were no longer to be equated. Holyoake took it as permission by the rank and file to carry on "business as usual."

A History of the Fleet Street House, published in 1857, and a follow-up report after the November meeting,[79] failed to squelch growing suspicion in Investigator quarters that Holyoake was building his own castle on the ruins of freethought. He was creating Holyoakites--not freethinkers.[80] What was worst, as Holyoakites, they smelled of

---

the Fleet Street House, Part II, for 1857; (Three reports are all part of the Holyoake Pamphlet Collection, Bishopsgate Institute, London.)

[76]See Maughan, "Report of the Committee of Inquiry on '147,'" pp. 122-23; Letter from John Maughan to M. Merritt, November 18, 1877, Holyoake Collection, Bishopsgate Institute.

[77]Maughan, "Report of the Committee of Inquiry . . . ," p. 123.

[78]Ibid.; "'Fleet Street House,' Explanations and Inquiries," Investigator IV (1857-58): 133; British Secular Institute of Communication and Propagandism, Report of the Fleet Street House, Part II, for 1857.

[79]See The History of the Fleet Street House, Report of the Fleet Street House, Part II, Secular Instit Report, 1858-59; The 'Fleet Street House;' a Circular by the Promoters of Freethought (London: 147 Fl Street, 1858).

[80]J. Maughan, "George Jacob Holyoake and Customary Reticences," Investigator V (1858-59): 9-11; "Collins," "Party Criticisms," Investigator V (1858-59): 12-13; J. Maughan, "Analysis of the Fleet

religion.[81] Holyoake had fallen away. A measure of censure, supported by the Fleet Street Promoters and a majority of the London Secular Society, spurred Holyoake to resign as President of the London Secular Society in 1858.[82] In his place, they elected as President a young firebrand who had only recently assumed the editorship of the Investigator.[83] Holyoake, himself, had first introduced him to the London lecture circuit; the man--Charles Bradlaugh.[84]

On the Fleet Street question, Holyoake and Bradlaugh had met as unequals. Charles Bradlaugh was the new Investigator editor--the protégé of Robert Cooper. If Holyoake had underestimated his opponent in 1858, he would see his strength in their ensuing struggles for domination of the freethought movement in the 1860's and 1870's.

Both were strong-willed, "self-made" men, and both were charismatic motivators of people. Both professed sacrificial commitment to the cause of working class reform, and both chose to work primarily through established channels for achieving that improvement. Finally, both

---

Street House," Investigator V (1858-59): 21-22.

[81]J. P. Adams, "Suggestions to Secularists," p. 37.

[82]J. Maughan, "Half-yearly meeting of the London Secular Society," Investigator V (1858-59): 25-27. See also follow-up letter of explanation delineating Holyoake's professions that do not measure up to his practice--Maughan, "Profession and Practice," Investigator V (1858-59): 36-38; "The New Position of the Fleet Street House," Investigator V (1858-59): 54-55.

[83]Maughan, "Half-yearly Meeting of the London Secular Society," p. 27.

[84]Holyoake, "Life and Career of Charles Bradlaugh," Freethinker's Magazine (1891): 3.

believed in the power of words and ideas to effect significant and lasting social and political change.

Despite their common bonds, their efforts to cooperate on practical matters were hopeless. Their temporary liaison to edit the **National Reformer** in the early 1860's ended in a lawsuit that left all of their subsequent interaction tainted with bitterness and self-righteousness.

They justified their separate paths in terms of their differing articulation of the freethought mission and plans for accomplishing that mission. Bradlaugh was ever the atheist and the agitator, Holyoake the Secularist and the accommodator. They made use of the same issues that had divided Owen from Southwell and Holyoake, and then Holyoake from Robert Cooper and the **Investigator** militants. Was truth best served by tearing down or building up? Was it a sword to be wielded or a shield to give defense? Was freethought a battle to be won or a peace to be made? If either Bradlaugh or Holyoake had been more interested in serving the cause than in being right, he might have been freer to see the complementarity rather than the incompatibility of their positions, and cooperation might better have served their ends than persistent agitation.

Dealings between Holyoake and Bradlaugh had never been smooth. Even before they had met in 1857-58 over the Fleet Street controversy, Bradlaugh had come to question Holyoake's disinterestedness in the cause of freethought. He resented Holyoake's apparent effort to control freethought for the sake of appearance, especially his own. Bradlaugh never quite forgave Holyoake's refusal to print beyond the third number of Bradlaugh's **The Bible, What It Is!** on the grounds that it glorified immorality, and implicated Holyoake and freethought as a whole. In Bradlaugh's mind, Holyoake's responsibilities as printer for freethought did not include censureship. Furthermore, Bradlaugh suspected that the rejection carried personal overtones, for he noted that Holyoake showed no consistency in executing a policy of printing only works that reflected the majority stand within freethought.[85]

In the spring of 1861, Holyoake had condemned Bradlaugh's behavior over oath-taking as inconsistent and compromising. Atheists, unlike Quakers and Jews, were not given the prerogative of "affirming" instead of "swearing" in an English court. Thus, they were placed in the difficult position of having to choose between perjuring themselves in swearing by a deity in whom they did not believe, or being discounted as credible witnesses in a court of law. After being denied permission to affirm, Bradlaugh, much to Holyoake's disgust, had chosen to swear an oath.[86] In Holyoake's words:

> . . . it is 'idle' in Mr. Bradlaugh to say that he 'should take the oath,' as though that was a thing within his power. With his opinions and position, it is seriously inconsistent in him to take it and it is not in his power to do so the moment his opinions become known to the Court.[87]

The freethinkers were as pious and critical of one another as were any

---

[85]"Iconoclast," "To the Editor of the Investigator," Investigator IV (1857-58): 135. See also Bradlaugh to Wm. Hilton, Bolton, Bradlaugh Papers, #69, National Secular Society Collection, Bishopsgate Institute, London.

[86]See discussion in Reasoner XXVI (April 21, 1861, April 28, 1861, May 12, 1861, May 19, 1861, May 26, 1861.) For Bradlaugh's response, see "Mr. Holyoake and the Oath Question," National Reformer II (May 11, 1861): 1.

[87]See Editor's note, Reasoner XXVI (1861): 248.

of the legalistic religious circles that the freethinkers so despised.

Given their rather stormy initial contacts, it is not at first obvious why Bradlaugh and Holyoake would choose to embark on a cooperative venture such as producing the National Reformer. There is no certain answer, except that several circumstances coincided in 1860- 61 to make the experiment appear opportune. Bradlaugh, writing as "Iconoclast," and Joseph Barker had begun editing the National Reformer in April 1860 as a continuation of the Investigator's approach to freethought journalism. An editorial parting of the ways that Bradlaugh attributed to personality[88] and Barker to principle[89] resulted in Barker's dismissal in August of 1861. So, in the fall of 1861, Bradlaugh had no partner. Just two months before Barker's dismissal, Holyoake had announced his intention of taking a leave of absence after nineteen years of editing the Reasoner.[90] Holyoake was without a job.[91] Finally, Barker's pretentions to represent orthodox freethought had

---

[88] "Fair Play," National Reformer III (September 28, 1861): 1. Interestingly, it was the "personality of too high principles" and its resulting arrogance and intolerance that was Barker's downfall, according to the Reformer. See "Quasimodo," "Men, Not Principles--What Then?" National Reformer III (November 2, 1861): 1; "Quasimodo," "The Unbounded Virtue Party," National Reformer III (November 23, 1861): 1.

[89] Joseph Barker, "Personalities," National Reformer II (August 31, 1861): 1.

[90] Holyoake, "Leave of Absence," Reasoner XXVI (1861): 349.

[91] There is no indication that Holyoake rushed to the National Reformer out of panic. In his resignation, he noted his plans to stay in contact with readers through the Counsellor, another small journal published by the Reasoner company. Furthermore, before joining the Reformer, he apparently had first considered beginning a new journal The Secular World. (Holyoake, "One Paper and One Party," National Reformer III (November 23, 1861): 5.

offended Holyoake as much as Bradlaugh.

The "marriage" of Bradlaugh and Holyoake was one of mutual convenience designed primarily to close ranks against Joseph Barker. In his explanation of the decision to the *National Reformer* readers in November of 1861, Holyoake very uncharacteristically emphasized the complementarity of "Secular principles" and "Freethought criticism"--all the while, of course, protesting his consistency. Said Holyoake:

> As I have always taught, the agitation of Critical Freethought ought to go on. Secular principles are, as I conceive them, *supplementary* to Freethought criticism, giving it a definite and ethical aim; and both can proceed side by side in one paper with logical propriety and practical usefulness . . .[92]

Just after explaining that "Of Mr Barker personally I have no disrespectful word to say," Holyoake proceeded to accuse him of "misunderstanding and misrepresenting us," of engaging in the "cant of virtue," of "think[ing] like a baby," "reason[ing] like a scold," and "writ[ing] like an enemy."[93]

Holyoake self-deceptively gloried in the unity of the freethought movement that Barker had failed to destroy.[94] In reality, the Barker issue highlighted freethought's weakness more than its strength. It was a fragile thread that, in uniting shared antagonisms, held Bradlaugh and Holyoake together in a brief unity of common self-protection. The issue at stake, the question of the proper relationship between birth control and freethought, would appear again in the movement in 1877, and then,

---

[92] Ibid.

[93] Ibid.

[94] Ibid.

Holyoake would be playing Barker's part.[95] But that is to get ahead of the story. In 1861, Holyoake informed the *Reformer*'s readers that:

> . . . three pages of space will be accorded to me . . . for the most unreserved exposition, illustration, and defence of Secular principles, and on terms which, under the circumstances, I regard as liberal.[96]

With an optimism that anyone who knew Bradlaugh and Holyoake must surely have regarded as laughable, Holyoake suggested that, since the united party had so long been desired, the arrangement for a shared editorship would no doubt be permanent.[97] The freethinkers celebrated the newfound

---

[95] Material relating to the Bradlaugh/Holyoake arbitration of 1862 suggests that, even at this point of "cooperation," Holyoake stood closer to Barker than Bradlaugh on the question of birth control. Holyoake clearly preferred that Bradlaugh minimize the emphasis on Malthusianism in material associated with the Secular position. See "Mr. Bradlaugh and Mr. G. J. Holyoake Arbitration"--Minutes of the meeting February 27, 1863, Bradlaugh Papers #100, National Secular Society Collection, Bishopsgate Institute, London.

[96] Holyoake, "One Paper and One Party," p. 5.

[97] Ibid.--Controversy between Barker and Bradlaugh on the birth control issue, as well as on the question of Barker's renascent theism, persisted long after Holyoake had left the **National Reformer** for his own reasons. Though the Bradlaugh-Barker conflict did not affect the movement as a whole, largely because Barker was less a public figure in his own right than Holyoake, it furnishes one more example of the delicate tension between principle and personality in the freethought movement. See articles such as "The Tendency of Freethought," **National Reformer** V (March 19, 1864): 9-10; "Iconoclast," "Joseph Barker and Iconoclast," **National Reformer** VI (November 12, 1865): 717; "Joseph Barker on Atheism," **National Reformer** VII (May 6, 1866): 273. Barker's penchant for changing sides whenever he felt so led became something of a joke at the **National Reformer**. See "Joseph Barker," **National Reformer** VII (June 17, 1866): 377; "Joseph Barker in His Original Character," **National Reformer** VIII (August 26, 1866): 134; "Melampus," "Joseph Barker versus Himself," **National Reformer** VIII (December 9, 1866): 369- 70; "Discussion Between Joseph Barker and Mr. Bradlaugh on Atheism," **National Reformer** XVIII (September 24, 1871): 193-94. The fact that Barker chose Bradlaugh rather than Holyoake as his principal adversary is difficult to interpret. It may be purely an accident of personality; it may reflect the fact that Barker and Holyoake did appear to have more in common in the 1860's than Barker and Bradlaugh; or, it may reflect a

accord at a gala Christmas Day Soiree, and looked forward to the "union of effort" between "Iconoclast" and Mr. Holyoake for the "better organization of the Secular Party."[98]

The union proved short-lived. In March 1862, in a series of events which suggests that neither Bradlaugh nor Holyoake would have been easygoing partners in any enterprise, the venture came to an abrupt end. Apparently Bradlaugh had first tendered his own resignation to the Board of the **National Reformer** after a dispute over his right to override a recommendation from the Board on size and frequency of publication. He even submitted Holyoake's name as a possible replacement, though, according to Bradlaugh's later testimony, it was only because he thought the Board had already sided with Holyoake against him.[99] After Holyoake and the Board had begun proceeding upon that suggestion, Bradlaugh changed his mind and wanted to be reinstated as sole editor, without Holyoake as Chief Contributor. According to Holyoake, Bradlaugh had promised to pay him for the rest of the contract period, but then later made the fulfillment of the **Reformer**'s contract contingent upon Holyoake's submission of two columns of print which Bradlaugh could edit and print at his discretion. At that point, when Holyoake demanded his two guineas per week without the modified copy requirement, Bradlaugh

---

perception that Bradlaugh, not Holyoake, was the rival to beat in the freethought movement of the 1860's and 1870's.

[98]Holyoake, "One Paper and One Party," **National Reformer** III (December 14, 1861): 5.

[99]Mr. Bradlaugh and Mr. Holyoake Arbitration, Arbitration minutes for February 27, 1863, p. 3; See also March 3, 1863 session.

invited arbitration.[100] The crucial question in the arbitration was who had finally precipitated the actual break, whether Holyoake by withdrawing his copy, or Bradlaugh by refusing it.[101]

The proceedings dragged out until July 1863 when the arbitrators decided for Holyoake.[102] Because Holyoake had continued to fulfill his obligation of providing copy until his copy had been refused by Bradlaugh, Bradlaugh, according to arbitrator Shaen, had clearly been the one to break the November 1861 agreement, and thus, should compensate Holyoake for breach of contract.[103] But the real question of the irreconcilable interpretations of the November 1861 agreement had never been addressed.[104] At stake was whether or not the two giants of freethought could work together harmoniously. Each proved too jealous of his own autonomy to be capable of surrendering to any meaningful

---

[100]For an account from Holyoake's perspective of the circumstances surrounding Holyoake's leaving, see: **Mr. Holyoake's Disconnection with the 'National Reformer and the Correspondence which accounts for it**, 1863 Pamphlet Box 5, Holyoake Collection, Bishopsgate. See also Dodworth, (Chairman of **Reformer** Board of Directors) **Letters to the Shareholders of the 'National Reformer' Co., Giving An Account of the way in which the editor elected at the March meeting**, 1862. Printed by requirement of several shareholders.

[101]Mr. Bradlaugh and Mr. Holyoake Arbitration, Arbitration minutes for February 17, 1863, pp. 1-5.

[102]See Bradlaugh Papers #89-150, National Secular Society Collection, Bishopsgate Institute, London. Includes correspondence between lawyers and freethinkers and minutes of arbitration sessions.

[103]Bradlaugh Papers 139a, Announcement of Shaen's award, July 7, 1863.

[104]Mr. Bradlaugh and Mr. Holyoake Arbitration, Arbitration Minutes for March 3, 1863 and April 10, 1863.

lasting united venture.[105] The entire freethought movement was the loser.

Throughout the 1860's, the two leaders maintained their adversarial stance, each keeping a fairly cagey watch on the activities of his opponent. Holyoake, after an aborted effort to kick off a new journal, the Secular World, resumed publication of the Reasoner. Both kept heavy itineraries of speaking engagements on behalf of freethought, despite Bradlaugh's time-out to make a bid for a Northampton Parliamentary seat in 1868.

The men criticized each other primarily for their different views on how best to propagate freethought and on whether atheism was essential to Secularism. Holyoake viewed Bradlaugh as a self-seeking rabblerouser, always ready to create a scene that would enhance his visibility, regardless of the damage to freethought.[106] It is in this light that Holyoake will judge the storm over Bradlaugh's entry to Parliament in the 1880's.[107] Holyoake even suggested that Bradlaugh's decision to use the pseudonym "Iconoclast" was one purely of effect,

---

[105] In arbitration, Bradlaugh denied any suggestion of intended parity between Holyoake and himself. (Mr. Bradlaugh and Mr. Holyoake Arbitration, Arbitration minutes for February 27, 1863, p. 1.) Holyoake, on the other hand, claimed he had been led to expect editorial independence in his section of the paper. (Ibid., Arbitration minutes for April 10, 1863, pp. 5-9.)

[106] See Holyoake's discussion of Bradlaugh's behavior at Wigan-- Reasoner, XXVI (1861): 243.

[107] Holyoake, "The Warpath of Opinion: Strange things seen Therein as Shown in the 'Life of Bradlaugh,'" (Leicester: Cooperative Printing Society, Ltd., 1896), 41-54.

designed to draw attention.[108] To Bradlaugh and the *Reformer* freethinkers, Holyoake was a toady to the Establishment, compromising principles whenever it proved advantageous. He had lost his former zeal for denouncing scriptural and theological error and had betrayed the cause of atheism that remained associated with his name.[109]

The proper place of atheism in a Secular world view had long interested both Holyoake and Bradlaugh. In 1857, Holyoake recorded the occasion of one of his lectures on "A Definition of Secularism, and of its Sphere of Controversy--in Answer to those who construe Secularism into mere Negative Atheism." "Iconoclast" was the respondent.[110]

The two came to represent in the 1860's the two faces of freethought, the first representing devotion primarily to undermining theological orthodoxy, the second representing efforts to create a morally just world irrespective of theology. Holyoake, in contrasting his position to Bradlaugh's, declared that he, Holyoake, "sought to test Christianity by its moral defects rather than its theological errors." Bradlaugh, as one of the "mere Church fighters, . . . found it livelier to discover errors than the truths which should replace them, and more popular to destroy than construct."[111]

---

[108] Ibid., p. 16.

[109] "Freethought Advocacy," *National Reformer*, VI (1865): 225; Charles Bradlaugh, "To George Jacob Holyoake," *National Reformer* V (1864): 201-2.

[110] Holyoake Diaries, July 26, 1857, Holyoake Collection, Bishopsgate Institute, London.

[111] Holyoake, *The Warpath of Opinion*, p. 16; See also Holyoake to Editor of *National Reformer*, *National Reformer* X (1867): 394-95; Holyoake, "A Word By the Wary," *Reasoner* XXX (1871-72): 68-69.

The controversy peaked in a two-day debate on the nature of Secularism announced for March 10 and 11, 1870 at New Hall of Science, City Road. The following propositions were to be the basis for the discussion:

1) The Principles of Secularism do not include Atheism.

2) Secular Criticism does not include Scepticism.[112]

Holyoake was to argue the affirmative and Bradlaugh the negative.

The central question of the debate itself was, practically, whether undoing Theism was a prerequisite to Secularism, and theoretically, whether Atheism was, *ipso facto*, a part of Secularism. Holyoake's chief contention was that Bradlaugh's position, by focusing on theology, actually glorified the enemy's position.[113] Furthermore, like Christianity, dogmatic Atheism claimed too much.[114] It assumed a certainty of spiritual matters of which humans were incapable. Bradlaugh accused Holyoake of failing to acknowledge that, for the atheists, de-Christianizing is not an end in itself.[115] He believed that Holyoake had betrayed his own position[116] and had failed to admit

---

[112]"Debate on Secularism," *National Reformer* XV (1870): 150. For a full account of the debate, see *Secularism, Scepticism, and Atheism*. Verbatim Report of the Proceedings of a Two Nights' Public Debate-- Between G. J. Holyoake and C. Bradlaugh. (Revised by, and published with the concurrence of, both disputants), (London: Austin & Co., 1870).

[113]Ibid., pp. 65, 68.

[114]Ibid., pp. v, 7.

[115]Ibid., pp. 27, 28, 30.

[116]Ibid., pp. vi, 12.

the logical implications of a Secularist order.[117]

The points at issue were not resolved. They were not intended to be. The controversy was, in one sense, an end in itself. It showed off both Holyoake and Bradlaugh to great advantage. It clarified the lines of thought on questions of import to the entire freethought movement.[118] Furthermore, and perhaps most important, to have argued away the truths asserted by either Holyoake or Bradlaugh would have killed the dialogue and the tension, and in so doing, have sapped some of the life of the freethought movement itself. For, by 1870, with no blasphemy arrests and fewer religious disabilities to fuel the freethought fires of enthusiasm, it was debate on just such internal matters as the role of atheism on which freethought agitation depended for its survival.

---

[117]Ibid., pp. vii, 16.

[118]See George Foote's discussion of the importance of this debate, especially in highlighting the need for a restatement of the Secular position. George W. Foote, Secularism Restated; with a Review of the Several Expositions of C[ ] Bradlaugh and George Jacob Holyoake. (London: W. J. Ramsey, 1874).

IV

Theologizing and dogmatizing did serve to establish and maintain individual "territory" within the freethought movement. But to view these phenomena solely as instruments of powermongering is not to comprehend truly at all. The freethinkers, however self-aggrandizing, seriously believed that they were participating in something bigger than themselves, and consciously sought only to see that mission realized. Prior to realizing a mission, however, one must know what the mission is. Of the specifics of their assignment, the freethinkers were not at all certain. It is partly as a result of this effort to articulate what they were about that freethought assumed a creedal and dogmatic aspect.

Freethought was an attitude before it was a position. People became freethinkers because of how they felt about the state of their own lives and of Victorian society at large. But while feelings inspire action, they do not readily lend themselves to the organization necessary for accomplishing specific actions. As Holyoake said in an early Reasoner, ". . . There can be no unity without knowing what is to be united about."[1] Attitudes cannot be institutionalized. The search for a satisfactory working statement of self-identification proved a necessary, though never-ending, endeavor of the freethought movement.

---

[1] Holyoake, "Why Have We Had No Revolution in England?" Reasoner VII (1849-50): 3.

Clearly, freethinkers felt the need to be organized. The call for clarification of goals, better communication among local freethought bodies, and national coordination of policy and programs was a persistent theme throughout the Victorian period. There are perhaps no better concise statements of the plight of freethought than the following *Investigator* excerpt:

> We have spoken of Freethinking. What are we to understand by the term? Does it mean the absence of all restraint--thinking without reference to any standard of authority whatever? If this really constituted Freethinking, it would be like going to sea without rudder, chart, compass, or anchor, destined to drift hither and thither, helpless and hopeless.[2]

Naturally, enthusiastic feelings of belonging to something worthwhile were strongest when attention was focused on some common object. Thus, freethought societies flourished in response to the wave of blasphemy prosecutions in the 1840's, and later in the 1880's at the time of Bradlaugh's struggle to enter Parliament. Zeal ebbed during and after demoralizing episodes of intra-party squabbling such as after the collapse of Harmony Hall in the 1840's and after the Fleet Street crisis of the 1850's. These struggles were, no doubt, both cause and effect of declining enthusiasm for freethought agitation.

But though the expressions of despondency may be more focused after such identifiable controversies, the feeling was never far away that freethought was floundering for lack of unified policy and clear vision.[3]

---

[2] J. Maughan, "Freethinking, Its Sphere, Power, Necessity, and Results," *Investigator* V (1858-59): 34.

[3] See for example: "To the Members and Friends of the Rational Society," *Herald of Progress* (1845-46): 108; "Secularism, and Its

While freethinkers lamented the absence of a sound theoretical basis for organization, they proceeded to organize, nonetheless. They were not the sort to wait for a perfect plan of action before taking action. In addition to the numerous local Eclectic Institutes, Halls of Science, and Freethought Societies,[4] several more comprehensive efforts at organization should be noted. In response to the Rational Society's decision to prohibit theological discussion, freethinkers of the early 1840's founded the "Theological Association" to pursue the following goals:

> Free Inquiry into the Religious Ideas--Religious Systems--and Modes of Worship--their Origin, Progress, Present State, and Prospects--

---

Aims"--substance of a lecture by R. Cooper to the London Secular Society, July 15, 1855, London Investigator II (1855-56): 97; Preface to Volumes V & VI, Investigator (1858-59); Holyoake, "The Problem of Secular Unity Illustrated," Reasoner XXIII (1858): 105-6; Letter from J. H. McGuire to Investigator, I (1854-55): 45; J. P. Adams, "Suggestions to Secularists," Investigator IV (1857-58): 36; "Report of the Society of Materialists," appended to January 1858 issue of Investigator V (1858-59): 3; C. F. Nicholls to the Editor of the Reasoner, "The Personal and Moral Director of Secularism," Reasoner XIII (1852): 187-89; Holyoake, "Further Reasons Why Freethinkers Should Organize," Reasoner XII (1851-52): 145; "The Question of Organisation," National Reformer III (December 7, 1861): 1; See discussion of Child's letter and merits of national organization versus local organisation, National Reformer IV (August 15, 1863): 7; G. W. Foote, Secularism Restated; with a Review of the Several Expositions of Charles Bradlaugh and G. J. Holyoake (London: W. J. Ramsey, 1874), 3.

[4]For a complete cataloguing of the various branches, see appendices to E. Royle, "George Jacob Holyoake and the Secularist Movement in Britain, 1841-1861" (Ph.D. dissertation, Cambridge University, 1968); Royle, Victorian Infidels -- The Origins of the British Secular Movement 1791-1866 (Manchester: University Press, 1974); Royle, Radicals, Secularists, and Republicans: Popular Freethought in Britain, 1866-1915 (Manchester: University Press, 1980).

with a view to the discovery and Promulgation of Truth, and the overthrow of error.[5]

Following the confused era of the Harmony Hall project, a number of renegades from Owenism organized the "Society for the Promulgation of Naturalism" under the umbrella of Holyoake's *Reasoner*.[6] In 1853, the London Secular Society was founded at Hall of Science, City Road.[7] It was through leadership in this organization that Holyoake, but especially Charles Bradlaugh, gained a national following. Holyoake's Fleet Street House, also in London, might well be seen as an effort, albeit less formal, to give expression to the idea of a cohesive national freethought movement.[8]

Two conferences, one at Manchester in 1852, the second at Stockport in 1854, brought together delegates from freethought societies around England and Scotland to discuss national strategy and objectives. Twenty groups sent reports or delegates to Manchester.[9] Only fourteen had representatives at Stockport.[10] More than anything, these

---

[5] "Theological Association," *Oracle of Reason* II (1842-43): 47. This article includes a more complete discussion of the Association's intended activities.

[6] See "Manifesto of Principles and Objects of the Society for the Promulgation of Naturalism," *Reasoner* I (1846): 252-54.

[7] See "Objects and Rules (Pro tem.) of the London Secular Society," *Reasoner* XIV (1853): 364-65.

[8] The January 1, 1854 *Reasoner* announces the opening of Fleet Street House. In its words, "Thanks to the zeal, confidence, and exertions of co-workers throughout the country, we attain to actual organization." "No. 147 Fleet Street," *Reasoner* XVI (1854): 1.

[9] "The First Secular Conference for the Organisation of Freethinkers," Report II, *Reasoner* XIII (1852): 305-8.

[10] "Secular Conference," *Reasoner* XVII (1854): 51-53.

gatherings served to assess the state of freethought in the early 1850's.

Finally, in 1866, a dream came true. A National Secular Society became a reality. Under the aegis of the *National Reformer*, and the presidency of Charles Bradlaugh, a program and a plan for national organization began to take shape.[11] That the National Secular Society did not immediately meet the approval of British freethinkers is suggested by the annotated principles published in the *National Reformer* in the fall of 1867. The clarifications were apparently intended to smooth over possible "misunderstandings" that might hinder Secularists from attending the upcoming Bradford conference of the National Secular Society.[12]

The problem with trying to organize freethinkers was that freethought could mean anything one chose it to mean. Several features inherent in the nature of freethought contributed to the difficulty of setting limits on what precisely it was, and what it was not. These same features made such a delineation absolutely essential if freethought as a movement was to accomplish anything of consequence. As the *National Reformer* well stated:

> Freethought people are very unlikely to organize--no radicals or democrats ever make much of concerted action. The reason is, that

---

[11] See "Proposed Programme for the National Secular Society," *National Reformer* VIII (1866): 169; "National Secular Society," *National Reformer* VIII (1866): 201; "Suggestions for a 'National Secular Society,'" *National Reformer* VIII (1866): 202.

[12] "National Secular Society," *National Reformer* X (1867): 234.

every Freethinker is a law maker, every democrat is a king in his way.[13]

The very term "freethought" implies an effort to escape from something deemed to be imprisoning. It has a negative sort of meaning, for it cannot be understood apart from that from which it represents a flight. Thus, it was always easier for the freethinkers to say what they were not, than what they were. Such a position places an organizational effort in the very unenviable situation of depending for its raison d'être on the very institutions which it is theoretically committed to destroy.

Freethinkers, in general, being discontented with the status quo, were committed to working class reform. What specifically that meant varied with each individual. According to the "Constitution and Objects of Secular Societies," published at the conclusion of the 1852 Manchester Conference, the three objects of Secular Societies were:

> 1) To promote primary attention to secular subjects; 2) To teach that Science is the providence of Life, and to warn men that 'absolute' spiritual dependency in human affairs may involve material destruction; and 3) The inculcation of Morals independently of Revealed Religion, by basing them on secular considerations more immediate, more demonstrative, and universal than those furnished by Scriptural Theology.[14]

Exactly how these aims were to be translated into daily policy and procedures was not at all obvious. Furthermore, active commitment to

---

[13] "The Question of Organisation," National Reformer III (December 7, 1861): 1.

[14] "Constitution and Objects of Secular Societies," Supplement to Reasoner XIII (1852): following 352. For an expression of frustration over the effort to arrive at a common understanding of the practical outworking of a slate of goals proposed for a union of London Secular Societies, see "To the Editor of the Investigator" from J. Maughan, Investigator V (1858-59): 205.

reform plus commitment to individual freedom necessarily involves one in the classic liberal dilemma of the extent to which people should be forced to be "free," or be coerced to seek their own "best interest."

Finally, as has already been discussed in the previous chapter, freethought as an organization suffered because freethought is, at its core, anti-organizational. The freethought movement sought to systematize a body of ideas and individuals that were inherently "anti-system." In one sense, the moment it organized, freethought abandoned its first principle. That the freethinkers themselves seemed so little troubled about this dilemma is no doubt a tribute to their inexorable faith in the self-revealing power of truth through reason. If men were free, they would all, of necessity, come to the same truth. Growing out of this was the sincere belief that what they were doing as freethinkers was purer--more disinterested--and therefore, exempt from the interfering personal biases that tainted others' efforts at articulating truth. It was other people, after all, not freethinkers, who built systems. As one freethinker, J. P. Adams, explained the situation:

> We are no system builders, for systems as a rule are the contrivances of the few for the delusion of the many. The facts of nature are open to all, and all that is necessary for the guidance, the safety, the order, and the general good of society is, that each should seek a knowledge of those facts, and act in obedience to them.[15]

Because they had no clear internal delimiting characteristics, the freethinkers necessarily expended a great deal of energy establishing

---

[15] J. P. Adams, "The Present Aspect of Freethought," *National Reformer* IV (August 8, 1863): 1. For another statement of the "exceptional" nature of freethought, see J. Watts, "Who Are Freethinkers?" *National Reformer* III (December 7, 1861): 2.

appropriate boundaries between themselves and a host of other religious, intellectual, political and socio-economic movements at work contemporaneously in Victorian England. It was not at all easy to tell which affiliations compromised the cause of freethought, and therefore should be avoided, and which were precisely the sort of concerns that the freethinkers should be about. Furthermore, no two freethinkers marked the boundaries in the same place. In the realm of religion and philosophy, freethinkers appeared to share some ground with sceptics,[16] Christian Socialists,[17] deists,[18] pantheists,[19] and positivists.[20]

---

[16] For examples of freethought concern over distinguishing their cause from scepticism, see the 1870 debate between Bradlaugh and Holyoake (footnote 112, chapter III); and "Atheos," "The Atheist Distinguished from the Scoffer," Movement II (1845): 92-93.

[17] For discussion on the relation of Secularism to Christian Socialism, see G. J. Holyoake, "Aspects of Christian Socialism," Reasoner X (1850-51): 265-66.

[18] On the relation of freethought to deism, see: Joseph B. Lear, "Deists," Oracle of Reason I (1841-42): 393-95; M. Q. Ryall, "Anatomy of Heterodoxies," Oracle of Reason II (1842-43): 125-27; C. Southwell, "Atheism and Deism," Movement II (1845): 43-45; C. Southwell, "Atheism and Deism," (Concluded) Movement II (1845): 51-53; C. Southwell, "The God of Nature and the God of the Bible Identical," (III) Movement I (1843-44): 244-48; "Atheos," "The Mustard Seed of Deism," Reasoner Tract IX, Reasoner IX (1850): after 102.

[19] For discussions on the relation of freethought to pantheism, see several articles and Holyoake commentary in Movement II (1845): 97-100; Wm. Maccall, "Pantheism and Secularism: A Lecture," (I) Reasoner XVI (1854): 280-82; W. H. N., "The Relation of Pantheism to Secularism," Reasoner XVI (1854): 13; F. B. B., "Pantheism and Secularism," Reasoner XVI (1854): 140-41; G. W. Foote, "Atheism and Pantheism," National Reformer XVIII (1871): 353-54.

[20] On positivism, see, for example, "'The Positive Philosophy of Auguste Comte,'" (II) Reasoner XV (1853): 375-76; Reviews of "The 'Positive Philosophy of Auguste Comte'" from Times 12/23/1853 and Weekly Dispatch, 12/18/1853, printed in Reasoner XVI (1854): 8-9; "New Society of Positivists in Paris" from "Paris Correspondent of the Atlas" printed in Reasoner XV (1853): 261-62.

Robert Owen associated with spiritualists toward the end of his life. Holyoake and Barker had, at one point, been Unitarians, and carried with them admiration for that tradition. Annie Besant and Charles Bradlaugh, later in their careers, mingled with Theosophists and others of the Eastern mystical ilk. The freethinkers were quick to rebuff any effort to equate freethought with any of these movements. Nonetheless, the family resemblances were sufficiently strong to cause confusion, both within and without the freethought movement.

Freethought shared personnel, if not explicit ideology, with numerous political causes of the day. These included agitation for an unstamped press, for freedom of thought and expression, for freedom of publication,[21] for the right of affirmation, for Sabbath Reform, and for republicanism, including the institution of universal suffrage. Some freethinkers, notably George Julian Harney, were Chartists.[22] Many were aspiring Utilitarian-liberals, sympathizers of John Stuart Mill and Jeremy Bentham. Nor did they restrict their concern to England. Holyoake, especially, solicited active support for the cause of Italian independence, and sympathized with liberal rebels in Poland.

There was a persistent strain of Socialism--the Utopian variety--in che freethought movement. It was most pronounced in the early years as

---

[21]The Anti-Persecution Union, which was devoted to fighting government interference with freedom of expression, shared official journals with the Holyoakites in 1844-1845. The complete title of the **Movement** was the **Movement, Anti-Persecution Gazette, and Register of Progress: a Weekly Journal of Republican Politics, Anti-Theology, & Utilitarian Morals**.

[22]For examples of attitudes toward Chartists, see note on tea-party at Lyne Dock Tavern, <u>Oracle of Reason</u> II (1842-43): 336; Holyoake, "The Integrity of Chartist Orators," <u>Reasoner</u> VII (1849-50): 225.

a result of Owenism, and in the years after 1870 when Holyoake devoted an increasing proportion of his time and energy to the development of effective cooperativism.[23] Though the freethinkers tended to support the "radical" side of rural economic organization, they became surprisingly conservative on matters relating to the development of urban working class consciousness. They favored association for education, recreation, and mutual financial assistance, but were less than enthusiastic about movements such as trade unionism[24] that sought to achieve economic advancement through manipulation of power or obstructive activities. It should be noted that objections to trade unionism were to the adversarial spirit that it represented. There was little question of their support of trade unions as a right of workingmen who had no alternatives for achieving their goals.

---

[23]For discussion of socialism, concordism, and the cooperative tradition, see: W. Oldham, "Doctrines of the Concordists," a series in Movement I (1843-44): e.g. 21-22, 110-11, 182-83; Holyoake, "Examinations of the Doctrines of the Concordists," (I) Movement I (1843-44): 302-3; Holyoake, "Examinations of the Doctrines of the Concordists," (II) Movement I (1844-45): 317-18; Holyoake, Notebook in Holyoake Manuscript Collection on "English Cooperation in French Literature," done at the request of Guillaumin & Co. of Rue Richelieu, Paris, 1902, Holyoake Collection, Bishopsgate Institute, London; Holyoake, "Co-Operation Distinct From Secularism," Reasoner XXX (1871): 33-35. Note that Reasoner XXX calls itself the Reasoner: A Secular and Co-Operative Review.

[24]See Holyoake, The Advantages and Disadvantages of Trades Unions, substance of a lecture to the Trades' Unionists of Sheffield (Sheffield: Hardcastle Printer, n.d.); "Caractacus," "Trades Unions," National Reformer III (September 7, 1861): 1; "Caractacus," "Trades Unions: A Defense," National Reformer III (November 23, 1861): 5; M. Q. Ryall, "The Industrious Orders, and 'Trade Unions' in Particular," Movement II (1845): 33-36.

Social issues were perhaps the most controversial, particularly the questions of teetotalism[25] and Malthusianism.[26] It would seem logical that anyone interested in promoting working class advancement would advocate means of limiting two of the greatest drains of the Victorian workman's pocketbook--alcohol and children. But the freethinkers were interested, not just in what they accomplished among the working classes, but in how that appeared to the rest of English society. They were scrupulously moral--some would even say Puritanical--another of their agenda items being to eradicate the common notion that to abolish the Established Church would be to unleash moral upheaval and social chaos on Victorian England.

The two goals clashed head-on in the matter of birth control. Birth control still connoted moral license, and thus could not be officially espoused by freethinkers who placed a premium on the queen of Victorian moral values--"respectability." At this point, one clearly

---

[25]For a discussion of the temperance question, see "The Bible and Teetotalism," *Reasoner* XVII (1854): 203-4; "Deficiencies of the Temperance Agitation," from *Christian Witness* No. 36, p. 592, printed in *Reasoner* IX (1856): 89; "The Maine Law Not a Moral Necessity," *Reasoner*, XX (1856): 113; "The Temperance Question," *National Reformer* X (1867): 290-91; "The Drink Trade and the Temperance Movement," *National Reformer* II (May 11, 1861): 1-2.

[26]On Malthusianism, see, for example, "Malthusian League," *National Reformer* IX (1867): 313-14; "The Malthusian Theory," *National Reformer* V (1864): 506-7; Review of *The Elements of Social Science; or Physical, Sexual, and Natural Religion*, *Investigator* IV (1857-58): 77-79. It was this book that Joseph Barker so condemned in his rift with Bradlaugh in 1861 over their differences in freethought moral policy. The most extensive discussion of the Malthusian question actually came after 1877, when Bradlaugh espoused the cause of E. Truelove's publication of Knowlton's *The Natural Fruits of Philosophy*. Though Bradlaugh argued that he was merely supporting the principle of freedom of publication, Holyoake thought his action an unnecessary tainting of the secular cause. (MacKay, *Biography of Charles Bradlaugh*, p. 29.)

sees the extent to which at least some of the freethinkers were as hypocritical as the Establishment they denounced.

The concerns for working class welfare and appearances conveniently coincided on the matter of teetotalism, but the two conflicted with a third value of freethought--freedom. How was it promoting self-discipline and moral responsibility in the long run to legislate against alcohol consumption? That was only bypassing and, in fact, deterring the self-policing that should be the mark of the truly free mature English workman.

The lack of an internally cohesive and consistent body of thought upon which to build a program was one of the freethinkers' greatest frustrations. It kept their energy divided in a dozen directions. Ironically, however, it is exactly this fluid nature of freethought that allowed its disciples to meddle in a multitude of causes at once, that accounts for most of the lasting and remembered contributions of the freethought movement. If a person in this century has even heard of the two leading working class freethinkers of Victorian England, it is probably because Holyoake espoused cooperativism and Bradlaugh insisted on getting into Parliament. The **Reasoner**, the **National Reformer**, and the National Secular Society are long since forgotten.

In addition to opening freethought to the demands of innumerable tangential reform movements in Victorian England, its initially weak theoretical foundation left freethinkers vulnerable to the whims and idiosyncracies of the personalities which it attracted. As was made clear in the preceding chapter, the movement was always somewhat in danger of being shaped in the image and for the purposes of the latest individual who had succeeded in commanding freethinkers' respect through sheer dint of personal presence and charisma.[27]

Thus, though everything in the nature and outworking of freethought militated against a strong sense of self-definition, its survival as a vital organization depended on just such a channelling of energy. It is toward that end that organizational efforts were directed. And it is in that process that freethought became a dogma.

In general, the problem of self-definition was whether freethought should have a positive or negative identify. Should it be known for what it was for, or against, for belief in "something," or "not something." Two schools of thinking, with corresponding implications in practical policy, operated in the movement for the duration of its existence. Perhaps nothing highlights the nature and distinguishing characteristics of the two positions any better than observing G. J. Holyoake's pilgrimage from the radical wing of the "negativist" school to the conservative wing of the "affirmativist" school.

It was around three types of issues that the two creedal positions developed: first, use of language in identifying themselves; second, views of epistemological certainty; and third, appropriate assignment of organizational priorities.

Language is crucial in a movement committed to propagation, for language is the conveyer of the message to be communicated. If words do not have the same connotation to the receiver that they had to the

---

[27]For a brief discussion illustrating the freethinkers' own awareness of their tendency to degenerate into factions inspired by personality differences, see "Our Policy," **National Reformer** III (September 14, 1861): 1.

sender, the message is obscured and the meaning lost. In teleological terms, it matters not at all what the speaker meant. It was the "affirmative" freethinkers who first took issue with freethought language. They were concerned on two grounds. First, words like "atheism" and "infidelity" implied a negative spirit. Furthermore, they were worn out. Holyoake noted in his diary the possibility of substituting "Netheism" for the term "atheism" and adds that the popular meaning of a term is of the "utmost importance" in the advocacy of truth.[28] Second, these words connoted a continuity and dependence upon the very systems that freethought repudiated. Holyoake, especially, did not like the judgment implied in the terms, "infidel" and "unbeliever." In a letter to the Morning Chronicle, he objected to that newspaper's identification of the Reasoner as an "infidel work":

> As the term 'infidel' in its derivation and application, is used to mean **faithfulness**, those who merely reject what to them are erroneous dogmas, and are yet faithful to truth and conscience, cannot, without injustice, be represented as **infidels**. We never entered into any obligation to be of the Christian Religion. We are free, as all men ought to be, to use our own discretion in the matter. Opinions are not the property of society, they are the children of evidence and of conscience, and society has no right to brand those who follow what to them is the truth . . .[29]

In the early 1850's, Holyoake made a point of initiating a supposedly new development of freethought to be known as "Secularism." He assured

---

[28] Holyoake Diaries, January 13, 1856, Holyoake Collection, Bishopsgate Institute, London.

[29] Holyoake to the Editor of the Morning Chronicle as printed in Reasoner VIII (1850): 69; For other examples of Holyoake's objections to "negative" freethought language, see Editorial "Cosmism and Atheism," Reasoner I (1846): 49: "Influence of the Pulpit in the Nineteenth Century," Reasoner III (1847): 345; The Report of the Four Nights' Public Discussion at Bradford between George Jacob Holyoake and John Bowes (London: E. Ward, W. Horsell, J. Watson, 1950): 45.

Reasoner readers that:

> We have not abandoned any principles--we have only reached a fuller development--the positive side of them, and a name implying that advancement is needed . . . We mean not to be ambiguous--so far from that, we would always wish to mean something intelligible.[30]

He objected to those who said that Secularism meant nothing peculiar since all people recognized certain non-sacred spheres of life and were in that sense, "Secularists." What distinguished "Secularists," according to Holyoake, was that, where others applied the term "secular" as an adjective to describe spheres of life, "Secularists apply it to the nature of all knowledge." It expresses a belief about what can be known, and therefore, of what can, with reason, be acted upon in this world.[31]

Not all freethinkers looked with kindness on Holyoake's claiming of the term "Secularism" as his own, nor of the separatism that it implied. The "negativists" were never as certain as Holyoake of the chasm that supposedly separated "affirmative" from "negative" freethinkers, nor of the essentially negative character of their own part of the movement.[32] It was one of Holyoake's "negative" antagonists who reminded him that, in any case, it was George Lewes, and not Holyoake, who had first articulated the notion of "positive freethought."[33] From 1852 on,

---

[30]Holyoake, "The Seculars--The Propriety of Their Name," Reasoner XIII (1852): 177-78.

[31]Ibid.

[32]See Investigator I (1854-55): 55-56; Investigator IV (1857-58): Preface, especially extract from Investigator I (1854-55).

[33]J. P. Adams, "Suggestions to Secularists," Investigator IV (1857- 58): 37.

Holyoake rather consistently used "positive" terminology to refer to his system. Not strangely, the "negativists," who claimed to be opposed to system building anyway, persisted in moving freely between the "positive" language of secularism and the "negative" terminology of freethought and atheism.

Apart from the recorded dialogue among the freethinkers, their concern for the image-carrying ability of language is no doubt reflected in the names of their journals--especially in the alternations in those names--and in certain of the pseudonyms--notably "Iconoclast"--by which various freethinkers chose to be known. The *Oracle of Reason* was, from start to finish, subtitled "Or Philosophy Vindicated," The *Movement*, also, was consistently the *Movement and Anti-Persecution Gazette*. The *London Investigator* became in 1857, with the beginning of volume IV, the *Investigator*--"A Monthly Journal of Secularism." It is particularly interesting that the basically anti-Holyoake *Investigator* had incorporated Holyoake's terminology in its title. Perhaps this is merely confirmation that they were not resigned to his claiming that territory and excluding them from it. The *Investigator*'s offspring, the *National Reformer*, also, from volume III on, made use of "affirmative" language in its subtitle "Secular Advocate and Freethought Journal."

It is with the *Reasoner* that the changes become more interesting. The *Reasoner*: A Weekly Journal--Utilitarian, Republican, and Communist, changed in 1850 to become the *Reasoner and Theological Examiner*. Volume XIII, beginning in June of 1852, dropped the "and Theological Examiner." After being just the *Reasoner* for half a year, the journal added to its title in volume XIV, "and Secular Gazette." Volume XVI was entitled the

<u>Reasoner</u>: Gazette of Secularism. In March, 1855, the name changed to the <u>Reasoner and London Tribune</u>. Volume XXI came out in 1856 as the <u>Reasoner--</u> Journal of Freethought and Positive Philosophy. In 1858, the old title the <u>Reasoner</u>: Gazette of Secularism returned in volume XXII. Volume XXV, 1860, was again "Journal of Freethought and Positive Philosophy." In January 1865, the <u>Reasoner</u> became "A Utilitarian and Secular Journal." In August, 1865, it changed to the <u>Reasoner</u>: A Political and Secular Review. Finally, when the <u>Reasoner</u> reappeared briefly in 1871, it had assumed a new interest, or more accurately, resurrected an old one. It was entitled the <u>Reasoner</u>: A Secular and Co-Operative Review.

This parade of variations may indicate nothing more than the vacilatory character of the <u>Reasoner</u>'s editor, or his excessive sensitivity to impression. It would be irresponsible to say anything with certainty on such scanty evidence, but perhaps it at least suggests that creating a positive system of freethought, as Holyoake sought to do, was a much shakier business than taking a stand in direct opposition to--and therefore, being supported by--an existing institution.

Within the freethought movement, even more fundamental than the language question was the question of epistemology. What sorts of things, and how much could one know with certainty? In other words, what exactly is open to reason? For those committed to rational living, this was an essential question, for what one knew would determine what one should and would do.

To the freethinkers, it was an issue of whether one should be an "affirmative" or a "negative" atheist.[34] The outsider would probably define the two positions as agnosticism versus atheism. Both "affirmative" and "negative" freethinkers argued that they did not actively assert the probability, or even the possibility, of a deity, such as the orthodox or even the deists defined "deity." But where the "negative" atheists explicitly denied the possibility of a God,[35] the "affirmative" atheists denied that absolute knowledge about such matters was possible.[36] They argued that, since no certain knowledge is possible about the non-material realm, the reasonable action is to behave with no base of reference in that world at all. Act as if it does not exist, for that is all one knows. Matter exists. That is clear. Whether there is anything else becomes quite irrelevant. How to live in this life is our concern. The "whys" are for the idle speculator--not for the freethinker. Furthermore, the "affirmative" atheists saw the "negative" atheists as giving the believers altogether

---

[34]For evidence of concern over the question of epistemology, see series by C. Southwell, "Sentimental Theists, and Natural Theology," (I, II, III), Movement I (1843-44): 34-35, 43-45, 52-55; M. Q. Ryall, "The Principles of Naturalism," Movement I (1843-44): 2, 11-12; "The Battle of the Choryphaei," Movement I (1843-44): 293-96, 307-12, 319-25; Holyoake, The Trial of Theism (London: Holyoake and Co., 1858).

[35]See for example W. Chilton, "Is There No God?" Oracle of Reason I (1841-42): 295-97; Chilton, "Definition of Atheism," Reasoner IX (1850): 127-29; Chilton, "Theistical Versus Atheistical Logic," Reasoner IX (1850): 307-9.

[36]Holyoake to Dr. Kalley, (V), Movement I (1843-44): 341-45; "Mr. Holyoake to Mr. O'Brien," Reasoner VII (1849-50): 289-91; W. E. B., "The Creation of the World," Reasoner IX (1850): 165; Holyoake, "Is There a God?" (XVII), Oracle of Reason I (1841-42): 243. For an example of public opinion on the issue, see "Letter to Editor," Birmingham Daily Gazette, October 14, 1869 commenting on Holyoake's Secular Education. Miscellaneous Envelope "Secularism," Holyoake Collection, Bishopsgate.

too much territory. Only a statement free of theological assertions--even negative ones--could release Secularists from dependence on their opponents. Holyoake re-introduced the Reasoner in 1864 as a publication

> to further enforce the distinctions and applications of that New Form of Freethought, which . . . raising no issue and permitting none, save as to the fact and quality of moral guidance--would recast the whole tone of controversy, hitherto mostly calumnious, fretful and fruitless.

He criticized the practice of attacking Christianity as "a sign of creative incapacity" and suggested that the "Negationist," who has no need of principles, is "apt to substitute illicit invective, which the ignorant or vicious, or irresponsible can equally contribute, for patient and energetic exposition, which can alone establish the dominion of ideas."[37]

One should note at this point that the "negative" atheists objected to that label. In their minds, they were the ones, not the "affirmative" atheists, who had maintained some content and therefore a

---

[37]Holyoake, Pamphlet announcing Reasoner (1864) Envelope #3, Holyoake Collection, Bishopsgate. For additional information on Secularism, see Christianity and Secularism: Report of a Public Discussion between the Rev. Brewin Grant and G. J. Holyoake (London: Ward & Co., 1853), esp. 221-23; Christianity versus Secularism: A Public Discussion in Newcastle-on-Tyne between the Rev. J. H. Rutherford and Mr. G. J. Holyoake (London: Ward & Co., 1854), 3-4; Mr. Geo. J. Holyoake's Three Lectures in Heywood in answer to Mr. E. Grubb's Lectures Entitled "Infidelity Unmasked" (Heywood: A Whitworth, 1852), Pamphlet Box #3, Holyoake Collection, Bishopsgate; Holyoake, The Positive Side of Free Inquiry (Reasoner Tract, 1852), Pamphlet Box #3 Holyoake Collection, Bishopsgate; Holyoake, The Organization of Freethinkers (London: James Watson, 1852), Pamphlet Box #3, Holyoake Collection, Bishopsgate; Holyoake, The Principles of Secularism Briefly Explained (London: Holyoake & Co., 1859); Holyoake, The Logic of Life (London: News agents' Newspaper & Pub. Co., 1861). On the matter of atheists being occupied with theist agenda, see Holyoake clipping from Secular Review, August 28, 1880 from Miscellaneous Envelope in Holyoake Papers on Secularism, Bishopsgate.

truly positive aspect to their atheism.[38] They knew where the boundaries were. The "affirmative" atheists had left the realm unprotected. Moreover, they hardly recognized the enemy.[39] The "negative" atheists knew that an atheist must be a materialist. They also knew that an atheist must be as much an apologist for atheism as the believer was for theism. To be an atheist, one must think it reasonable to disbelieve in God.

The "negative" atheists seemed less troubled than the "affirmative" atheists by their supposed re-active position. William Chilton openly acknowledged that active disbelief <u>does</u> depend on the prior existence of a theist position.[40] After all, if theism had not previously created a false and unjust foundation for Victorian England, there would be no need of making an issue of a-theism. The sort of "dependence" on orthodoxy of which the "affirmative" camp accused the "negative" atheists was to the "negativists" far less compromising to the cause than the openness that the "affirmative" atheists implicitly exhibited toward the theists.[41]

---

[38]See <u>Secularism, Scepticism, and Atheism, Verbatim Report of the Proceedings of a Two Nights' Public Debate Between G. J. Holyoake and C. Bradlaugh</u> (London: Austin & Co., 1870), 27-34. "Iconoclast," <u>A Plea for Atheism</u> (London: Austin & Co., 1864), 1-2.

[39]Robert Cooper, <u>Investigator</u> I (1854-55): 1 reprinted in "Anthony Collins," Editorial. <u>Investigator</u> IV (1857-58): 1.

[40]Chilton, "Is There No God?; Definition of Atheism." (See note 35). See also M. Q. Ryall, "The Principles of Naturalism" (II) <u>Movement</u> I (1843-44): 11.

[41]M. Q. Ryall, "The Incomprehensible God of a Socialist," <u>Oracle of Reason</u> I (1841-42): 302; Southwell to Editor of <u>Investigator</u> I (1854- 55): 27; Unsigned response to Holyoake's reaction to Cooper's speech on secularism, <u>Investigator</u>, II (1855-56): 145-46; "Anthony Collins,"

The extent of one's rational, and therefore certain, knowledge was important because of its perceived implications for the establishing of practical priorities. Since all the freethinkers were supposedly committed to the amelioration of the working class, what mattered ultimately was determining the most effective expenditure of energy for achieving that end.

The "negative" freethinkers argued that, since the Establishment was upheld by orthodoxy, and since orthodoxy was false, the shortest root to changing the status quo was to shake the foundation. The "affirmative" freethinkers countered that, though they did not think orthodoxy to be true, neither could they prove it false. Since all theological knowledge was outside the realm of reason, the most direct path to human improvement was to bypass theological concerns altogether. Construct a pattern for the "good life" apart from orthodoxy, and orthodoxy would die of its own accord.

In short, the question became, "Must the old be removed before the new can come?" The affirmative freethinkers said "No;" the negativists, "Yes."

While eschewing the adjective "negative," and protesting their belief that morality is the essence of truth,[42] the negativists asserted that a truly moral world could be attained only when truth is allowed free rein. At present, truth is shackled by the political and religious

---

Editor's Address, Investigator IV (1857-58): 1. "Collins" identifies Chilton, Jackson, Haigh, Bowker, M'Guire as being of his "party."

[42]"Anthony Collins," "Letters to Young Men," (II) Investigator V (1858-59): 44-46.

Establishment, and must be freed. According to one *Investigator* correspondent:

> The great labour of the earnest reformer, whether social or political, appears to me to be Iconoclasticism. Ghastly religious systems, slowly dying amidst their gaudy wealth, with their half-paralyzed limbs galvanized into a spasmodic and unnatural activity, stand in the way of all progress in either direction. The Bible is a millstone around the neck of truth, the Church a gravestone on the bosom of inquiry, while popular ideas on the subject of Deity have rendered the open expression of opinion dangerous, and its general reception for the present impracticable. Our labour then is to aim at the destruction of existing errors on these topics, and to widen the narrow and obstructed path before us. At the present day destruction is pre-eminently the work of the theological reformer.[43]

For the "negativists," destruction was clearly a means to an end, but it was a necessary means. Bradlaugh likened the task to pulling up weeds so that seed could grow. His work was not a substitute, but a necessary pre-requisite to sowing seed.[44] Or, in a different analogy, he compared theology to an empire that demanded universal allegiance. In that territory, it would be foolish to deny the relevance of one's belief to one's happiness. In his words, "independence can only be achieved by Secularistic resistance to theistic teachings--that is by the promulgation of atheistic views.[45] Thomas Paterson expressed similar conviction in the *Oracle*, "Let every one recollect that on the destruction of _religion_ depends our liberty, for _religion and liberty_

---

[43] Henry Tyrrell to Robert Cooper, "The Path Before Us," *Investigator* V (1858-59): 49-50.

[44] Bradlaugh's editorial in *Investigator* V (1858-59): 121 cited in Bonner, I: 79-80.

[45] Bradlaugh, *National Reformer* I (February 2, 1861) cited in Tribe, *President Bradlaugh*, 34.

can never co-exist.[46]

The "affirmative" freethinkers viewed their emphasis on construction as a more advanced stage of freethought than mere negativism. It was an effort to move beyond the categories and, therefore, the limitations of religion, and build a world on new terms. One Reasoner writer said:

> We have to a considerable extent, emerged from the war phase. The rough manners of the camp still cling to many of us. Having conquered our right to speak to ourselves and to those who are not with us, we have yet, most of us, to learn how to speak--to speak so as to persuade. To 'beat down our opponents' argument' is easy and often done--we are generally prepared for that; to 'put better arguments in their place' is not so easy . . .[47]

Holyoake, self-declared articulator of "affirmative" atheism, viewed "Secularism" as the belief that gives primary consideration to the experiences of this life, that seeks truth through reason and science, and finally, that pursues the building of a moral world grounded in human nature, utility, and intelligence. "Pure Moralism is a term which might be used as descriptive of the pervading characteristic of Secularism."[48]

In criticizing a recent Robert Cooper publication devoted to the negative side of freethought, Holyoake exhorted readers that the negative perspective "should be carefully and vigorously persecuted." He went on to discuss the necessity of developing, simultaneously with

---

[46]T. Paterson, "Politics for Politicians," (III), Oracle of Reason II (1842-43): 190. For further statements advocating priority on tearing down the old, see "Is There a God?" (XXII), Oracle of Reason I (1841-42): 321-23; J. C. F., "Policies of Socialism, and the Policy of the Socialists," Oracle of Reason I (1841-42): 161-63.

[47]C. F. Nicholls, "The Future of Secularism," Reasoner XII (1851- 52): 188.

[48]Holyoake, "Outlines of Secularism," Reasoner XVI (1854): 17-19.

negativism, a set of "<u>positive</u> principles." <u>Destruction</u> will be all the more effective if <u>construction</u> goes on with it.⁴⁹

What emerged, in effect was a division between "theological" atheists and "moral" atheists--if the adjectives are understood, not as character descriptions, but as labels of priority commitment. Both factions were, of course, interested in both theology and morality. It was a matter of disagreement over which area--being set on the right course--would most like bring the other along with it.

Inter-related with this question of priorities are two other controversial matters that had both theoretical and practical implications for the institutional development of freethought. First, how should freethinkers address the freewill/determinism paradox in human experience. Second, how does one find a balanced policy that gives due recognition to both the power of truth and the power of error.

Freethinkers found themselves in the same dilemma as any group that attempts to "solve" the "problem" of human freewill. On the one hand, they sought to protect man from the weight of guilt under which Christianity had placed him. Toward that end, they stressed the determinism of circumstances.⁵⁰ Man is the passive respondent to his

---

⁴⁹Holyoake, "Provincial Organisation," <u>Reasoner</u> XVII (1854): 417.

⁵⁰<u>Christianity versus Secularism--A Public Discussion in Newcastle- on-Tyne between the Rev. J. H. Rutherford and Mr. G. J. Holyoake</u> (London: Ward & Co., 1854). Note qualification to position--"All men ought to be judged primarily with reference to the condition in which they are placed; but, irrespective of condition we call that man virtuous who acts usefully towards himself and others, and that vicious who abuses his privileges, and neglects opportunit of doing good to himself and others," p. 26. See also W., "The New Argument 'A Posteriori' for the Existence of God." (I), <u>Oracle of Reason</u> I (1841- 42): 317; C. Southwell, "Response to 'An Investigator,'" <u>Oracle of</u>

environment. If he does not respond in a certain way, it is because there was not sufficient stimulation in his surroundings to evoke that response. Hidden in the midst of these assumptions was the notion that reason, if allowed unfettered reign, would convince man of the rationality, and therefore the desirability, of the good life. Therefore, if man was not behaving rationally, which included morally, it was a result of insufficient rational impetus. In any case, man was not to blame, and was not accountable.

On the other hand, freethinkers asserted man's autonomy in the universe, and his responsibility, once knowing the law of determinism, so to order the society that all men might be "determined" to know, and therefore to do, the good. Determinism was to the freethinkers a doctrine of freedom, not of bondage.[51]

The freethinkers do not explain how some are able to rise above their state, and take charge of their condition for themselves and for the benefit of society. Like the Christians they so despised, who blamed man as if he were free while simultaneously preaching predestination, the freethinkers addressed the working classes as if they were free to choose to rise above their condition, while inculcating them with a logical position that would appear to make such a

---

Reason I (1841-42): 102; "Proposed Act of Incorporation of the Colony of 'Equality,'" Herald of Progress, (1845-46): 65-67; Holyoake, The Trial of Theism (London: Holyoake & Co., 1858), 174; Holyoake, Rationalism: A Treatise for the Times (London: J. Watson, 1845), 9-10.

[51]"Proposed Act of Incorporation of the Colony of 'Equality,'" 66; Holyoake, "The Philosophy of Forbearance," Oracle of Reason I (1841-42): 121; Holyoake, Rationalism: A Treatise for the Times, 9-19; Holyoake, The Trial of Theism, 5; Henry Travis, "The 'Can't Help It' Fallacy," National Reformer, XI (1868): 330-31.

transcendence impossible.

Not surprisingly, this dilemma was never resolved. Both the "constructive" and "destructive" freethinkers lived with the apparent contradictions of their position. Nevertheless, each tended consciously to emphasize one side of the dichotomy. The "affirmative" freethinkers asserted their belief in determinism by concentrating on building a rational society that fostered goodness by rationally reinforcing good and discouraging evil in this world. "Good" was that which promoted utility and happiness. The "negative" freethinkers, by focusing on the rational discrediting of theology, through lectures, debates, and tract distribution, implicitly affirmed man's ability to discern truth from error, and therein to be responsible and accountable for choosing truth.

It hardly need be pointed out that, in the very act of emphasizing one aspect of the truth, each side merely deepened the paradox. For the harder one worked to build a rational society that would "order" goodness, the more he is assuming the freedom of someone, at least, to rise above his circumstances. The more one proclaimed truth with accountability, assuming he believed in a just cosmos, the more he is affirming the self-authenticating power of the truth and its "power" over error.

Developing a position that exhibited proper respect for both truth and error was especially important in coming to a policy about proselytizing. If one had utmost faith in truth's ability to reveal itself to the true seeker, then he would tend to favor a "passive"

approach to propagandizing. Proclaim truth and error will fall.[52]
Another might well argue that, if a barrier or error is distorting
truth, then vigorous aggression against the false is essential that
truth might be able to be rightly perceived.[53] To those who advocated
"calm," "formidable" adherence to truth,[54] the aggressive denunciators
of error seemed almost to be courting persecution for its own sake.[55]
From the latter's perspective, however, silence was merely failure to
deal with reality, or, even worse, cowardice.[56] The "affirmative" and
"negative" atheists might be loosely associated respectively with these
two positions.

G. J. Holyoake's passage from one school to another is no doubt
more important for what it suggests about Holyoake than about the nature
of freethought. Nevertheless, his experience does serve to illuminate

---

[52]C. S. M., "A Few Hints to Secularists," *Reasoner* XXV (1860): 29; Holyoake, "Outline of Secular Policy in Topics of Debate," *Reasoner* XXIII (1858): 169; Holyoake, "Self-Made Obstacles in the way of Progress," *Reasoner* XVII (1854): 148-51; Holyoake, "Another Series of the *Reasoner*," *Reasoner* VI (1849): 370-71.

[53]"Special Papers," *National Reformer* III (March 29, 1862): 5; C. Southwell, "Mr. Southwell's Reply to the 'Vindicatory Chapter,'" *Reasoner* IV (1847-48): 19-23; "Our Policy," *Investigator* V (1858-59): 124-25.

[54]Holyoake, "Self-made Obstacles in the way of Progress," p. 151.

[55]"Spectator," "Atheism and Deism: A Manuel of the Accredited Writings of Opponents," *Reasoner* XII (1851-52): 2-4; "Exaltada," "Freethinking Not a Disqualification," *Reasoner* XI (1851): 151-52; Holyoake, "Introduction to the Seventh Volume: An Epilogue," *Reasoner* VII (1849-50): ii-iii; "Omnipax," "How Christianity Should Be Attacked," *Oracle of Reason* II (1842-43): 119-20.

[56]For support of aggressive combatting of error, see W. Chilton, "Admirable Defence of Messrs. Southwell, Holyoake, Paterson, Finlay, M'Neil, and Miss Roalfe," *Movement* I (1843-44): 393-94; "Revival of Persecution in Hull-Public Meeting," *Movement* I (1843-44): 434.

some of the distinctions between the two positions by showing the
reasons why a freethinker at any one point might choose to belong to one
side over the other. Furthermore, he embodies in his thought and
actions the paradoxes that suggest that, though the freethinkers
themselves, at times, saw the approaches as opposites, the
affirmativists and negativists were not nearly as different as they
seemed.[57]

Holyoake came to freethought in search of freedom to be a seeker.
But he was not a seeker for its own sake; Holyoake truly wanted to find.
He wanted a cause big enough to accommodate him, and in whose service he
might find himself, or make his name, depending upon how one reads his
character.

In his <u>Oracle</u> and <u>Movement</u> periods, Holyoake was essentially a
"negationist." He argued against Owen for the inextricability of
atheism from socialism. During this time, his tenure in Gloucester Gaol
fed his anti-establishment leanings, and provided plenty of specific
details from personal experience with which to season his derision of
orthodox religion as practiced in nineteenth-century England.

Following the slump associated with Queenwood in the second half of
the 1840's, Holyoake deliberately sought to show that the cause of

---

[57]For samples of Holyoake's earlier more atheistic writing, see:
Holyoake, "Is There a God?" (X), <u>Oracle of Reason</u> I (1841-42): 130-31;
Holyoake, "Is There a God?" (IX), <u>Oracle of Reason</u> I (1841-42): 118-19;
Holyoake, "Mr. Owen's Thirteenth and Fifteenth Addresses," <u>Oracle of Reason</u> I
(1841-42): 97-98; Holyoake, "Is There a God?" (XIX), <u>Oracle of Reason</u> I
(1841-42): 275; Holyoake, "Discussion on the Question 'Is Belief in a
Deity of Any Kind Morally Beneficial?'" <u>Oracle of Reason</u> II (1842-43): 362-
63; "On the Commencement of our Second Volume," <u>Movement</u> II (1845): 1.

freethought was bigger than the vicissitudes of changing personalities and specific projects. In short, it was something worth believing in. The short-lived Herald of Progress and its successor the Reasoner represent Holyoake's effort to fill the desperate need for a permanent foundation of principles upon which freethought could take a stand.[58] It is during this period that he began to speak of the cause of "Secularism" rather than atheism or freethought. From that point, Holyoake never wavered from advocating a statement of freethought that focused on what the movement was for, rather than on what it was against. It was a system with principles that would be valid in their own right, long after the orthodox English Establishment had lost its sway.

This pilgrimage from the "negative" to the "affirmative" school can be understood from a number of perspectives. Certainly, it seemed logical to realize that, if freethought were to be an institution, rather than a reaction, it needed to rest upon an independent body of thought. Blasphemy charges were few and far between after 1845. Clearly, the movement could not derive its life from the "flames" of its martyrs.[59] Not all Holyoake's colleagues agreed that systemization was

---

[58]Holyoake, "Delineations of Atheism," Reasoner I (1846): 145-46; Preface, Reasoner I (1846): iii; Holyoake, "An Answer to 'Our Servant Jones,'" Reasoner X (1851): 337-39; See especially Holyoake, "Mr. Southwell's New Pamphlet Examined," Reasoner XIII (1852): 115 in which Holyoake specifically states that the Reasoner has been supporting "affirmative" unbelief since Reasoner, No. 19; Holyoake, Editorial, Herald of Progress (1845-46): 1. In Reasoner III (1847): i, Holyoake denies that he has "sold out" to Belief. According to Holyoake, "We tell Christianity, face to face, of her hollowness and untruth." (i.)

[59]Holyoake, "Going Fogging," Reasoner XXX (1871-72): 17. Though this is written much later, it illustrates at least how Holyoake

a proper end of freethought. They were in the business of tearing down dogma and creed, not of building it up. The goal of freethought was a world of political, social, and economic justice--not a new system of thought. Holyoake's opponents painted the development in rather unflattering light. Holyoake was obviously setting up a new "sect" with the intention of being a new "pope."[60] "Secularism" was a cover for the personal aggrandizement of G. J. Holyoake. It was something to give him a peculiar identify within freethought.

Without totally discounting either Holyoake's sincere interest in the welfare of freethought, or his power and influence, it seems that one must probe further for a complete explanation of Holyoake's espousal of "affirmative" atheism. Regarding the second explanation, it would seem that, if all Holyoake had wanted was influence within freethought, he could have gained that as effectively with a negative platform, as with an affirmative one, in the 1840's.

Formulating and personifying Secularism was above all a personal matter for Holyoake. It was an effort to get the "best of both worlds" in Victorian England. Holyoake had found in freethought the freedom to think as he chose. He had polished his tools of argument and perfected an apologetic to justify his own misgivings with the existing orthodox Establishment. But having "arrived" in freethought, he found that it was not enough. Holyoake was a creature of the old order more than even

articulated what he was doing in establishing Secularism. Moral actions required a principled foundation and Secularism provided those principles.

[60]Those who expressed most distrust of Holyoake's motives were Southwell, R. Cooper, and others associated with the <u>Investigator</u>.

he was perhaps willing to admit. While being free to question its foibles, Holyoake sought desperately to be "respectable" in Victorian society. He consciously cultivated contacts with the middle and upper classes.[61] He never tired of pushing on the working classes the raw materials of "respectability," such as education and good grammar.[62] For, in the end, Holyoake wanted to find a niche for himself in Victorian England that he could occupy with integrity, and then bring the working class along with him, far more than he really wanted to destroy Victorian England. Continuing to peddle iconoclastic atheism could never have brought Holyoake back into the mainstream of the society in which he most wanted acceptance. It smacked of civil disobedience and raised the spectre of working class revolt. Above all, it connoted in the minds of Victorians the imminent collapse of all morality, order, and decency--the very foundation on which their society rested. So, as Holyoake viewed the situation, to continue to use provocative language that communicated a very different message than that which he intended to communicate was akin to telling a lie. If

---

[61]It is impossible to read Holyoake's diaries and look at his scrapbooks of letters and signatures of Victorian notables without detecting his delight in being associated with "respectable" people.

[62]See for example Holyoake, The Handbook of Grammar (London: J. Watson, 1846); Holyoake, Practical Grammar: Intended for the use of those who have little time for Study (London: J. Watson, 1847); Holyoake, The Child's Ladder of Knowledge (London: F. Farrah, 1864); Holyoake, The Child's Second Letter Book for teaching Reading and Writing at Once (London: James Watson, 1854); Holyoake, "Instruction-- Rational and Scholastic," Movement I (1843-44): 257-58; Holyoake, "Instruction--Rational and Scholastic," (II), Movement I (1843-44): 265-66.

they were offended by the form, they would not receive the substance.[63]

Besides wanting the acceptance of the old order, Holyoake also wanted the security of its beliefs. He could not accept the content of the dogma, but he envied the certainty. During the 1850's, Holyoake cultivated a friendship with Francis Newman that was openly based, at least partly, on Holyoake's interest in Newman's theology.[64] It was this apparent pursuit of a belief system as an end in itself that most distinguished Holyoake from the other freethinkers.

Secularism seemed to integrate the differing aspirations and the various stages of Holyoake's journey. It was a system of principles founded on the surest sources of truth known to man--reason and science. It preserved morality, utility, and human nature. It freed man from the bogies of the afterlife, and the present tyrannies that rested on manipulation of guilt and fear at the thought of that uncertain future.[65]

Having said this, it is significant that, at no time, did Holyoake repudiate his disbelief in a deity.[66] In fact, he would argue that his

---

[63] Holyoake, "Another Series of the Reasoner" Reasoner VI (1849): 369-72.

[64] For other indications of his interest in some positive belief system, see Holyoake, "Lewes's 'Comte' and Leigh Hunt's 'Religion of the Heart,'" Reasoner XV (1853): 273-75; Holyoake, "Utilitarian Reveries," Reasoner IV (1847-48): 1-4.

[65] Holyoake, "Papers on Secularism," Reasoner XVI (1854): 81-82; "First Anniversary of the London Secular Society," Reasoner XVI (1854): 369-74; Holyoake, Principles of Secularism (London: Holyoake and Co., 1859); Holyoake, "The Policy of Secularism in Advocacy and Controversy," Reasoner XXIII (1858): 153.

[66] Though never affirming belief in God, he does sometimes appear to try to minimize the intensity of his former disbelief in God. See for

own life had been remarkably consistent.[67] He had simply adapted his emphases to his current understanding and to the needs of the time. And though he never tired of deriding the "mere" negativists, Holyoake would be hard pressed to show that they were not as actively involved in building as in tearing down.[68] Somewhat ironically, it was the arch "negativist" Charles Bradlaugh who succeeded in getting into Parliament and who seriously pursued such policies as republicanism and Malthusianism--policies that would have created a much "newer" England than Holyoake dreamed of, or even desired.

All the freethinkers shared this curious mixture of resentment at the "system" for its treatment of them, and repudiation of the ideological foundations of the system, but at the same time an unmistakable affinity for the system, and desire to make it work for them more than a desire to destroy it. That they had these feelings in common made them Victorian working class freethinkers. That they needed

example Holyoake, "The Limits of Atheism," Reasoner XXVI (1860): 160.

[67] Christianity and Secularism: Report of a Public Discussion between the Rev. Brewin Grant, B. A. and Geo. Jacob Holyoake, Esq. (Ed. of the Reasoner) (London: Ward & Co., 1853): esp. 221; Holyoake, Last Trial by Jury for Atheism, 99-100; "On the Commencement of our 2nd Volume," Movement II (1845): 1; Holyoake, "Justice," Oracle of Reason I (1841-42): 186; Holyoake, "Delineations of Atheism," Reasoner I (1846): 145-46.

[68] Chilton even at one point seems to modify his dogmatic denial of Deity. See W. Chilton, "Creation of the World--Reply to 'An Admirer of Truth,'" Reasoner IX (1850): 115; Christopher Charles "Real Religion versus Popular Religion," Investigator V (1858-59): 188-90; (In this article, Charles sounds like a Holyoakite in the sense that he makes Secularism a "religion" of morality, and calls it the real religion.); J. Barker, Investigator I (1854-55): 13; "Principles, Constitution, and Objects of the West Riding Secular Union," Investigator, I (1854-55): 264.

to formulate a "position" to survive, and that the position was necessarily forged in controversy, in an atmosphere of personal jockeying for influence, tended to accentuate the differences and obscure the underlying unity that had drawn the freethinkers into a movement in the first place.

In the end, each of the "schools" in its own way took on part of the character of the established Christianity they were both rejecting. The "affirmative" atheists preserved a religion. They might be viewed as being primarily concerned with the aspects of orthodoxy that were "not right" as opposed to those that were "not true."[69] They sought to retain and purify the morality while bypassing the theology. As Holyoake writes in "Secularism Distinguished from Atheism and Orthodoxy:"

> The difference between Atheism and Secularism may be put thus. Atheism is the negation of Theism--Secularism is the inculcation of Natural Morality; which is true, irrespective of the views of the sects. Its principles are independent of dogmas both of Atheists and Theists.[70]

The negative atheists were those who considered "not true" a much more insidious problem than "not right." The "false" must be purged from the land before any "right" can be profitably established. If the affirmative atheists developed a religion, the negativists were more zealously religious. Where the moralists produced a dogma, the

---

[69] For example of apparent primary concern for morality, see "Reply of Mr. Holyoake to the Rev. Richard Chester," Reasoner IX (1850): 159; At times, Holyoake appears to be defending God from Christian's moral blasphemy. See "The Newcastle Debate--Christianity versus Secularism," Reasoner XV (1853): 407.

[70] Holyoake, "Secularism Distinguished From Atheism and Orthodoxy," Reasoner XXIII (1858): 146.

a-theologians were far more dogmatic. Moreover, both schools led to a peculiar kind of certainty that gave to both the "affirmers" and the "negaters" a "positive" identity--something to be about.

Ironically, coming to a sense of "self" was life-threatening for freethought. Clearly, to survive and be effective, they needed an agenda and a presuppositional foundation upon which to justify that agenda. But neither the affirmative or negative orientation was totally satisfactory. Each, while answering somewhat the need for a direction of operation, created new dilemmas.

The negationists offered a clearly defined policy, but it was so very dependent on enemy initiative. It drew its enthusiasm from their persecution. It drew its rhetoric from their dogma and their mistakes. The freethinkers' own strength varied in direct proportion to the strength of the opponent. Freethought agitation inspired orthodox zeal which, in turn, provoked further intensified freethought activity. The negationists were in the rather uncomfortable position of flourishing and fading as the enemy flourished and faded. To destroy the enemy was to destroy themselves. For the negationist, the freethought mission was, in the end, a kamikaze mission. For some, that self-extinction would not have been too great a price to pay for the annihilation of the enemy. But the survival instinct is strong for institutions, as for individuals, and the "affirmative" atheists clearly wanted to outlive their antagonists. They wanted a system independent of Christianity that could stand on its own merit.

The "affirmative" freethinkers could have achieved this, except that they were themselves, but in a different way from the "negationists," also intricately intertwined with the orthodoxy they repudiated. True, they had rejected some of the presuppositional foundations. Nevertheless, to the degree that the positive freethinkers chose to focus on what they affirmed, rather than on what they denied, they were choosing to focus on the very values, standards, and aspirations that they shared with "establishment" Victorian England.[71] They seemed oblivious to the fact that, in such a large measure, the freethinkers had equated "reasoned" society with Victorian Society purged of its vices. Thus, the more they emphasized the "positive" life of morality, the more difficult it became to distinguish between freethought and Victorian Christianity. Secularism claimed to have no interest in theology, and Victorian Christianity was very concerned about morality. What would hinder a person from belonging to both parties?[72]

If the "negationists" strengthened the enemy by attacking him, the affirmative freethinkers, by not attacking, weakened themselves. The more they blended in Victorian society, that is, the more they became "respectable," the less of uniqueness they had to offer. Interestingly, in his early days, few were more critical of freethinkers seeking respectability than the father of "Affirmative Atheism," G. J. Holyoake. The institutional elevation that cut the reformer from the masses was to

---

[71] For an example of their own testimony on this matter, see "The Rev. C. Williams on Secularism," **National Reformer** II (April 20, 1861): 3.

[72] For indication of concern among the freethinkers for this matter of uniqueness, see E. Gottheil, "Can a Christian Accept Secularism and Retain His Religion?" **Investigator** IV (1857-58): 91.

be avoided at all costs. It had been Owen's downfall. Socialism, according to Holyoake "has drawn around itself a conventional circle, over which the poor man cannot step."[73]

The freethinkers, including Holyoake, struggled with this dilemma resulting from the fact that success in promoting improvement cuts one off from those who need help the most.[74] That Holyoake eventually had to contend with the same accusations he had made against Owen is perhaps evidence of his success in reform work, but at the same time, evidence that he also had failed to find a resolution to the "respectability gap."[75] Furthermore, once he had arrived, it is unlikely that Holyoake would have been interested in closing the gap, if it had meant his own going even part way.

Thus, both the negationists and the affirmativists, in proportion to their success, worked themselves out of a distinct position in Victorian Society. They were both, though in different ways, parasites, at the mercy of the life of the host.

That is to move to the perspective of the twentieth-century spectator. It did not appear nearly so glum to the Victorian freethinkers. In the mid-nineteenth century, they had, as a result of

---

[73] Holyoake, "Men of Business," Movement I (1843-44): 373.

[74] Holyoake, "Socialism," Movement I (1843-44): 41; W. Chilton, "You will Injure Our Cause," Oracle of Reason I (1841-42): 254-55; John Cramp, Gen. Sec., "To the Members of the Rational Society," Herald of Progress (1845-46): 37.

[75] Holyoake, "The Progress of Secular Organisation," Reasoner XV (1853): 337. Holyoake would come to defend the advantages of "respectability." See No. 5 by Holyoake in J. Watts and "Iconoclast," (eds.), Half-Hours With Freethinkers (London: Watts & Co., 1864).

years of struggle and hard work, come of age. Whether as an "affirmativist" or a "negationist," or as some combination of the two, they had something to be about. They had bookshops, and their own publications. They had a national institution with a network of local societies. Freethought had moved from being an attitude to an organization. It had a hierarchy of dignitaries. It had a bureaucracy of sorts. It had a creed. Freethought was a force to be reckoned with. Unbeknownst to contemporaries, at this very point of institutional triumph, and in part because of this triumph, freethought was in danger of losing its soul.

V

The freethinkers had their feet in two worlds. Furthermore, they seemed to like it that way. To switch metaphors, they wanted freedom from the orthodox moorings, but they clearly did not want to, or be thought to want to, drift out to sea. Holyoake assured his readers that "freethinking does not . . . lead to Anarchy in Thought."[1] In a later Reasoner editorial, he summarizes the Secular position:

> We are freethinkers, not in the sense of caprice or wantonness, but in the sense of thinking for ourselves, and, where necessary, without the permission of church or state, and without any fear of eternal perdition for so doing. Honest thinking can bring no condemnation from a just God, whether it agrees with or differs from the orthodox. We do not feel called upon to agree with the Bible, but to agree with the truth, whether we find it in the Bible or out of it. We consider the book of Nature a higher and more reliable book than the Book of the Jewish prophets or of the Jewish fishermen. We are not freethinkers in the sense of being lawless thinkers, or licentious thinkers, as some suppose—but freethinkers in the sense of being self-thinkers. . . . The self-thinker feels bound to follow the truth wherever he may find it, and wherever it may lead; he feels bound to study nature, to recognize facts, to follow reason and experience.[2]

While purporting to be striving to rid society of "godism," as a means to greater political, social, and economic justice, the

---

[1] Holyoake, "Modern Freethinking: Its Definition, Sphere, and Defence," Reasoner XII (1851-52): 81.

[2] Holyoake, "Self-thinking and Secular Morals," Reasoner XVII (1854): 160.

freethinkers ended up defending most of the ends toward which Christianity, in theory, is directed. While claiming to denounce the system itself, they succeeded to a remarkable degree, in reality, in affirming the system and seeking to eliminate merely its abuses.

Because of the religious backgrounds of many of the freethinkers, their concern for hypocrisy and falsehood in contemporary orthodoxy, and their need for an operational policy, the freethinkers created a movement that, in addition to being preoccupied with the categories and terms of its opposition, took on a creedal form of its own in the very process of organizing to combat creeds and the narrowness they represented.

This formation of a dogma, which was, at first, an effect of the freethinkers' effort to mobilize, became itself a cause of further systemization and ritualization as freethought increasingly acquired the character of the religion it claimed to despise. What had begun as a by-product of the need to harness undisciplined zeal became an end in itself as freethinkers sought to preserve and propagate the "fellowship of the unchained." Freethought, one might argue, served as a stopping-off point for travellers on the road from one world view to another. It eased the shock of coming to terms with the possibility that, not only one's answers, but one's questions had become totally irrelevant. Freethought, in effect, developed into a transitional belief system that not only permitted organized agitation against outworn orthodoxy, but also increased the appeal of the movement to those looking for alternative ways of obtaining the perceived advantages of religion without its liabilities.

Militant freethought, in essence, gave new answers to old questions. The answers claimed to free the working classes from bondage to the old order of tyranny and superstition. For some, in a sense, they did that. In reality, however, it is the questions one asks, as much as the answers one accepts, that determine the parameters of one's world view. The fact that the questions were framed in the terms of the mind-set from which they sought freedom kept the freethinkers forever partially in that world, and limited their appeal to those in Victorian society who also were struggling with the same questions.

Of prime importance to all the freethinkers at some point, and to some of them throughout their lives, was the matter of the character of ultimate reality.[3] Is there a God? If so, what is His relation to the Cosmos? What is His nature? That such knowledge was perceived to be significant for the living of one's life, and that it was thought to be obtainable, testify to the distance that separated freethinkers from the unself-conscious "Secularists" of our own day, and even of Victorian England.

---

[3] For examples of discussions centering on the nature of ultimate reality, see: G. Baillie, "Materialism," **Reasoner** V (1848): 217-20; C. Southwell, "Atheism and Deism," **Movement** II (1845): 43-45, 51-53; "Atheos," "The Atheist Distinguished from the Scoffer," **Movement** II (1845): 92-93; Holyoake, "The Philosophic Type of Religion, Developed by Professor Newman: Stated and Examined," **Reasoner** XI (1851): 83-86; "Iconoclast," "A Plea for Atheism," (3-part series), **National Reformer** VI (1865): 1, 17, 33; C. Southwell, "Alphabet of Materialism," **Movement** I (1843-44): 449-51; II (1845): 1-4, 17-19, 81-83; William Maccall, "The Living God," (5 parts), **Reasoner** XIV (1853): 388-90, 404-6; XV (1853): 6-7, 38-39, 70-72; William Gillespie and Charles Bradlaugh debated the question of atheism intermittently in the **National Reformer** from "Debate on Atheism," **National Reformer** X (1867): 289-90 to "The Debate on Atheism, 'Gillespie v. Bradlaugh' Last Paper," **National Reformer** XIII (1869): 129-30.

The freethinkers made certainty in theological matters the goal after which to seek, and the measure of one's presuppositions about the universe.[4] Furthermore, as with the orthodox, the question of ultimate reality was one that had to be dealt with, one way or another, before one could proceed with daily living. In 1882, G. J. Holyoake published a work, which, perhaps more explicitly than anything else, captures the Janus-like character that freethought had become. According to <u>Secularism a Religion Which Gives Heaven No Trouble</u>, what man needs is a religion of certitude;[5] Secularism fills that need in seeking "to transact the business of humanity on purely mercantile principles. It engages only in that class of transactions the <u>issue of which can be tested by the experience</u> of this life."[6] "Science and Utilitarian Morality are Kings in that country, the Land of Certitude, and rule there by right of conquest over error and superstition."[7]

Now it is true that the freethinkers, when pressed on the issue, very often denied that they did or could affirm with certitude that there was no God. Rather, they sought merely to establish that the burden of proof on the question of an Ultimate Being rested with those who affirmed His existence and not with those who questioned it.[8]

---

[4]Holyoake, "The Critics of Atheism," (II), <u>Reasoner</u> XX (1856): 25.

[5]Holyoake, <u>Secularism a Religion Which Gives Heaven No Trouble</u> (London: Watts & Co. 1882), p. 6.

[6]<u>Ibid</u>., p. 7.

[7]<u>Ibid</u>., p. 8.

[8]See, for example, "M.," "Is There a God?" (XVIII), <u>Oracle of Reason</u> I (1841-42): 251; "Iconoclast," "A Plea for Atheism," <u>National Reformer</u> V (1864): 10-12.

The orthodox would no doubt have insisted that the proof was already in.

Furthermore, the "affirmative" freethinkers did seek increasingly to discard the emphasis on theology by focusing solely on matters that pertain to this life. But even this move incorporated an implicit deliberate resolution of theological issues--that is, the decision to ignore them--that would be foreign to most twentieth-century citizens.[9]

Thus, to the question of the nature of ultimate reality, freethinkers provided a qualified, if not an outright materialistic answer. Clearly, there was not sufficient evidence to merit belief in a personal, or even an impersonal, Deity, such as the Christians or Deists posited.[10] Therefore, for all practical purposes, such a Being did not exist; at least one must live life without taking Him into consideration.[11] Furthermore, an explanation of the universe that accepted matter as the ultimate reality was equally as defensible and perhaps even more satisfactory than those explanations that presupposed matter an intermediate, rather than a final, cause.[12] Of at least

---

[9]See, for example Holyoake, "Perils of Neutral Ideas," Reasoner XXX (1871-72): 1-2; Holyoake, "Going Fogging," Reasoner XXX (1871-72): 17-18.

[10]See, for example, "M.," "Is There a God?" (XX), Oracle of Reason II (1842-43): 125-27; Holyoake, "To Dr. Kalley," (V), Movement I (1843-44): 341-45.

[11]T. Paterson, "Little Faith, Much Gain," Oracle of Reason II (1842-43): 81; "Iconoclast," "A Plea for Atheism," National Reformer V (1864): 11-12; "Secularism as a System of Truth and Morality," National Reformer XVI (1870): 211; Holyoake, "Secularism a Method of Thought and Action," Reasoner XXX (1871-72): 49-50; Holyoake, "A Short History of Secularism," Reasoner XXX (1871-72): 225-26.

[12]C. Southwell, "The Free Inquirer's Why and Because," (III), Oracle of Reason I (1841-42): 245; "Is There a God?" (XXIII), Oracle of Reason I (1841-42): 371; See note under "Library of Reason," Oracle of

two things the freethinkers were certain--their own existence, and that of the world around them.[13]

Having rejected the orthodox God as the basis of reality, the freethinkers still wanted to know the truth and they still wanted an authoritative guide to life. What is perhaps even more remarkable than their asking for an authority is their obvious belief that such an authority was available and that it would make itself known to the true seeker. The following poem from the National Reformer illustrates well the hopes of at least one freethinker in this regard:

The Chief Good:

What is the greatest good?
To love the Truth with undivided heart;
To seek it with unwavering purpose;
With fearlessness of soul prepar'd to brave
The fury of a world, for that world's good,
To trample down the mental despotism
Which seeks to chain the soul's immortal powers
Within the narrow limits of a creed
Set forth by earthly tyrants. Only demons
Need a chain, not the freeborn soul of man.
Its native element is liberty;
Take that away, and she becomes a weak
And sickly thing, that languishes, and lives
A crippled fragment of humanity--
Mean, despicable, servile; frighten'd oft
At some strange truth, and shuddering quick returns
Within her little world. So the caged bird,
Ignorant of freedom's glorious life,
Deems her narrow prison no confinement,
The broad blue sky, the verdant trees, and flowers
That bloom in nature's pride, ne'er yet recall'd

Reason II (1842-43): 239; Ryall, "Principles of Naturalism," Movement I (1843-44): 2, 19-20; Holyoake, "To Dr. Kalley," (V), 343; "Iconoclast," "A Plea for Atheism," National Reformer VI (1865): 1-3; Holyoake, "Examination of the Doctrines of the Concordists," (I), Movement I (1843-44): 302.

[13]"Materialism," Oracle of Reason II (1842-43): 65-66; M. Q. Ryall, "The Principles of Naturalism," (II), Movement I (1843-44): 10.

> Its glorious destiny. And if, perchance,
> It gets beyond the customary bounds,
> Bewildered at the sight, with beating heart
> And fluttering wings she hurries back, and spurns
> The proffered liberty.
>
> What is the greatest good?
> To love the Truth--not for ourselves alone;
> There is a nobler end, to lift up truth that all
> Diseased by Error's venom'd sting, may look
> And live; that Mercy, Joy, and Love may reign
> Triumphant o'er the hearts of all.
> G. H. S.[14]

In the Enlightenment tradition, reason was, for the freethinkers, the source of all truth.[15] As one freethinker expressed it:

> Whatever expedites the business of reasoning expedites the common business of life, and hastens the adjustment of that great question--the relation of man to the external world--in which human happiness is involved.[16]

Reason was the new revelation--the true gospel. Reason alone could dispel prejudice, topple tyranny, and break through the darkness of superstition. The *Reasoner* begins volume IV singing her praises:

> Men are now beginning to suspect all causes which reason will not serve . . . The pike will fall. The musket will be grounded. Liberty's true champion is Reason. At its voice prejudice is

---

[14] G. H. S., "The Chief Good," *National Reformer* I (June 2, 1860): 4.

[15] Holyoake, "A New Estimate of Christianity's Historical Evidences," *Movement* I (1843-44): 281-83; "Undecimus," *The New Testament--No. 2* (*Reasoner Tract No. 55*), *Reasoner* X (1850-51): following 438, p. 4 of tract; Holyoake, "Truths to Teach," *Reasoner* XII (1851-52): 1; Holyoake, "Secularism an Induction not an Invention," *Reasoner* XXIII (1858): 9-10; *Secularism, Scepticism, and Atheism: Verbatim Report of the Proceedings of a Two-Nights Public Debate between G. J. Holyoake and C. Bradlaugh*, p. 4; Holyoake, *The Policy and Resources of Freethinking*, 1848 (Pamphlet Box #1) Holyoake Collection, Bishopsgate, p. 2.

[16] Holyoake, "A New Estimate of Christianity's Historical Evidences," p. 281.

enlightened, clamour is hushed, violence is stilled, tyranny is confounded, and the advance the people make knows no reaction.[17]

It was his increased reasoning capacity that gave man his edge over the animals. To have reason, and to use it rightly, was to be strong. To be without reason was to be weak and miserable.[18]

Closely allied with reason was science,[19] the methodology through which man transferred the experiences of this world into rational categories, which, in turn, enabled him to harness the phenomena of the universe for the progress and happiness of mankind. Science was, to the Secularists, the new Providence.[20]

If one asked for criteria of "reasonableness," one would no doubt be told that it was to be determined by utility. What was useful, what was efficient, what contributed to human improvement--these things were "reasonable." To reply that such criteria merely pushed one step back the element of subjectivity in their absolute principle would have seemed inappropriate. To the Victorians, such measures seemed obvious, and, notwithstanding the departure from a strictly rational-empirical epistemology, matters of simple intuition.[21]

---

[17]Introduction to Reasoner IV (1847-48): i.

[18]C. Southwell, "The Free Inquirer's Why and Because," (XVI), Oracle of Reason II (1842-43): 205.

[19]Holyoake, "Secularism in the Cabinet," Reasoner XV (1853): 355- 57; John Watts, "The Providence of Life," National Reformer VI (1865): 589-90; Holyoake, The Trial of Theism (London: Holyoake & Co., 1858), p. 175; Holyoake, The Principles of Secularism Briefly Explained (London: Holyoake & Co., 1859) p. 14.

[20]Holyoake, "The Policy and Resources of Freethinking," Reasoner IV (1847-48): 296.

[21]Holyoake, "The Moral Remains of the Bible," (Chapter 1), Reasoner

The freethinkers seemed quite untroubled by the fact that, very often, reasonable human beings differed on matters of judgment and interpretation. Indeed, the movement, by its very nature, fostered diversity. What reconciled for the freethinkers their simultaneous espousing of the right of private judgment and the infallibility of Universal Reason was their belief that truth as reason possessed both the inclination and the power to vindicate itself.[22]

In what appears almost to contradict the foregoing confidence in reason, the freethinkers also believed that, if reason did not appear to be operating effectively in a person or in a situation, it was being inhibited from doing so by the forces of tyranny and superstition.[23] Thus, reason was both captive and liberator vis à vis the powers of ignorance and fear. For the freethinkers, spreading Enlightenment was a process of introducing reason to itself. Reason external to an individual would recognize itself inside the shell of fear and darkness that encased the British working man. The reunion of the two would result in the liberation of the individual in question and restore him to harmony with the universe. Most immediately, that would mean freedom

---

V (1848): 21; C. D., "Discussion on the Question 'Is Belief in a Deity of any Kind Morally Beneficial?'" Oracle of Reason II (1842-43): 363.

[22]Holyoake, "Expectations of Readers," Reasoner VI (1849): 209; "Ion," "The Advantages of Criticism, and Mr. Macready's Treatment in America," Reasoner VI (1849): 354; The Report of the Four Nights Public Discussion at Bradford between George J. Holyoake and John Bowes (London: E. Ward, W. Horsell, and J. Watson, 1850), p. 44; Holyoake, "Remarks on Mr. Search's Letter," Reasoner V (1848): 338.

[23]"Hints on Politics, II," Oracle of Reason II (1842-43): 42; C. D., "Discussion on the Question 'Is a Belief in a Deity of any Kind Morally Beneficial?'" p. 364; Holyoake, "A New Estimate of Christianity's Historical Evidences," p. 283.

to think for himself, to pursue self-improvement, and thereby, to contribute usefully to the edification of society.

This belief in reason's irresistible power to convince of truth relieved the individual from fear of believing--and therefore behaving--wrongly. If he did not believe a certain way, it was the result of insufficient freedom for reason to be itself. The individual in pursuit of truth could only be as he was. Whereas Christianity demanded that one believe "rightly," thereby limiting the right to be a seeker, freethought asked only that one believe "sincerely."[24]

Thus, freethinkers proclaimed to the Victorians a sure guide to progress and happiness in this world. The Reasoner stated:

> It is not the spreading of certain doctrines of belief or disbelief, so much as diffusing a taste for education personal, practical, and independent. It is to teach men to think for themselves, and to give a resolute reason for the "faith that is in them." It is to lead them by inductive steps to knowledge, until they stand alone and reason on life unfettered, and act on humanity with the purpose of progress.[25]

On the matter of social morality, the freethinkers determined to beat orthodoxy at its own game. It is almost a truism that respectable Victorians feared disorder among the masses far more than they feared atheism. Guarding the faith was a means to keeping the peace, for, at that point, morality without a religious base was thought to be a contradiction in terms. It was left to the freethinkers to assert that

---

[24]Holyoake, "Distinction Between Secular Rights and Christian Rights," Reasoner XIX (1855): 185; Holyoake, "Self-Thinking and Secular Morals," Reasoner XVII (1854): 162.

[25]Holyoake, "Expectations of Readers," p. 209.

such was, in fact, not the case.[26]

The freethinkers, too, wanted morality, law, and order. As a matter of fact, they prided themselves on upholding orthodox morality better than the Establishment.[27] After all, cultivating justice, thrift, goodness, and honesty was in the best interest of the working classes, both internally, and in terms of how they would be perceived by other classes of English society. Furthermore, it was in the name of the standard of morality common to the realm that freethinkers fought for redress of political and social grievances of the working classes. To have berated the standard would have been to sabotage the cause.

The problem, according to the freethinkers, was not with morality, but with the way in which morality fit into the orthodox system. The orthodox had erred on two counts. First, they had judged morality by religion, and goodness by orthodoxy, rather than vice versa.[28] An act was good, not because it was mandated by a creed. Rather, it was true to the extent that it was good--that is, to the degree that it contributed to human welfare. According to one Oracle writer, even the question of God's existence must be decided on a moral basis: "It must

---

[26]"Meetings," (Nottingham), Investigator V (1858-59): 183; M. Q. Ryall, "Anatomy of Heterodoxies," Oracle of Reason II (1842-43): 82-83; "Christopher," "Religion, Atheism, and Art," Reasoner, XI (1851): 118; C. Watts, "Atheistic Morality," National Reformer VIII (1866): 33-34.

[27]"Mr. Holyoake and His Lecture," Reasoner V (1848): 452. For further evidence of desire for moral system, see Holyoake, "The Philosophic Type of Religion," (Conclusion), Reasoner, XI (1851): 100.

[28]Holyoake, "Relation of Christianity to Morality and to Progress," Reasoner V (1848): 353-58; Holyoake, "The Logic of Death," Reasoner VIII (1850): 34; T. S. M., "Is There No God?" Oracle of Reason I (1841-42): 373-74; "Mr. Holyoake's Reply to the Rev. Dr. Kerns, of St. James's Church," Reasoner X (1850-51): 459.

be ultimately settled by its own intrinsic merits; that is whether it be for the good of mankind to believe in a god of any kind or no."[29] Thomas Paterson, in "Religion Destructive of Morality," suggests that religion actually inhibited morality by its promoting of intolerance in the name of truth, by its associating reasonable morality with irrational religion, and by its focusing on abstraction rather than on the reality of this world.[30]

Second, the Establishment had made the Christian religion the basis of English morality.[31] In doing so, it was necessarily promoting good for inferior reasons--for fear of hell, for the hope of eternal reward--and not for its own sake.[32] Furthermore, in directing believers' attention to the world to come, the orthodox implicitly, and sometimes even explicitly, hampered efforts to make life in this world the very best that it could be. Finally, they were grounding British morality in a religion that was itself immoral. The freethinkers were only too ready to point out choice passages from scripture--especially the Old Testament--to confirm their contention that Christianity, if anything, promoted immorality by giving it such extensive coverage in its canon.

---

[29] T. S. M., "Is There No God?" p. 373.

[30] T. Paterson, "Religion Destructive of Morality," Oracle of Reason II (1842-43): 138.

[31] T. Paterson, "The Christian Religion," Oracle of Reason I (1841- 42): 336; "Supernaturalism Considered as a Question of Moral Influence," (I), Oracle of Reason II (1842-43): 3-5; W. J. B., "Goddism and Thuggism," Oracle of Reason II (1842-43): 114-17; "B," (Subscriber), "The Moralities of Christ and the Philosophers," Reasoner XIV (1853): 181-84.

[32] "Defence of the Civil Rights of Atheists," Reasoner XI (1851): 307-10.

G. J. Holyoake went so far as to print an edited version of the scriptures that would render them useful for moral instruction. "The Moral Remains of the Bible--A Version of the scriptures not 'authorised,' but suitable to be read in 'churches' and Sunday Schools," took Old Testament narratives and re-worked them to illustrate values like "fraternity," "friendship," and "hospitality."[33] In a reply to a subscriber who apparently had argued for the indispensability of Christianity to morality, Holyoake commented on the immorality at the very core of orthodoxy:

> He seems to forget, that Christianity had its birth in immorality. Does he not remember the miraculous conception? unnatural, impossible, and contrary to all scientific knowledge. Does he forget that God's vengeance was appeased by a vicarious sacrifice-- or will he say that these are not parts of Christianity, when the mass of Christians hold them as the bulwark of their faith.[34]

In the minds of the freethinkers, morality should take precedence over religion, for it transcended religion.[35] At one point, the Reasoner described the task of anti-religious work as "rescuing morality" from the "ruins of theological arguments."[36] Religion was a

---

[33] See series by Holyoake, "The Moral Remains of the Bible," Reasoner V (1848): beginning 21. Not to be outdone, "Panthea" suggested a moral version of Handel's Messiah that would exalt "Liberty, the People's Messiah." "Panthea," "Music for the People," Reasoner VI (1849): 69-72.

[34] Editor. "Further Reply to Mr. Norrington," Reasoner XI (1851): 216.

[35] Freethinkers reminded the Establishment quite regularly that morality did not originate with the Christian religion. See, for example, Holyoake, "Relation of Christianity to Morality and Progress," Reasoner V (1848): 357.

[36] Holyoake, "Influence of the Pulpit in the 19th Century," Reasoner III (1847): 345.

matter of private concern and should not be allowed to infringe on morality which was in the true public interest.[37] Indeed, morality was the only religion considered worthy of rational, secular man.[38] The touchstone of morality was utility.[39] Whatever contributed to man's happiness and progress in this world was good. Given this measuring rod, and the freethinkers' assessment of religion, it is quite understandable that orthodoxy fell far short of qualifying for any citations of moral excellence from freethought.

Finally, the freethinkers, despite their professed materialism, clearly espoused a metaphysical explanation of the nature and purpose of man. To be sure, it was grounded in the physical world. Nevertheless, it presupposed categories that one is hard pressed to verify on empirical grounds.[40]

The freethinkers decried the injustice of the Christian system that called a man depraved, then laid on him a burden of requirements that he

---

[37] Holyoake, Reasoner I (1846): 147.

[38] Holyoake, "Self-Thinking and Secular Morals," Reasoner XVII (1854): 161-62; "Secularism as a System of Thought and Morality," National Reformer XVI (1870): 193-97, 210-12.

[39] "Meetings," (Nottingham), Investigator V (1858-59): 183; C. Watts, "Christian and Secular Morals," National Reformer VI (1865): 113-14; C. Watts, "Atheistic Morality," National Reformer VIII (1866): 34; C. Watts, "Utilitarian Basis of Morality," National Reformer XV (1870): 5-6, 21.

[40] For a particularly intriguing juxtaposition of the "old" metaphysics and "new" materialism, see Holyoake, "Utilitarian Reveries," Reasoner IV (1847-48): 1-4. The series by F. B. Barton on "The Constitution of Man" is interesting for its effort to affirm the priority of environment in explaining human behavior, but at the same time, to account for the differences among human behaviors that do not seem attributable to circumstances. See F. B. Barton, "The Constitution of Man," Reasoner XIII (1852): 23-26, 39-42, 71-74, 87-90, 103-6.

could not possibly meet, given his nature, only to punish him in the end for not meeting the requirements. According to the freethinkers, man is the necessary product of his circumstances. He is, by nature, a moral, national progressive being, for that is the character of the universe.[41] Any deviant behavior is, therefore, the result of insufficient penetration of goodness and truth from outside, which is a result of insufficient freedom to be exposed to truth. "When men have proved all things," paraphrased Holyoake, "they will hold fast to the good."[42] Man himself is not to blame for his shortcomings. In this world, man's proper duty is pursuit of physical and moral reform for their own sake.[43] As the Reasoner put it: ". . . it is his mission, his province, his duty and his interest, to improve and to please. The attributes which Rationalism prescribes to man are perennial discretion

---

[41] W. J. B., "The Supremacy of Man Examined," Movement I (1843-44): 212-13; "Anniversary of the Storming of the Bastille," Movement I (1843-44): 255-56; F. B. Barton, "The Doctrine of the Resurrection," (Concluded), Reasoner XII (1851-52): 439; "On Secular Standards of Morality," Reasoner XVI (1854): 91; The Report of the Four Nights Public Discussion at Bradford between Holyoake and Bowes, esp. 66, 110; C. Charles, "Real Religion versus Popular Religion," Investigator V (1858-59): 188-90; "Secularist and Theological Ideas of Responsibility," Reasoner XX (1856): 153.

[42] "The Chances of Obtaining an English Republic by Moral Means," Reasoner IV (1847-48): 283.

[43] C. Charles, "Real Religion versus Popular Religion," Investigator V (1858-59): 190; Christianity and Secularism Report of a Public Discussion Between the Rev. Brewin Grant and Geo. Jacob Holyoake (London: Ward & Co., 1853), p. 221-22; Secularism, Scepticism, and Atheism, Two Nights Public Debate Between G. J. Holyoake and C. Bradlaugh (London: Austin & Co., 1870), esp. 4. See also series on "The Affirmations of Secularism," Reasoner XXII (1857): 148, 164ff., 171; and series "The Religion of Duty," Reasoner XXV (1860): 244ff., 254ff., 264ff., 269ff., 278ff., 295; "Freethought: Its Advocacy and Its Tendency," National Reformer VI (1865): 345.

and kindness."[44] As man comes to understand the forces at work in the universe, he will be able to manage them. According to Holyoake:

> His [man's] relation to the external world, and the conditions of fraternity with his fellows, are the physical and social problems he has to solve. He sees the strength of passion and the educative forces of circumstances, and he studies them to control them. The affairs of men are a process which he seeks to wisely regulate, not blindly and violently thwart.[45]

Ironically, the freethinkers succeeded in constructing a morality of "works" as demanding as any system of Christian legalism. There was no faith versus works controversy as in orthodoxy, for, in freethought, one's "justification" was obtained through conduct or not at all.[46]

The freethinkers failed to address the contradiction embodied in their simultaneous adherence to belief in a naturalistic predetermined character of man, and belief in the necessity of striving to liberate that nature from bondage to ignorance and tyranny. Man is simultaneously freed from the burden of being responsible for what he is, and given the burden of being totally responsible for what he is to become. The freethinkers argued that the causation of will worked in their favor, not to their detriment. For, if one understands the operation of cause and effect in the past, one can predict its operation, and therefore, to some extent, control its operation in the future.[47] Nevertheless, if man is what he is by nature at present, how

---

[44]Holyoake, "Utilitarian Reveries," Reasoner IV (1847-48): 3.

[45]Holyoake, The Logic of Death (London: J. Watson, 1850), p. 13.

[46]Holyoake, "Outlines of Secularism," Reasoner XVI (1854): 17.

[47]"The Causation of the Will," Reasoner XX (1856): 161; "Process of Responsibility by Causation," Reasoner XX (1856): 169; "Philosophical Necessity the Hope of the Future," National Reformer V

can he be different in the future? Furthermore, if what he is, is in some way not what he is supposed to be, then there have been introduced elements of both moral perversity and evaluation in the system, that neither arise out of a naturalistic system, nor fit well within it.

Freethought had its own "problem of evil," that was every bit as thorny as that of the orthodox. To blame ignorance and tyranny is only to push the question back further. Whence appeared ignorance and tyranny, except from mankind, who, according to freethinkers, should have, in the natural state, served only truth and reason.[48] Furthermore, the freedom with which freethinkers criticized one another, not to mention outsiders, suggests that, in practice, if not in theory, they held individuals very much responsible for their own behavior.

If organized freethought retained "old" questions, even more did it retain the "old" forms of orthodoxy. Institutionally at least, freethought increasingly became the mirror image of the very Established religion that it had despised and rejected. Both the character of the

---

(1864): 602; "Moral Freedom and Causation," **National Reformer** VI (1865): 741, 765.

[48]For one example of the effort to explain "sin" without reference to the supernatural, see "Conversations on Bible Difficulties between Brown and Robinson," **Reasoner** XVII (1854): 249. Sin is, according to this article,
"the inherent native properties of the natural constitution of the human mind, roused into activity either for what we call good or evil, by external circumstances and internal excitement."
See also R. Otley, "The Crisis," **Investigator** IV (1857-58): 121-22; C. Southwell, "The Free Inquirer's Why and Because," (X), **Oracle of Reason** 1 (1841-42): 429-30.

belief system, and the nature of its practice clearly reflected the family likeness of orthodoxy.

First, the movement owned a dogma. They believed that they alone disinterestedly served truth, and that there was truth to serve.[49] Serving truth meant living according to reason and the senses.[50] It meant living morally.[51] It meant focusing on this world--on the "hows" of life rather than the "whys."[52]

> A secularist, said Robert Cooper, is one who believes that his duties pertain to the world he does know--not to the world he does not know. Not that he has any objection 'to live again,' especially if he can do more good than now; but he considers his duties pertaining to any other existence can only commence when he enters upon that existence. While here, his obligations lie here. The mistake of mankind has been that they have been quarrelling as to who will have the right to be happy in another world, instead of rendering all happy in this. Secularism corrects this error.[53]

Holyoake goes so far as even to speak of a "doctrinal basis" of

---

[49] Holyoake, *The Logic of Life, Deduced from the Principle of Freethought* (London: Newsagents' Newspapers & Pub. Co., 1861); "The New Year's Festival of the London Secular Society," *Reasoner* XVI (1854): 37.

[50] Holyoake, "Modern Freethinking: Its Definition, Sphere, and Defence," *Reasoner* XII (1851-52): 81; "Abstract of Principles of Secularism," Adopted by the National Secular Association, *National Reformer* III (January 18, 1862): 2; C. Charles, "Secularism: What It Is," *National Reformer* XIII (1869): 241-42; 265-66.

[51] "New Forms of Freethought," *Reasoner* XXIII (1858): 34; R. Cooper, "The Logic of Atheism," *Investigator* IV (1857-58): 115; Holyoake, "Outline of Secular Principles," *Reasoner* XXIII (1858): 89; "A Brief Statement of Secular Principles," *National Reformer* IV (September 12, 1863): 5/(September 19, 1863): 5; "Secularism, Belief, and Morals," *National Reformer* V (1864): 265.

[52] Holyoake, *Reasoner* XVIII (1855): 97; R. Cooper "Secularism, and Its Aims," *Investigator* II (1855-56): 97; Holyoake, "The Separateness of Secularism," *Reasoner* XXX (1871-72): 36-37.

[53] R. Cooper, "Secularism and Its Aims," p. 97.

secularism. According to this chief spokesman of the movement, it is that

> justification by conduct is a higher and more reliable truth than justification by faith; its object of study is the order rather than the origin of nature . . . its practical result is the discovery that science is the providence of man, and the development of truth is a protection against false dependence; its theory of morals, that there exist guarantees of morality in human nature, in utility, and intelligence; its sphere of controversy, the criticism of sacred books and existing religion, only in those respects in which they seem to contradict ascertained moral truths, and are impediments to rational progress.[54]

Serving truth meant also, in theory at least, being always open-minded and maintaining the conditions that permitted new infusions of truth.[55] Nevertheless, this openness was not to be confused with scepticism.[56] Freethinking was not "anarchy in thought."[57] Neither did it want to become so enamored with the seeking that it delayed forever the finding. Said Holyoake:

> Discussion is a great discoverer of truth, but it is a very great mistake when people give us discussion instead of the truth. Auguste Comte has usefully pointed out how some persons have so mistaken the uses of free inquiry, that they think it criminal to come to a conclusion.[58]

Freethought was a way of knowing. It was a methodology. But

---

[54]*Christianity versus Secularism--A Public Discussion between Rev. J. H. Rutherford and Mr. G. J. Holyoake* (London: Ward & Co., 1854), p. 4.

[55]Holyoake, *Reasoner* XVIII (1855): 97; Holyoake, "Outline of Secular Principles," *Reasoner* XXIII (1858): 90.

[56]For a clear statement of the methodological limitations of freethought, see Holyoake, "Freethought--Its Conditions, Agreements, and Secular Results," *Reasoner* XXX (1871-72): 243-49.

[57]Holyoake, "Modern Freethinking: Its Definition, Sphere, and Defence," *Reasoner* XII (1851-52): 81.

[58]Holyoake, "Secular Propositions," *Reasoner* XVI (1854): 193.

freethinkers doggedly resisted the tendency for the methodology to become an end in itself, rather than a means to knowing. They sought freedom of thought only so that they might freely choose to take a position.

The creed of freethought might be summarized thus: reason, science, morality, and progress in this life.[59] Since choosing to believe certain things implies necessarily choosing *not* to believe certain other things, adopting dogma meant for the freethinkers adopting its accompanying intolerance. When confronted with an accusation of bigotry, Holyoake, while confessing to intolerance, attempted to save face by asserting that, unlike the Christians, he would seek no means of changing his opponent's mind other than expressing his own opinion.[60]

For all their talk of freethought, the freethinkers were especially critical of groups within their ranks who chose to think differently from the majority. Furthermore, since it is the intolerant who are most cognizant of, and most offended by, intolerance in someone else, the more dogmatic the movement became, the more it deplored the closemindedness of those who did not think exactly like themselves.

---

[59]For a concise, yet thorough and representative statement of the dogma of freethought, see Holyoake, Secularism--The Practical Philosophy of the People (London: Holyoake & Co., 1854). See also "Lionel Holdreth," "The Creed of a Secularist," Reasoner XX (1856): 41-42; "Holdreth," "The Affirmations of Secularism," Reasoner XXII (1857): 140-41; "Atheism, Its Policy and Logic," National Reformer III (1861- 62): 5; "Proposed Programme for the National Secular Society," National Reformer VIII (1866): 169; C. Watts, "The Philosophy of Secularism," National Reformer XIV (1869): 19, 34-35; F. Neale, "The Doctrines of Atheism," National Reformer XIX (1872): 241-42.

[60]Holyoake, "Colloquies on Religion and Religious Education," Oracle of Reason I (1841-42): 362.

Paradoxically, railing against internal dogmatism is evidence, as much of an increasing overall sense of freethought "orthodoxy," as of the movement's efforts to avoid all creedal formulations. At one point, William Chilton accused the Newcastle Branch of freethinkers of the "cant of infidelity." The article's title expresses very clearly his position--"The Newcastle Society of Bigots & Superstitionists, for the overthrow of all superstitions--But Their Own."[61]

If there is "orthodoxy," there must also be heterodoxy, and following closely on the heels of the dogma of freethought were its heresies. One listing of the "Agreements and Conditions of Secular Free Thought" suggested five matters that were capable of making one a freethought heretic: 1) disregarding reason as a test of truth; 2) believing in the natural depravity of man; 3) believing that sincerity might be eternally punished; 4) distrusting that God would be the God of the honest; and 5) believing something other than service to humanity as the highest creed.[62]

Apart from these generally accepted measures of right thinking, there were other matters of tension within the movement that, according to some freethinkers, could also be made touchstones of party loyalty. Suggesting that someone was becoming soft on religion was tantamount to an accusation of betrayal. This was a frequent charge against those who, like the later Owen and Holyoake, appeared to be cultivating

---

[61] W. Chilton, "The Newcastle Society of Bigots and Superstitionists, for the overthrow of all superstitions--But Their Own," Oracle of Reason II (1842-43): 337.

[62] Holyoake, "Freethought--Its Conditions, Agreements, and Secular Results," Reasoner XXX (1871-72): 249.

sociability with the "respectable."[63] Anyone whose atheism rested on reaction to personal experience, rather than on principles gleaned through reason, might be suspected of the heresy of "pseudo-atheism."[64] This was, in a sense, only a form of the larger category of errant thinking that made truth in any way dependent on personality rather than principle.

Apart from espousing dogma like the Established Church, freethinkers also adopted a moral system like the Church. Reference has already been made at several points to the similarities and differences in the two systems. Perhaps the most striking feature that distinguished freethought morality from Christian morality was its preference for "sincere" behavior over "right" behavior. One might even say that, to the freethinker, the only right behavior was "sincere" behavior. Given their disgust with the hypocrisy of the Establishment, it is not strange that they would judge virtue by motive rather than by outcome. Furthermore, given their faith in reason and the basic goodness of man, "sincerity" was a sure guarantee that the results would be as pure as the motive behind them. Of one thing at least, the freethinkers wanted to be certain. That is that no one would be able reasonably to mouth the platitude that the end of the orthodox Establishment would be the end of morality in England.

---

[63] J. P. Adams, "Suggestions to Secularists," Investigator IV (1857-58): 37.

[64] T. Paterson, "Pseudo-Atheism," Oracle of Reason I (1841-42): 409; Holyoake, "The Religious Views of the Leader," Reasoner X (1850-51): 385-87; Holyoake, "The Socialist God," Oracle of Reason II (1842-43): 211; "Why Are We Atheists?" Oracle of Reason I (1841-42): 318-20.

Freethinkers, despite their insistence on living only by what they knew irrevocably to be true, nevertheless spoke of their "faith." According to the Herald of Progress, the fundamental "faith and hope" of the rationalist was his belief that "Progression is the peculiar attribute of man, and an indication of his ultimate destiny."[65] An earlier issue added to this that, based on this belief, the "Social Reformers'" practice will be to further, by all means in his power, man's "improvability" and to "accelerate" his "ultimate happy destiny."[66] "Eugene," writing for the Reasoner, confesses that "Yes, the Infidel does hope--in humanity, in the eternal laws of progress, and in the prospect that Goodness, Providence, and Truth will triumph."[67] Even the hard "negativist" Robert Cooper acknowledged his "faith" in truth, liberty, progress, and the glorious future of this world.[68]

To make a point of this is not to suggest that they viewed their own faith as "blind" faith. Their "faith," after all, was built on the evidence of reason and the senses, unlike the faith of the religious establishment. Nevertheless, it seems significant that, in describing their espousal of a world view, freethinkers frequently resorted to the language of religion.

Finally, freethinkers, like the Church, anticipated a millennium as

---

[65] "Our Motto," Herald of Progress (1845-46): 121.

[66] "Our Motto," (II), Herald of Progress (1845-46): 17.

[67] "Eugene," "Skeptical Hope," Reasoner I (1846): 211.

[68] R. Cooper, Investigator I (1854-55): 182.

the reward of their labors.[69] As one local enthusiast expressed it:

> Our attention is mainly directed to mental and moral improvement, and the propagation of the social views, thus preparing ourselves for the advent of that glorious day, that shall yet dawn upon the human race, it may be that that day we shall never see but though the sun that shall light the reapers to the harvest, shall shine on our graves, yet we have this consolation left, that we are sowing the seed that future generations shall reap and enjoy.[70]

Granted, it was a millennium in this world, and the motivation to bring it in was the hope, not of one's own happiness, but that of posterity.[71] Furthermore, belief in that future utopia rested on a naturalistically based tendency toward progress and improvement in this world, rather than on any supernatural intervention.[72] Finally, one must not over-emphasize the unique proximity of freethought to Christianity on this point, for the notion of a future idyllic state is a common motif in secular utopian literature as well as the scriptures. Many of the freethinkers had been Owenite Socialists, so from that connection alone, they no doubt derived familiarity with the millennial ideal. Giving due consideration to these qualifications, it is still worth noting as one further point of belief common to the "religions" of Christianity and organized freethought.

---

[69] See excerpt from "Whitechapel Branch," Herald of Progress (1845-46): 3; "The Present Condition of the Society, with its Objects and Prospects," Herald of Progress (1845-46): 41.

[70] Report from Lambeth, Herald of Progress, (1845-46): 7.

[71] It should be noted that Robert Owen actually announced the advent of the millennium in 1855. Though Owen never considered himself a secularist, the strong Owenite loyalties latent in the freethought movement prompted the Investigator to make note of the announcement as if Owen were one of their own. See Investigator I (1854-55): 163-64.

[72] S. D. Collet, "Social Reformers in America," Herald of Progress (1845-46): 36.

A person familiar with the routines and jargon of Victorian orthodoxy could have moved quite comfortably into the community life of Victorian freethought. That this is both cause and effect of the tendency of organized freethought to serve a transitional function in the lives of disillusioned orthodox disciples has already been mentioned. Not only did the similarity ease the way out of orthodoxy. It might equally serve as a half-way point on the way in. For those freethinkers without orthodox backgrounds, organized freethought could provide many of the sociological benefits of religion and do so in the name of progress and reform. Besides, in the working class districts of England, to have received these benefits at the hand of freethought would have been much more in keeping with class culture than to have received them at the hands of the Establishment.

Coming into freethought, like coming into orthodoxy, was a conversion experience. G. J. Holyoake lamented the double standard in Victorian society that honored the one conversion and not the other. As he said:

> With sincere persons, the transition from one system of belief to another is generally, if not always, a vital struggle. To make the transition completely, and act upon it consistently, is ever honourable and pleasing. Christians frequently do this--why should not Atheists generally follow the example? The reason probably is, that in them it would be deemed presumption. A bold and consistent convert is held in honour among believers--let the same be done among unbelievers . . . That course which in the Christian is respected as a duty, in the Atheist is held to be vanity. . . . Yet where is the difference? Moral courage, consistency and frankness are as beautiful in the Atheist as in the Christian.[73]

In both Christianity and freethought, notwithstanding

---

[73]Holyoake, "Christian Presumption," *Movement* I (1843-44): 361.

predestination and necessitarianism respectively, the individual was, in the end, responsible for choosing his destiny. Upon that decision rested his happiness and usefulness in this world, and both the Christians and the freethinkers believed that their side was the "true" side on which to be.

It was a logical extension of this conviction of the duty of individual responsibility that freethinkers insisted on the absolute right of free inquiry and free expression.[74] The only responsible and honest choice was the free choice. Paradoxically, the surest means of society's guaranteeing the "right choice" was to give truth the maximum freedom to operate--which is only a different way of saying to give individuals absolutely unrestricted freedom to search for truth wherever it led. The faith of the freethinkers in the integrity of truth and the individual was unshakable, and would no doubt appear naive to those of us in the twentieth century who have seen the social power of the grand lie.

What made the freethought case especially interesting is their insistence that all they were doing was carrying the Protestant right of private judgment to its logical conclusion.[75] Then, as if it were not

---

[74]Holyoake, "Why?" Reasoner I (1846): 145-46; Holyoake, "The Better to Be Safe System," Oracle of Reason I (1841-42): 281-82; T. Paterson, "Pseudo-atheism," Oracle of Reason I (1841-42): 409-10; T. Paterson, "Politics for Politicians," (IV), Oracle of Reason II (1842- 43): 250; Holyoake, Introduction to the Seventh Volume, Reasoner VII (1849-50): iv-v. "Features of the Reasoner," Reasoner XVI (1854): 227; "First Anniversary of the London Secular Society," Reasoner XVI (1854): 372; Holyoake, "The Conduct of Discussion," Reasoner XXI (1856): 33; T. Evans, "Free Inquiry and Discussion," National Reformer III (May 17, 1862): 6.

[75]W. J. B., "The Right of Private Judgment," Oracle of Reason II

insult enough to accuse the orthodox of betraying their own principles, the freethinkers, on occasion, came out appearing to defend the honor of God, against the orthodox effort to protect His dignity by harboring false teaching in His name. In Holyoake's words:

> Men who would not face their dancing-masters with a false step, nor their classical professors with a false quantity, will face Heaven with a <u>false proposition</u>. The student who dare not take up to his mathematical tutor a problem he does not understand, will take up to God a creed he never did understand, and never expects to understand. The believer who cannot impose on his professor, thinks to escape the detection of Deity.[76]

Once one was "converted," freethought, too, had its tests of zeal and commitment. At one point, the Glasgow branch of the Utilitarian Society suggested that the "moral fitness" of all prospective members should be certified by two current members of the society.[77] This sense that too many half-hearted freethinkers had joined the ranks prompted advocacy in London, as well, of a stiffer examination of membership candidates.[78] Talk of the need for sacrifice for the "cause" and the need to motivate flagging zeal was frequently heard, especially in the early days when disillusion set in after the Harmony Hall fiasco.[79]

(1842-43): 177.

[76] Holyoake, "Aspects of Theism," <u>Reasoner</u> XXII (1857): 137. See also "Freedom of Opinion," <u>National Reformer</u> IV (January 10, 1863): 5.

[77] "Glasgow," <u>Herald of Progress</u> (1845-46): 110.

[78] W. Chilton, "Socialist Errors and Rationalist Remedies," <u>Reasoner</u> I (1846): 121.

[79] "To the General Secretary from Samuel Houghton," <u>Herald of Progress</u> (1845-46): 46; "The People's Hall for Free Discussion," <u>Herald of Progress</u> (1845-46): 70; "To the Editor of the <u>Herald of Progress</u> from John Carter," <u>Herald of Progress</u> (1845-46): 71; "To the Members and Friends of the Rational Society," <u>Herald of Progress</u> (1845-46): 84; "The Coming Congress," <u>Herald of Progress</u> (1845-46): 97.

Later on, Holyoake acknowledged the importance of the "warm heart" as well as the "cool head" in sustaining secular enthusiasm. He is careful to distinguish freethought zeal from the zeal of the ordinary enthusiast. Where the latter is "blind," the zeal of the freethinker is "perceptive."[80] Articles on the need for "Secularist Churches" to foster secular commitment and the need for "constant advocacy" suggest that keeping up the spirit remained a concern of the freethought movement as it was for the zealous among the orthodox.[81]

When their fervency was heated, freethinkers could be as self-righteous about their integrity as any orthodox believer--perhaps even more so, because, in the case of the freethinker, the self-righteousness was fueled by a penchant for martyrdom.[82] To be a freethinker in Victorian England was to be among the righteous few.

If the requirements for admission to freethought fellowship resembled those of orthodoxy, so did life within the fellowship. Even the language of the freethinkers was replete with Biblical phrases. The meanings of many metaphors designed to communicate to Victorian readers would escape most twentieth-century minds. How many today would catch the warning contained in the statement that "it is impossible to keep

---

[80]Holyoake, "New Secular Book Depot, No. 147, Fleet Street," <u>Reasoner</u> XV (1853): 306-7.

[81]F. Neale, "The Necessity of Constant Advocacy," <u>National Reformer</u> XVIII (1871): 283-84; "Scotus," "Suggestions for Secularist Churches," <u>National Reformer</u> V (1864): 273-74.

[82]"Iconoclast," "My Summer Campaign," <u>Investigator</u> V (1858-59): 108; W. Chilton, "Admirable Defence of Messrs. Southwell, Holyoake, Paterson, Finlay, M'Neil, and Miss Roalfe," <u>Movement</u> I (1843-44): 393-94.

out the Aachens that worm themselves into every camp"?[83] Other Biblical allusions melted into freethought writings include "kicking against pricks";[84] "salvation draweth nigh";[85] "when I would do good evil is with me";[86] and "there is room for us in the vineyard."[87] One writer spoke of The Central Secular Society sitting "under its own vine and its own fig tree, none daring to make it afraid."[88] A report from Sheffield noted that a Mr. Biltcliffe will be delivering a lecture on the "text," "I am not ashamed of Secularism, for it is the power of good to those who believe."[89] At one point, "Iconoclast" is reported to have lectured to a "respectable" audience on the subject, "What Shall a Man do to be saved?"[90]

All of this proves nothing conclusive except to suggest further that organized freethought shared more than it would have liked to admit with Establishment Victorian England. One cannot argue convincingly from silence. Nevertheless, it seems even more telling that the use of

---

[83]"Correspondence," (Edinburgh) Herald of Progress (1845-46), p. 45.

[84]C. Southwell, "The Scotch God War," Oracle of Reason II (1842-43): 391.

[85]Notice re: Joiners Trade Society, Herald of Progress (1845-46): 43.

[86]"President's Address to the Members of the Rational Society," Herald of Progress, (1845-46): 60.

[87]Herald of Progress (1845-46): 76.

[88]Holyoake, Reasoner XX (1856): 121 cited by John Maughan, "Profession versus Practice," Investigator V (1858-59): 38.

[89]"Meetings, &c.," (Sheffield), Investigator V (1858-59): 112.

[90]"Meetings, &c.," (Northampton), Investigator V (1858-59): 208.

these phrases appears so unself-conscious and natural. Surely, if the freethinkers had thought themselves to be attesting even to the latent Christian influence of language, they would have sought to eradicate such evidence from their communication immediately.

The freethinkers had no wish to leave new converts without the benefit of further instruction in the ways of freethought. One subscriber wrote to the Reasoner of the danger of freethought spreading too fast. Drawing a parallel to the progress of Christianity in India, "S. B." suggested that, unless new freethinkers became grounded in their new faith and studied its implications for daily life, they would succeed in being nothing more than bigoted freethinkers. "Instead of becoming a good Freethinker, he [will be] after all nothing but a spoiled Christian."[91] Much of this instruction took place in the informal network of social and inspirational activities planned in the various Halls of Science. But, apart from this, there was a recognized need for some sort of formal educational institution in which freethinkers could be trained to be the very best representatives of their faith that they could be.[92] Holyoake, especially, realized that, in addition to instructing converts, freethought schools were essential for the proper education of "second-generation freethinkers." A movement must have a school if it is to survive.[93] In his effort to

---

[91]S. B. "To the Editor of the Reasoner," "Precaution in Freethought," Reasoner XXVII (1865): 38-39.

[92]Hugh Fulton, "A Secular School," National Reformer V (1864): 390-91; Austin Holyoake, "The Training of Secular Advocates," National Reformer XIII (1869): 292.

[93]Holyoake, "Christian Testimony in Favour of Atheism," Reasoner IX

provide appropriate "secular" education, Holyoake published Child's First Word Book, The Child's Ladder of Knowledge, and The Child's Second Letter Book for teaching Reading and Writing at Once.[94] At one point, he "borrowed" a "catechism of Religion for the use of Young Children" and, adapted it for the moral instruction of "secular children." He sought to exonerate his plagiarism by assuring his readers that "we are sure Mr. Crosskey is a man wise and liberal enough to be pleased that any portion of his labour should furnish guidance or pleasure to others, whether of his church or not."[95] One of Holyoake's more creative ideas in the pursuit of Secular educational institutions was his suggestion, after passage of the Forster Education Bill in 1870, to seek money from the government for atheist schools. "Being a denomination," they were "equally entitled to state endowment with any other denomination."[96]

The freethought community provided one with the same sense of "belonging" that one might find in any religious fellowship. One enterprising freethinker even suggested that selling and wearing identical gold brooches would both raise funds for the movement and provide freethinkers a way to recognize each other immediately, even

---

(1850): 121; Holyoake, "Progress of Atheism," Reasoner IX (1850): 278.

[94] Holyoake, Child's First Word Book (London: Fleet St. House, 1854); Holyoake, The Child's Ladder of Knowledge (London: F. Farrah, 1864); Holyoake, The Child's Second Letter Book for Teaching Reading and Writing at Once (London: James Watson, 1853).

[95] Holyoake, "A Catechism for Little Children," Reasoner XVI (1854): 241-44.

[96] Holyoake, "Principles of an Atheistic School," Reasoner, XXX (1871-72): 97-98.

though strangers by name.[97]

Also, the "schedule" of community life and the sorts of activities that constituted that life differed little from what one would have found in the ordinary Victorian parish calendar. Sunday mornings and evenings were the normal meeting times for lectures. They could be counted on. Mid-week lectures were less regular, but by no means infrequent.[98]

The societies organized opportunities for recreation and fellowship. Secular tea parties were a common occurrence and, on festive occasions, might be accompanied by a dinner or ball. The freethinkers celebrated English holidays, though taking care to separate themselves from the usual significance of these holidays. At a "Family Tea Party," announced for December 28 at the John Street Literary and Scientific Institution, the lecture was entitled, "Mythological Origin of Christmas Eve."[99] Especially appreciated were the Sunday afternoon excursions to places of interest in and around London.[100] A report of an outing by the London Secular Society to Broxbourne included

---

[97]"Dover," Herald of Progress (1845-46): 450.

[98]Complete lists of all lecture times and topics were a regular feature of all the freethought journals. Usually the back page of each issue was reserved for such announcements. In addition, the societies often printed single-sheet flyers for wider distribution outside the circle of journal subscribers.

[99]"General Literary and Scientific Institution," Herald of Progress, (1845-46): 40; Announcement for "Soiree and Ball," Herald of Progress (1845-46): 64.

[100]See announcements for "Hollingworth Excursion," Investigator IV (1857-58): 71; announcement for Rosherville Gardens outing, Movement I (1843-44): 224; and announcement for 8 hour sea side excursion in Reasoner XXVII (1865): 43.

acknowledgement of the good weather--which was "as on both occasions last year . . . of the best quality--real Secular sunshine."[101] How that differs from generic sunshine is left to the reader to determine. Some districts combined recreation and instruction in the annual "camp meeting," probably an idea borrowed from the Methodists.[102]

Freethought circles sought to be centers of education and culture.[103] Any subject perceived to contribute to the improvement of the English worker was legitimate. Typical topics included phrenology, writing, drawing, singing, literature, and French.

Some societies served as centers of cooperative business ventures and sources of mutual encouragement and financial support in times of unemployment and sickness.[104] No area of life was too insignificant to come under the umbrella of order and reason--as attested to by one organization entitled "The Manchester Rational Sick and Burial Association."[105]

Organized freethought provided all the social benefits that people seek in religious affiliation, and far more than the Victorian working

---

[101]"A.," "London Secular Society," Reasoner XVI (1854): 286.

[102]See "Atheos" from Huddersfield to Investigator, I (1854-55): 44.

[103]See "London-John Street," Herald of Progress (1845-46): 32. Again, as for the lectures, announcements would be made for these classes in the freethought journals.

[104]Herald of Progress (1845-46): 16; Announcement for "The London Co-Operative Building Society," Herald of Progress (1845-46): 56; "The Carpenters," Movement II (1845): 23. See suggestion to the Editor of the Herald of Progress, (1845-46): 112.

[105]"Sixth Annual Report of the Manchester Rational Sick and Burial Association," Reasoner IV (1847-48): 348-49.

classes would have found within Established Christianity. Furthermore, any inkling that joining the freethinkers might mean parting with, or escaping from, liturgy and form would soon be dispelled. Organized freethought had the dogma of religion. It had the community life of religion. It also had its ritual.

Freethinkers "worshipped." They even talked about it as "worship." Their work was worship.[106] Every contribution to truth, all publication of it, is an act of worship, according to Holyoake.[107] As a vehicle of worship, music was considered important. Freethinkers often sang "secular" hymns at their gatherings,[108] and a number of societies had regular choirs. Even at camp meeting, music was appreciated. A participant reported with pleasure the attendance of the Baildon Brass Band at the Shipley Glen camp meeting.[109]

Freethinkers had ceremonies appropriate to the calendar and to the various rites of passage of the human experience. In 1858, the London Secular Society reported having had its fifth annual New Year's Festival, complete with music, songs, and recitations.[110] Funerals had

---

[106]See, for example, Holyoake, The Trial of Theism (London: Holyoake & Co., 1858), p. 175.

[107]"The Secular Act of Worship," Reasoner XXVII (1865): 17.

[108]For references to the importance of hymn singing, see "Secular Progress," Investigator V (1858-59): 103; "What Should the People Sing?" Reasoner VI (1849): 18-19; "Panthea," "Music for the People," Reasoner VI (1849): 69-72; "The New Secular Hymn Book," National Reformer III (October 11, 1862): 3. For examples of secular poetry and hymns, see "The Banner of Faith," Oracle of Reason I (1841-42): 344; "Now Hark, Brothers, Hark," National Reformer XI (1868): 311.

[109]"Provincial Meetings," Investigator V (1858-59): 91.

[110]"London Secular Society," Investigator IV (1857-58): 128.

their appropriate hymns and orations.[111] Several freethinkers made a deliberate effort, late in the 1860's, to collect a series of marriage, burial, and naming services suitable to their beliefs. Austin Holyoake expressed the purpose of Secular ceremonies as providing the emotional element absent in a strict legal transaction without the superstition that is part of the Church's liturgy.[112] The result of Holyoake's and Watts' project was the publication of The Secularists's Manual of Songs and Ceremonies in 1871. It was announced to consist of "purely secular songs, recitations, and ceremonies."[113]

The freethinkers had "saints," and "martyrs," even scriptures. The Oracle of Reason, in a parody of orthodoxy, spoke of the four gospels of the blasphemers "acted, spoken, and written by martyrs to the cause," the "genuineness" and "authenticity" of which, no one will challenge. The four were Hetherington, Southwell, Holyoake, and Paterson.[114] The Investigator published an article on "The Martyrs of Secularism"-- arguing that, if the Church has viewed martyrdom as a vindication of truth in their own case, they should apply the same test of truth as they view the plight of freethinkers persecuted in Protestant England

---

[111]"Obituary," Investigator V (1858-59): 104.

[112]Austin Holyoake, "Secular Ceremonies," National Reformer XI (1868): 59-60. For the proposed secular burial service, see A. Holyoake, "Secular Ceremonies," National Reformer XII (1868): 313-14; The "Naming of Infants" ceremony can be found in C. Watts, "Secular Ceremonies," National Reformer XII (1868): 388-89.

[113]"The Secularist's Manual of Songs and Ceremonies," National Reformer XVIII (1871): 73.

[114]W. J. B., "Epistles--Not Paul's," Oracle of Reason II (1842-43): 193, 204, 209, 313, 330.

for their espousal of the right of private judgment.[115] Indeed, freethinkers, like martyrs of all ilks, read persecution as affirmation of the righteousness of their cause.[116]

There is no evidence that the freethinkers deliberately sought to mirror orthodox forms and institutions. If anything, they repudiated efforts to hold new substance in old forms.[117] Perhaps the phenomenon only testifies to the human tendency to excuse, or even to fail to see, in oneself the very thing that seems so objectionable in someone else.

Evidence of old forms was not limited to interaction within freethought. Organized freethought was, from its conception, a proselytizing movement. In its relations to the outside, perhaps more than anywhere, one sees the extent to which freethought exhibited the character of any aggressive organized religious belief system.

First, the movement clearly was imbued with a strong sense of mission. Freethinkers believed they possessed truth and were convinced of their duty to make it known, at any cost. Whether that task should take the form of tearing down the old or building the new was a matter of debate. But of the importance of the mission, there was no doubt.

---

[115] "The Martyrs of Secularism," Investigator I (1854-55): 81. On this matter, see also "Z" to the Editor of the Oracle of Reason II (1842-43): 31-32.

[116] J. Griffin H., "Christian Charity and Forbearance," Oracle of Reason I (1841-42): 397-99; Holyoake, "The Philosopher and the Screech- Owl," Reasoner XIII (1852): 97-99; "The Support of Freethought," Reasoner XIX (1855): 299.

[117] See, for example, Holyoake, "The Socialists' Banquets in Honour of Christ," Reasoner VI (1849): 34, in which Holyoake announces that "The time for religious symbols is passed; the republic must be the domain of truth and rational politics."

Freethinkers described the mission in different ways: as the "mighty cause of man's emancipation from superstition and delusion;"[118] as the task of "creating as everlasting development in all that is beautiful and good;"[119] as the job of "uprooting religion from the world, thence loosing the artificial bonds that hold society together, and creating a moral atmosphere that will preserve the moral life of the community."[120] Whatever words they used, the freethinkers shared the convictions that present political, social, and economic improvement of the working classes was of prime importance; that the chief obstacle to that advancement was the integrated political and ecclesiastical Establishment; and that the linchpin of that conglomerate was a false view of reality, intentionally perpetuated by the Establishment to insure their continued domination of Victorian society.

Second, the freethinkers recognized the necessity of developing a convincing apologetic for their vision of truth. The apologetics of freethought included both works that aimed at discrediting theism, and those that sought to present a convincing portrayal of atheism. Examples of the former include Bradlaugh's The Bible; What It Is[121] and Examination of the Four Gospels according to Matthew, Mark, Luke, &

---

[118]"Correspondence," (Edinburgh), Herald of Progress (1845-46): 54.

[119]J. R. "Secular Propaganda," National Reformer X (1867): 395.

[120]T. Paterson, "Pseudo-Atheism," Oracle of Reason I (1841-42): 410.

[121]C. Bradlaugh, The Bible; What It Is (London: Austin & Co., 1859).

John,[122] and Holyoake's *Paley Refuted In His Own Words*,[123] not to mention the numerous articles in freethought periodicals on the topic.[124] Writings that seek to argue for the truth of freethought include Bradlaugh's *Heresy: Its Utility and Morality--A Plea and a Justification*[125] and *A Plea for Atheism*,[126] as well as Holyoake *Principles of Secularism*;[127] *Secularism: The Affirmative Philosophy of the People*;[128] and *Secularism a Religion Which Gives Heaven No Trouble*.[129] Perhaps the best illustration of periodical apologetics is "Lionel Holdreth's" four-part series in the *Reasoner* entitled "Apology for the Secularists."[130]

---

[122]Bradlaugh, *Examination of the Four Gospels According to Matthew, Mark, Luke, & John With Remark on the Life and Death of the Meek & Lowly Jesus*, 1850. Bradlaugh Papers, National Secular Society Collection, Bishopsgate Institute.

[123]Holyoake, *Paley Refuted In His Own Words* (London: Hetherington, 1843).

[124]See, for example, "Taylor's Short and Easy Method With the Theist," *Reasoner* XVI (1854): 203f.

[125]C. Bradlaugh, *Heresy: Its Utility and Morality--A Plea and a Justification* 3rd. ed. (London: Freethought Co., 1882).

[126]C. Bradlaugh, *A Plea for Atheism* (London: Austin & Co., 1864).

[127]Holyoake, *Principles of Secularism* (London: Holyoake & Co., 1859).

[128]Holyoake, *Secularism: The Affirmative Philosophy of the People* (London: Holyoake & Co., 1854).

[129]Holyoake, *Secularism A Religion Which Gives Heaven No Trouble* (London: Watts & Co., 1882).

[130]"Lionel Holdreth," "Apology for the Secularists," *Reasoner* XXII (1857): 5, 9, 13, 17, 21. See also Joseph Barker, "Atheism," *National Reformer* I (July 21, 1860): 2; J. Watts, "The 'Apologist' on Secularism," *National Reformer* III (August 23, 1862): 1; "Why Are You a Secularist?" (II), *National Reformer* IV (January 31, 1863): 5-6; C.

Third, the movement developed a strategy for propagation. To say this is not at all to imply that the overall effort was well planned and systematically executed. Rather, it is to suggest that the accumulated endeavors of individuals and local societies reflected a movement-wide commitment to spreading the "good news" of freethought. It should be noted that such efforts commenced long before the organization of the National Secular Society and the resulting possibility of a nationally coherent propaganda policy. Any means of propagandizing that respected individual integrity was considered legitimate.

Some freethinkers argued for the one-on-one approach to proselytizing. In a letter to the Editor of the Oracle, "Omnipax" asserted that public propagandizing actually hindered the cause of freethought by promoting orthodox reaction. By working inconspicuously, freethinkers presented less of a perceived threat to order and decency, especially among the "passive religionists." Furthermore, private conversations allowed for sensitivity to individual perspective, and for slow and patient "extirpation" of religion. In the writer's words:

> A thing which has been stuffed into people from their earliest infancy is not to be cast out by means of a few smart arguments and cutting satires--it rarely gives way to anything but the undermining and incessant attacks of friends and acquaintances.[131]

Though "Omnipax's" is a difficult argument to denounce in any final sense, it did doom the cause to a far slower pace of proselytization

---

Watts, "A Defence of Secular Principles," National Reformer XIV (1869): 202, 247, 284.

[131]"Omnipax" to the Editor of the Oracle of Reason, "How Christianity Should Be Attacked," Oracle of Reason II (1842-43): 119- 20. (Quote from p. 119.)

than most freethinkers favored. Besides encouraging individual efforts, the movement actively promoted several forms of public propaganda. To facilitate this effort, and no doubt a carryover from the practice of the Owenite Rational Society, the freethinkers supported several full-time workers. Unlike the Owenites, the missionaries of freethought were self-appointed, owing to the late organization of a national freethought agitation. Except for their accountability as heads of freethought publications to their respective publication boards, these freethought leaders had very little check on their policies, schedules, or handling of finances. Also unlike the Owenite missionaries, the freethought lecturers were, by and large, unstationed. This transiency and independence of freethought leadership contributed to the persistent disunity of the movement and its propensity to splinter into factions associated with particular personalities. A plea for the establishment of regular lectureships reflects the recognition both of the need for full-time workers, and of the ineffective present arrangement. According to this *Reasoner* writer:

> Peripatetic lecturing will not do except for destruction of error and incitement of opinion. There is no construction possible with it--new truths cannot be established by it. The wandering speaker has his place, but it is that of a platform scout. He dogs the footsteps of the enemy and watches his progress and movements, but he can seldom give battle. The scout should belong to an army. He should have some headquarters to which he is to report what he discovers, and there should be generals in command who can act upon his information. In the present state of Free Thought we have nothing but scouts--there is no headquarters, no corps, no commanders.[132]

The exhortation went unheeded. Freethought persistently relied on

---

[132] "Secular Lectureships," *Reasoner* XXVII (1865): 17.

a national emphasis in propagation, even before the existence of an organizational and communicational network to make such a grand scale of operation as effective as it might have been.

The most consistent avenue of propagation was the freethought periodical. Though subscriber lists for any of the periodicals never reached more than a few thousand,[133] the journals, while they lasted, provided some measure of unity and continuity to a movement painfully lacking in both.

Apart from the periodicals, freethinkers also printed numerous pamphlets advertising lectures and advocating opinions on particular subjects.[134] Joseph Barker summed up the perceived advantage of tracts when he wrote:

> Tracts can go everywhere. Tracts never blush. Tracts know no fear. Tracts never stammer. Tracts never stick fast. Tracts never lose their temper. Tracts never tire. Tracts never die. Tracts can be multiplied without end by the press. Tracts can travel at little expense. They want nothing to eat. They require no lodgings . . .[135]

In the later 1840's, the Reasoner began a series of four-page tracts to be printed simultaneously in the Reasoner and as separate pieces of literature for wider distribution. An Infidel Tract Society was

---

[133] For complete figures on subscription lists see appendices in E. Royle, <u>Victorian Infidels--The Origins of the British Secular Movement 1791-1866</u> (Manchester: University Press, 1974).

[134] Copies of many of these pamphlets are available at Bishopsgate Institute from the Holyoake and National Secular Society Collections. Except where copies indicate which "1000" they were printed from, there is little evidence for determining numbers printed, or for assessing the extent of tract distribution.

[135] J. Barker, "Diffusion of Tracts," printed in <u>Reasoner</u> III (1847): 496. Perhaps Barker's background in the ministry left him with a fondness for tracts.

organized specifically to promote this form of freethought propagation.[136] In both the case of that society and the case of a similar "Secular Colporteur Society" in the Manchester area, lack of funds proved a serious hindrance to their efforts to sustain and expand their work.[137] With the tract distribution, as with all forms of proselytizing, so much depended on the sacrificial involvement of particular individuals. In London, the Secular Society announced that Bradlaugh's famous tract The Bible Not Reliable could be obtained upon request and the payment of 1s. 2d. per 100.[138] Charles Southwell suggested that, to minimize cost and to avoid the wastage of tracts resulting from their bad reputation, freethinking might consider lending tracts.[139] There is no indication that such a plan was implemented.

The most stationary geographic centers of the freethought movement were the book centers where individuals could pursue or purchase freethought literature. The dean of such centers, and also the most controversial, was Holyoake's operation at 147 Fleet Street in London. In addition to containing a reading room and Holyoake's printing press, the establishment housed meeting rooms for the London Secular Society. 147 Fleet Street facilitated the availability of freethought literature to Londoners. It also replaced James Watson's Queen's Head Passage

---

[136]See the announcement of its inception in Movement I (1843-44): 288.

[137]See "Infidel Tracts," Movement I (1843-44): 429; "Summary" Investigator IV (1857-58): 76.

[138]"London Secular Society's Propagandist Tracts," Investigator V (1858-59): 126.

[139]C. Southwell, "Tract Distribution," Reasoner IX (1850): 164-65.

printshop as the headquarters of freethought publishing during the 1850's. Finally, it became the locus of Holyoake's brand of "positive" atheism, and his center of personal power within the freethought movement.

Without denying the importance of the printed word for freethought propagandizing, it is quite safe to speculate that, in most working class neighbourhoods, the tongue proved even mightier than the pen in attracting an audience. The best publicized of propagandizing activities were the public services featuring a freethought advocate,[140] or better yet, a debate between a freethinker and an orthodox believer.[141] Some of the meetings were open-air meetings, like those held by contemporary believers in hopes of reaching the masses.[142] More common were the two-to-four evening lecture or debating series held in one of the London institutes and throughout the provinces. Accounts of both the lectures and debates are peppered with evidence of lively

---

[140]See appendix for examples of flyers advertising various lecture series.

[141]For examples of public debates, see: "Two Nights Public Discussion between Mr. Alexander Robertson and Mr. C. Bradlaugh on The Existence of God"--reported in the National Reformer XVI (July, 1870); Two Nights Debate in Newcastle between the Rev. A. J. Harrison and Mr. C. Bradlaugh on the topic "Secularism as a system of Truth and Morality," reported in the National Reformer XVI (September, 1870); Debate Between Father Ignatius and Mr. Bradlaugh, National Reformer XX (1872): 353ff.; Holyoake, "Evangelical Tone of the Cowper Street Debate," between Holyoake and Rev. Brewin Grant, Reasoner XIV (1853): 177-79; R. Cooper, "Mr. Robert Cooper and the Rev. Brewin Grant," Reasoner XIV (1853): 299-300; "The Newcastle Debate--Christianity v. Secularism" between Holyoake and Rev. J. H. Rutherford, reported in Reasoner XV (1853): 407ff.

[142]See "Atheistical Open Air Preaching," Reasoner XI (1851): 315. Also see report from the North London Open Air Secular Mission in "Reports of Meetings," National Reformer X (1867): 13.

audience participation. Listeners did not hesitate to express vocally either support or hearty disapproval. In the case of the debates, the participants themselves had no qualms about berating their opponents to the accompaniment of audience applause or guffaws of disgust. It is difficult to determine the impact of these gatherings on those who attended. No doubt most had rather decided opinions about the speakers and the topic of debate before coming to the meetings. About all that one could surmise with even a slight degree of certainty is that it appears that, at these gatherings, "a good time was had by all."

Apparently quite unconsciously, freethinkers succeeded in creating an institutional framework that both in spirit and form resembled the religious world from which they were seeking escape. In its perpetuation of religiosity, organized freethought cushioned for the renegade orthodox their departure from the faith. But, of course, freethought was more than a continuation of Established religion. Though it had retained the forms and the questions of orthodoxy, it had provided a new basis of motivation, new inspiration, and startling answers where the former ones had become worn out and inappropriate. Paradoxically, in these areas where it most represented a break from orthodoxy, freethought was most like her, for, in the process of perpetuating religiosity, freethought had itself created a positive belief system. In short, it had become a religion.

Tragically for the organized freethinkers, even the "affirmative" ones, their system had never completely extricated its own life from that of the Judeo-Christian Establishment which they, the freethinkers, had sentenced to death. In both its most negative and most positive forms, freethought organization depended on the continued existence of its enemy--in the former case, because it needed something to be against; in the latter case, because it needed the questions and categories of the old system to remain matters of vital public concern. While the old questions lived, freethought was an oasis of sanity and confidence in the midst of a society torn between clinging to the doubtful claims of orthodoxy, and facing the fearful prospect of living in an ungoverned, undisciplined universe. When the questions of God's existence, man's origin, man's purpose, and the "right" road to social harmony ceased to be relevant, so did the "faith" that had provided palatable answers. By its very nature, freethought could hardly outlive a single generation of converts. The better that generation accomplished its mission, the more likely the movement would be to die out in the next.

Conclusion

The British Secular Society, founded in 1866, still exists in England, but it cannot even afford a place to house its library. The organization has ceased to serve a useful function in a culture that has become more "secular" than the Victorian freethinkers thought possible and more "free" than even most of the freethinkers would have thought desirable.

As a theological and religious movement, freethought died out gradually after 1870. True, G. W. Foote continued to harp on the evils of Christianity through the pages of the Freethinker. Furthermore, in terms of actual numbers, membership in the National Secular Society peaked during the 1880's at the time of Bradlaugh's fight to enter Parliament as an atheist. The Freethought publishing company flourished during the 1870's and 1880's under Bradlaugh and Annie Besant. W. Stewart Ross, Charles Watts, and Charles MacKay perpetuated the Holyoake tradition of "affirmative" atheism in the Secular Review. Holyoake, himself, continued to write and travel as a Secularist speaker until his death in 1906. After Bradlaugh's death in 1890, his daughter Hypatia Bonner Bradlaugh, and J. M. Robertson continued to keep his name before the public as the "true" father of British freethought.

Nevertheless, though the organizational apparatus, the periodicals,

and the personalities remained the same after 1870, the spirit of
freethought gradually changed. It was increasingly preoccupied with
this world, rather than with the next. Bradlaugh was more interested in
gaining entrance to Parliament and in turning England into a republic
than in denouncing the immorality of the Old Testament. G. J. Holyoake
preferred to devote his attention to establishing cooperatives among the
working classes than to engaging in the intricacies of logical
refutation of Paley's **Natural Theology**. The freethinkers were interested in
Irish independence, in pacifism, in Secular education, in land reform,
in birth control, in promoting English liberalism throughout Europe.
The Church was left to care for itself.

That this transformation took place might be viewed as the very
success of the religious phase of the freethought movement. For, as has
been observed already, the freethinkers should have wanted nothing more
than to be able to stop discrediting the Establishment because there
were no more shackles of superstition and tyranny to be broken. To
argue for this explanation would be to claim too much for militant
freethought.

Its changing agenda and eventual irrelevance reflected much more
the inherently tentative nature of the religious element in freethought,
and the changes that were taking place in Victorian England, quite apart
from the labors of the freethinkers, and that made "religious"
freethought increasingly inappropriate.

The shift away from a theological orientation could have been the
salvation of the freethought movement as an organization. For, to the

extent that it separated itself from orthodoxy's issues, freethought guarded the possibility of outliving orthodoxy. That freethought did not go far enough in establishing a consistent, rational system that offered hope and true alternatives to the British working classes, meant that it could not compete with those emerging movements that did.

"Religious" freethought was, of necessity, a short-lived phenomenon for the very reasons that the movement had taken on a theological orientation in the first place. As a reaction, it depended upon clientele familiar with, and angry about, orthodoxy and its outworking in Victorian England. Furthermore, to the extent that the freethinkers' reaction was to the social disabilities caused by challenging orthodoxy, rather than to orthodoxy itself, that provocation was removed as individual freethinkers broke the respectability barrier of Victorian society. As a transitional step from a religious to a secular world view, freethought could survive only as long as there were people who thought that the old questions should and could be given new answers.

As a religion in its own right, freethought, in the form of Secularism, was guilty of many of the very things for which it had faulted Christianity. It became exclusive. It became dogmatic. A freethinker could no more admit the intellectual integrity of a believer than a believer could accept the moral integrity of a freethinker. Freethought accused Christianity of double-talk in its espousal of both the doctrines of pre-destination and individual responsibility. Freethought had its own freewill/determinism paradox to resolve in its proclamation of both necessitarianism and human capability--indeed, mandate--for realizing unending material improvement and moral progress.

The freethinkers could never quite agree which came first--man's circumstances or his ideas. To protect him from moral culpability, they insisted that he was determined by circumstances. On the other hand, to give him hope, they clung equally tenaciously to belief in the power of man's ideas to enable him to rise above his circumstances. The faith in reason is no more merited logically from the freethinkers' materialistic system than is the existence of a benevolent personal deity to be rationally derived exclusively from the "effect" of the physical universe. Secularism went beyond the terms of its own system in its emphasis on joy, love, and goodness. These are not essentially rational categories. If all that is meant by these terms is some aspect of the somewhat more rational criterion of utility--that is one thing. But it is clear that, despite their defense of the need to live only on the basis of what man knows by reason and the senses, the freethinkers were interested in something besides emotionless, calculated living. They conceded, in practice, and at apparently unguarded moments in writing, that man was more than a reasoning machine.

Freethought offered both too much and too little to survive the latter quarter of the nineteenth century with any degree of vitality. To the extent that its objectives were specific, they related to destroying the validity and the relevance of Christianity. The Church itself was doing rather a satisfactory job of accomplishing both of those ends. Furthermore, there was little enough Christian influence to start with among the working class at large. Freethought, as militant anti-orthodoxy, was wasting its energy fighting an enemy that, to the degree that he was viable at all, was already destroying himself quite effectively.

As a movement committed to human progress and material improvement, freethought offered nothing terribly unique. Morally and politically, freethought leaders were hardly distinguishable from Victorian middle-class liberals and radicals. Freethought wanted to give the working class the means to become "respectable." They were not interested in working class identity as an end in itself. Education, self-reliance, and cleanliness were the tickets of admission to true Victorian respectability. "Not wishing to enter" was not an acceptable excuse to the freethought leaders who had fought hard for their own place in the Establishment. Freethinkers were too "Christian," too "respectable," and too idealistic to be able to match the appeal of movements such as trade unionism that offered tangible material gains, and of Marxism that offered a scientific explanation of change and an identity to the working class as itself. Furthermore, and perhaps even more significant than these competing movements in accounting for the tepid appeal of Secularism, is the fact that the English working class is notorious for its preference for practical over theoretical causes. It might organize a Charter during a bad harvest year, or storm Hyde Park to demonstrate for extended suffrage. But to marshall sustained enthusiasm for such maxims as "that Science is the Providence of Life" would be quite out of character for the average English worker.

"Religious" freethought was, like Deism, a religion of the gaps. Freethinkers criticized the Deists for not following their positions to their logical conclusions. The deists were supposedly not as honest as the atheists, for they denied the implications of their materialism. One might well level the same charges at the freethinkers. They wanted the security of boundaries without their restrictions--or at least without any restrictions that they did not choose. By retaining reason and utility as absolutes, freethinkers sought to escape the paralysis of relativism, but they left themselves free to be the arbiters of what constituted reason and utility. To assume that ability and that disinterestedness was nothing other than an act of faith.

Militant freethought was a place to "camp," but not a place for building a home. Among the leadership, few devoted their entire lives to the movement. Several, including Southwell and Thomas Cooper, reconverted to some form of Christianity. Holyoake was intrigued by Comte's religion of Positivism, and by F. W. Newman's and Leigh Hunt's writings on religion. Annie Besant espoused the mystical theosophy of Madame Blavatsky, and even Bradlaugh developed a keen fascination for Far Eastern philosophy. Apart from their tendency to retrieve some form of supernatural interest after a time as materialist freethinkers, the leaders also devoted varying proportions of their energy to freethought at different points in their lives. Lesser figures such as Charles Watts, James Watson, and Austin Holyoake may have proved more consistently faithful to the cause of militant freethought than the two major leaders, G. J. Holyoake and Charles Bradlaugh.

Victorian freethought, though drawing some nourishment from the Enlightenment Radical tradition and Owenite Socialism, drew its strength primarily from the life--past and present--of its antagonist, the

English political and ecclesiastical Establishment. It thrived on orthodox moral and intellectual hypocrisy, on its betrayal of goodness and truth. As such, freethought, as a "religious" movement, was limited to the time frame of the image it reflected.

Assessing the significance of the movement is not as simple as it might appear, given its relatively defined chronological boundaries. Some of the goals of the freethinkers were realized in the course of the late nineteenth and early twentieth centuries. Blasphemy trials are a phenomenon of the past. The working classes are theoretically on a par legally and politically with the "respectable" classes. It is possible to receive a basic education without subscribing to the 39 Articles. Nevertheless, it is difficult to establish any significant causal link between these accomplishments and the efforts of the freethinkers. Perhaps the best that one can say is that they happened to espouse causes that were in line with contemporary rational and humanitarian sympathy for reform, and that would no doubt have succeeded quite apart from their own labors.

If one chose to, one could argue just as convincingly that, despite appearances, the deeper goals of the freethinkers were not achieved at all. England is still socially an hierarchical society. The working classes are still the working classes, and they have prospered, to the extent that they have prospered, not by climbing the ladder of respectability, as much as by commanding recognition for their position as it is. They have acquired a measure of power through economic and political leverage, more than through the "moral" leverage of cleanliness, proper grammar, and teetotalism. The working classes are not a bastion of intellectual ferment, and the motivating force of right thinking would seem now, as in the nineteenth century, to be overshadowed by more immediate and tangible considerations. Even on the matter of the cessation of blasphemy trials, one might insist that nothing really has changed. Suppressing blasphemy among the working classes in Victorian England was merely a function of maintaining law and order. Threats to the peace, and the status quo, though taking a different form in the twentieth century, are still met with the heavy hand of justice.

Whether one sees freethought vindicated depends on what one perceives to have been the essence of the freethought program, and what one chooses to see in subsequent developments. What is certain is that the freethinkers claimed too much for themselves. They were not averse to attributing to the greater cause of freethought all human progress and improvement, just as they had credited Christianity with all human folly and degradation.

In reality, it seems nearly impossible to prove that the mainstream of British history was affected significantly one way or another by the work of the militant freethinkers. They were on the fringes of society at large. As the movement aged, and mellowed, its less offensive style was matched by less persecution from the authorities, and its venom as a poison to British society was, thus, neutralized.

This is not to say that Victorian militant freethought is a movement without significance. But it is to suggest that its importance is other than what the freethinkers would have seen or desired it to be.

First of all, it is significant for its service to the lives of the individuals who participated in the movement. For them, it provided an avenue for venting personal frustration against the Establishment. It provided a stimulating forum for sorting through ideas. It provided the security of an organizational and metaphysical structure that fostered and channeled their energy toward self-improvement and social reform.

Second, the Freethinkers helped to make Enlightenment thought accessible to the English working classes. Through periodicals, lectures, and debates, the movement popularized the philosophes' gospel of reform based on Reason. In doing so, the freethinkers added an intellectual component to the tradition of British working class radicalism that is more often characterized by concern for practical over theoretical matters.

Third, the freethought movement is significant for the light it sheds upon, and the questions it raises about, the environment in which it took shape. The fact that the movement no longer has a following suggests something about the nature of the difference between England of the mid-nineteenth and England of the late-twentieth centuries. That freethought achieved some measure of vitality in Victorian England is testimony both to the strengths and to the weaknesses of Victorian Christianity. It had permeated society with its ideals, and it had so established itself as guarantor of the Victorian social and political order that, when the society fell short of the ideal, the Church was considered the necessary and appropriate sacrificial victim.

Fourth, the freethought movement is significant as the occasion of a missed opportunity for orthodoxy in its work among the working classes. Militant freethought, in a curious sort of way, could have been the Church's best insight and liaison into the British working class. Freethought inadvertently called the Church back to itself. In denouncing its shortcomings, freethought called for a re-commitment to compassion and truth whatever the cost in institutional terms. It called for a revival of the servant mentality. It called the Church back to practicalities and to the world where the people lived--away from the lofty other-worldly platitudes that permitted the Church to justify its betrayal of its ideals in the interest of succeeding in the this-worldly game of Establishment politics.

In short, the freethinkers invited the Church back to honesty, to goodness, and to humanity. Orthodoxy, in characteristic self-righteousness, responded at its worst. Either it showed itself in force or in dogmatism. Those who would take the time to debate the freethinkers only confirmed the stereotypical anti-intellectual, inconsiderate, presumptuous characteristics that freethinkers associated with orthodoxy. Whether they faced a Sir James Graham of the Establishment, or a Rev. Brewin Grant of the "enthusiastic" branch of Christian clergy, the freethinkers perceived that they had not been given an audience. They had not been heard. Furthermore, in designating themselves the religion of humanity, the Secularist freethinkers, by implication, had relegated orthodoxy to the side of inhumanity. Unfortunately for the orthodox, their response did little to refute that designation.

To mix metaphors, freethought was both the offspring and the parasite of an orthodoxy in distress. The roots of freethought were

Christian, but the movement drew its nourishment from the decay of orthodoxy, rather than from its health. As offspring and parasite, the health of freethought depended upon the survival of its parent and host. It could be relevant only as long as Christianity was relevant. Ironically, militant freethought is as uniquely and properly--though less characteristically--Victorian as outward piety, prudery, and "respectability." These phenomena belonged to the same world, and though apparent opposites, could not help but become anachronistic together.

APPENDIX

SAMPLE LECTURE ADVERTISEMENTS

SYLLABUS OF LECTURES

TO BE DELIVERED IN THE

HALL OF SCIENCE, MANCHESTER,

BY

G. JACOB HOLYOAKE, OF LONDON,

Editor of the "Movement."

The Sunday Morning Series will be INSTRUCTIONAL. The Sunday Evening Series will relate to SOCIALISM. The Wednesday Evening Series will be THEOLOGICAL. Those on Sunday Mornings will be chiefly addressed to YOUNG PERSONS; those on Sunday Evenings to the PUBLIC; and those on Wednesday Evenings to CHRISTIANS.

LECTURE I.—*Sunday Morning, June 23, 1844.*
THE ART OF ACQUIRING KNOWLEDGE.

LECTURE II.—*Sunday Evening, June 23.*
THE DISTINCTIVE FEATURE OF SOCIALISM ILLUSTRATED AND ENFORCED.

LECTURE III.—*Thursday Evening, June 27.*
A NEW ESTIMATE OF CHRISTIANITY'S HISTORICAL EVIDENCE.

LECTURE IV.—*Sunday Morning, June 30.*
HOW GREAT MEN ARE MANUFACTURED.

LECTURE V.—*Sunday Evening, June 30.*
THE INFLUENCE OF SOCIALISM ON THE THOUGHTS AND CONDUCT OF ITS PROFESSORS.

LECTURE VI.—*Wednesday Evening, July 3.*
THE RIGHT INTERPRETATION OF THE BIBLE DECIDED.

LECTURE VII.—*Sunday Morning, July 7.*
THE ELEMENTS OF LOGIC MADE EASY.

LECTURE VIII.—*Sunday Evening, July 7.*
THE VALUE OF BIOGRAPHY IN THE FORMATION OF INDIVIDUAL CHARACTER.
Illustrated by the Life and Writings of CHARLES REECE PEMBERTON.

LECTURE IX.—*Wednesday Evening, July 10.*
Refutation of the Great Argument for the Existence of God.
As propounded by Archdeacon PALEY, illustrated by Lord BROUGHAM, and enforced in the celebrated "Bridgewater Treatises."

LECTURE X.—*Sunday Morning, July 14.*
RHETORIC; OR, THE ART OF PUBLIC SPEAKING,
EXPLAINED TO YOUNG BEGINNERS.

LECTURE XI.—*Sunday Evening, July 14.*
THE CLAIMS OF SOCIALISM ON INDIVIDUAL ATTENTION
ASSERTED AND VINDICATED.

LECTURE XII.—*Wednesday Evening, July 17.*
SOCIETY AS IT WOULD BE WAS RELIGION WITHDRAWN FROM THE WORLD.

To commence on Sunday Mornings at Eleven, Evenings at Half-past Six, and Wednesday Evenings at Eight o'clock.

ADMISSION TO THE PUBLIC, ONE PENNY EACH LECTURE.

ABEL HEYWOOD, PRINTER, OLDHAM-STREET, MANCHESTER.

Utilitarian Society.
HALL OF SCIENCE,
NEAR FINSBURY SQUARE, CITY ROAD.

SUNDAY EVENING
LECTURES.

BY G. J. HOLYOAKE,
Editor of the 'REASONER.'

May 23. The Replies of Dr. CHALMERS, Rev. JAMES MARTINEAU, and PROFESSOR YOUNG to the Utilitarian Society.

May 30. [Conversational Tea Party. The Meeting will be Addressed by Mr. ROBERT COOPER, of Huddersfield, Mr. LUKE BURKE, Mr. HOLYOAKE, and others].

BY LUKE BURKE,
Late Editor of the 'PEOPLE'S PHRENOLOGICAL JOURNAL.'

June 6. A Demonstration of the Existence of a God, upon purely Philosophical Principles.

June 13. An Inquiry into the Nature and Attributes of a Deity, upon the same Principles.

BY 'EUGENE.'

June 20. The 'Snob Papers' in *Punch*.

DISCUSSION AFTER EACH LECTURE.
To Commence at 7½. Floor 2d., Gallery 4d.

For Objects and Principles of the Utilitarian Society, see No. 27 of the 'REASONER,' to be had at the Hall.

J. G. Hornblower, Printer, 77, Myddelton Street, Clerkenwell.

Utilitarian Society.
HALL OF SCIENCE,
NEAR FINSBURY SQUARE, CITY ROAD.

SUNDAY EVENING
LECTURES.

BY G. J. HOLYOAKE.
Editor of the REASONER.

November 21st, 1847.
Vulgarisms on Death, from Dr. CUMMINGS'S 'Manual of Christian Evidence.'

Nov. 28th.
Analysis of Puffing.

Dec. 5th.
The Logic of the 'Bottle,' or a Temperate Remonstrance to Teetotal Artists and Advocates.

Dec. 12th.
Examination of the Objections of the *Daily News* and *Athenæum* to the Institutions of the People.

Dec. 19th.
Moral Conventionalities of the Drama —The Rev. JAMES WHITE'S new Play of 'John Savile of Haysted.

DISCUSSION AFTER EACH LECTURE.

To Commence at 7.   Floor 2d., Gallery 3d.

For Objects and Principles of the Utilitarian Society, see No. 27 of the REASONER, to be had at the Hall.

Utilitarian Society.
HALL OF SCIENCE,
NEAR FINSBURY SQAURE, CITY ROAD.

SUNDAY EVENING
LECTURES.

BY G. J. HOLYOAKE,
Editor of the REASONER.

[In consequence of the Discussion arising out of Mr. Holyoake's outline Lecture on the 'Four Christs,' it has been deemed desirable to analyse each Christ separately, which will be done as follows:—]

Sept. 26. The 'Black'-Christ of Mythology, with remarks on the nature of History, and the difficulties of Historical Controversy.
Oct. 3. The Two-Natured Christ of the Churches.
 ,, 10. The Literal-Christ of Scripture.
 ,, 17. The Ideal-Christ of the Humanitarians.
 ,, 24. Lecture to City Missionaries, and Sunday School Teachers, in reply to the new work addressed to these parties by the Rev. John Cummings, D.D., entitled—'Is Christianity from God?' exposing the gross perversions of truth respecting celebrated Sceptics in this pretended 'Manual of Christian Evidence.'
 ,, 31. Second Lecture to do., including parallels between Dr. Cummings and Professor Smyth, and the Death-beds of Hobbes and Dr. Samuel Johnson.

NOVEMBER COURSE.
The Lectures of this month will continue the Moral Analysis of the Scriptures.

DISCUSSION AFTER EACH LECTURE.
To Commence at 7½. Floor 2d., Gallery 3d.

For Objects and Principles of the Utilitarian Society, see No. 27 of the 'REASONER,' to be had at the Hall.

Utilitarian Society.
HALL OF SCIENCE,
NEAR FINSBURY SQUARE, CITY ROAD.

SUNDAY EVENING
LECTURES.

July 11. EUGENE. Puseyism.

„ 18. Mr. SHORTER. Ancient and Modern Slavery, including (if then made known) an Examination of the Reason why Robert Dale Owen has recently Voted for Slavery in America.

„ 25. GEO. PICKESS. Life and Trial of Warren Hastings.

Aug. 2. G. J. HOLYOAKE. Moral Remains of the Old Testament.

„ – 9. EUGENE. Cromwell.

„ 16. J. P. DOUGLAS. Influence of Living Song Writers.

DISCUSSION AFTER EACH LECTURE.

Six speeches, of ten minutes each, are permitted in objection; and of the last three Speakers the President may be one. When two persons claim possession of the Chair at the same time, the preference is given to the Stranger.

To Commence at 7½. Floor 2d., Gallery 3d.

For Objects and Principles of the Utilitarian Society, see No. 27 of the 'REASONER,' to be had at the Hall.

J. G. Hornblower, Printer,] [77, Myddelton Street, Clerkenwell.

Lectures
BY
GEORGE JACOB HOLYOAKE,
FOR THE YEAR, 1853.

'REASONER' Office,
3, Queen's Head Passage.

I. Secularism the Positive Side of Free Inquiry.
II. Theory of Secular Morality.
III. Science the Providence of Life.
IV. Public Aim of Secularists.
V. The Progress of Reason in Religion.
VI. Truths Established in Recent Controversies.
VII. Secularism in the Pulpit, as set forth in 'Is it possible to make the Best of both Worlds?' by Thomas Binney.
VIII. Christian Secularism, Limited, Subordinate, and Contradictory.
IX. The Moral Innocency of rejecting Christianity where Conscientiously Disbelieved.
X. Morality before Christ.
XI. Moral Objections to Christianity.
XII. Do the Clergy approve Discussion?—in defence of the essay 'Why do the Clergy avoid it?'

Topics from the List of 1852.

Secular Education the Best for the Scholar and the Safest for the State.

Jesus Christ considered as an Example to Modern Reformers.

Roman Catholicism a Type of the Churches around us.

LITERARY INSTITUTION,
JOHN STREET, FITZROY SQUARE.

SYLLABUS OF ORATIONS
TO BE DELIVERED
ON SUNDAY EVENINGS.

CHARLES SOUTHWELL,
Editor of the 'Lancashire Beacon.'

Oct. 28.—The Cause of Progress, with special reference to recent proceedings in Lancashire.

THOMAS COOPER,
Author of the 'Purgatory of Suicides.'

Nov. 4.—The Genius of Shakspere—Hamlet.

GEORGE JACOB HOLYOAKE,
Editor of the 'Reasoner:'

Nov. 11.—Influence of the Writings of Robert Owen on Opinions and Practice.

(In the course of the evening, Mr. Holyoake will name a child, whose parents were resident at 'Harmony Hall.'

THOMAS COOPER,
Nov. 18.—Life and Genius of Milton.

The Apollonic Society, accompanied by the powerful Organ of the Institution, will perform a Choice Selection of Choral Music before and after each Oration.

To COMMENCE AT SEVEN O'CLOCK PRECISELY.

Admission: HALL 2d., GALLERY 3d.

FRIDAY EVENING LECTURES.
On Friday evenings, at half-past 8 precisely, JAMES BRONTERRE O'BRIEN, B.A., will Lecture on the 'Progress of Democracy at Home and Abroad.' Admission to Hall 1d., Gallery 2d.

A. & H. Holyoake, Printers, 3, Queen's-head Passage, Paternoster Row.

BIBLIOGRAPHY

PRIVATE PAPERS

London. Bishopsgate Institute. Bradlaugh Papers.

London. Bishopsgate Institute. George Jacob Holyoake Collection, including Holyoake's diaries, writings, letters, and scrapbooks, as well as contemporary miscellany about Holyoake.

GOVERNMENT DOCUMENTS

Great Britain. Parliament. Sessional Papers (Commons), 1852-53, "Census of Great Britain, 1851. Religious Worship in England and Wales," LXXXIX, 1852.

FREETHOUGHT PERIODICALS (1840-1872)

Herald of Progress (London), October 25, 1845-May 23, 1846.

(London) Investigator (London), April 1, 1854-August 1, 1859.

Movement (London), December 16, 1843-April 2, 1845.

National Reformer (London), April 14, 1860-December 29, 1872.

Oracle of Reason (London), November 6, 1841-December 2, 1843.

Reasoner (London), June 3, 1846-June 30, 1861; January 1, 1865-October 1, 1865; January 1, 1871-July, 1972.

CONTEMPORARY WRITINGS BY AND ABOUT FREETHINKERS

Answer to G. Jacob Holyoake's Pamphlet Entitled the "Logic of Death or Why Should the Atheist Fear to Die?" Dundee: James Duff, 1851.

Atheism Defended--Being a Review of a Tract Entitled "Holyoake Refuted"
by the author of the "Logic of Life." Newcastle-upon-Tyne: John
Ross, 1852.

"Atheos, Diagoras." Atheism Justified and Religion Superseded,
Reasonably, Summarily, and Conclusively. London: H. Hetherington,
1843.

Besant, Annie. Annie Besant--An Autobiography. London: T. Fisher
Unwin, 1893.

_____. A Selection of Social and Political Pamphlets by Annie
Besant. Edited by John Saville. New York: Augustus M. Kelley,
1970.

_____. Theosophy. London: T. C. and E. C. Jack, n.d.

Bradlaugh, Charles. The Bible; What It Is. London: Austin & Co.,
1917. [1856.]

_____. Examination of the Four Gospels according to Matthew, Mark,
Luke, & John with Remarks on the Life and Death of the Meek & Lowly
Jesus. Manuscript among the Bradlaugh Papers. Bishopsgate
Institute, 1850.

_____. A Few Words on the Christians' Creed. London: Charles
Bradlaugh, Jr., n.d.

_____. Freethinker's Textbook. London: Freethought Publishing Co.,
1876.

_____. Genesis. 3rd ed. London: A. & H. B. Bonner, 1882.

_____. Has Man a Soul? London: Freethought Publishing Co., 1884.

_____. Heresy: Its Utility and Morality--A Plea and a
Justification. 3rd ed. London: Freethought Co., 1882.

_____. A Plea for Atheism. London: Austin & Co., 1864.

_____. A Selection of the Political Pamphlets of Charles Bradlaugh.
Ed by John Saville. New York: Augustus M. Kelley, 1970.

_____. Theological Essays. London: R. Forder, 1891.

_____. When were our Gospels Written? London: Freethought
Publishing Co., 1881. [1867.]

Chew, Sanders. Mr. G. J. Holyoake Refuted in His Own Words. London:
Houlston and Stoneman, 1852.

Collet, Sophia Dobson. *George Jacob Holyoake and Modern Atheism--A Biographical and Critical Essay*. London: Trubner & Co., 1855.

_____. *Phases of Atheism*. London: John Watts, 1860.

Correspondence between Holyoake and Rutherford. Newcastle: Blackwell & Co., 1853.

Cowper, B. Harris. *The Logic of Life and Death or Words with the Unbeliever*. London: Elliot Stock, 1865.

Curzon, Frank. *The Gift of Life, or Why Should an Atheist Care to Live?* London: Houlston & Stoneman, 1853.

Dodworth, James. *Letter to the Shareholders of the "National Reformer" Co.* London: Printed by Request of Shareholders, 1862.

Foote, George William. *Secularism Restated: with a Review of the Several Expositions of Charles Bradlaugh and Geo. Jacob Holyoake*. London: W. J. Ramsey, 1874.

Harrison, J. *Holyoake Refuted; Being a Review of his Pretended Refutation of Paley*. Newcastle-on-Tyne: T. P. & W. Barkas, n.d.

Hetherington, Henry and Paterson, Thomas. *"The Man Paterson"--God versus Paterson--The Extraordinary Bow Street Police Report*. London: George Clarke, 1843.

The History of the Fleet Street House. London: Promoters of Freethought, 1856.

"G. J. Holyoake Exposed," *The Young Men's Magazine: A Monthly Journal of Religion, Literature, and Philosophy*, June, 1854, pp. 117-20.

Holyoake, G. J. and LeBlood, Robert. *The Appeal of the Distressed Operative Tailors to The Higher Classes and the Public*. London: Printed for the Writers, n.d.

Holyoake, George Jacob. *Bygones Worth Remembering*. 2 vols. New York: E. P. Dutton & Co., 1905.

_____. *Catholicism, The Religion of Fear*. London: J. Watson, 1850.

_____. *Child's First Word Book*. London: Fleet Street House, 1854.

_____. *The Child's Ladder of Knowledge*. London: F. Farrah, 1864.

_____. *The Child's Second Letter Book for Teaching Reading and Writing At Once*. London: James Watson, 1853.

_____. *Code of the Tenets or Governing Principles of the Society of Secularists Set Forth in 10 Articles*. London: Published for the Society of Secularists, 1881.

_____. *Cumming Wrong; Colenso Right--A Reply to the Rev. Dr. Cummings "Moses Right Colenso Wrong," by a London Zulu*. London: Farrah and Dunbar, n.d.

_____. *English Cooperation in French Literature*. Manuscript in Holyoake Collection, Bishopsgate, 1902.

_____. *English Secularism--A Confession of Belief*. Chicago: The Open Court Publishing Co., 1896.

_____. *Excluded Evidence on the Ground of Speculative Opinion*. London: London Book Store, 1865.

_____. *The Handbook of Grammar*. London: J. Watson, 1846.

_____. *The History of the Last Trial by Jury for Atheism in England*. London: James Watson, 1851.

_____. *The Liberal Situation: Necessity for a Qualified Franchise*. London: London Book Store, 1865.

_____. *Life and Career of Charles Bradlaugh*. Buffalo: Printed by Freethinkers' Magazine, 1891.

_____. *The Life and Character of Richard Carlile*. London: J. Watson, 1849.

_____. *The Limits of Atheism, or, Why Should the Skeptics be Outlaws?* London: J. A. Brook & Co., 1874.

_____. *Literary Institutions--Their Relation to Public Opinion*. London: Watson, 1849.

_____. *The Logic of Cooperation*. London: Trubner & Co., 1873.

_____. *The Logic of Death*. London: J. Watson, 1850.

_____. *A Logic of Facts: or Plain Hints on Reasoning*. London: J. Watson, 1848.

_____. *The Logic of Life, Deduced from the Principle of Freethought*. London: Newsagents' Newspaper & Publishing Co., 1861.

_____. *Mathematics No Mystery (or the Beauties and Uses of Euclid)*. 2nd ed. London: J. Watson, 1847.

_____. *My Religious Days*. n.p., 1901.

_____. *A New Defence of the Ballot--In Consequence of Mr. Mill's Objections to it*. London: London Book Store, 1868.

_____. *New Ideas of the Day*. London: Freethought Publishing Co., 1887.

_____. *1000 Shillings for European Freedom*. n.p., 1852.

_____. *The Organization of Freethinkers*. London: James Watson, 1852.

_____. *Organization: not of Arms--but Ideas*. London: J. Watson, 1853.

_____. *The Origin and Nature of Secularism; showing that where Freethought Commonly Ends Secularism Begins*. London: Watts &. Co., 1896.

_____. *The Outlaws of Freethought--The Policy Which May Secure an Affirmation Bill*. London: Holyoake & Co., 1861.

_____. *Partnerships of Industry: A Statement of the Co-Operative Case Divested of Sentimentality*. London: London Book Store, 1865.

_____. *Patriotism by Charity*. Leicester: Humberstone Gate Book Store, 1885.

_____. *Paley Refuted in His Own Words*. London: Hetherington, 1843.

_____. *The Philosophic Type of Religion, As Developed by Professor Newman--Stated, Examined, and Answered*. London: J. Watson, 1851.

_____. *Plain Words About Secularism*. n.p., 1882.

_____. *A Plea for Affirmation in Parliament*. London: Henry Cattell & Co., 1882.

_____. *The Positive Side of Free Inquiry*. *Reasoner* Tract., 1852.

_____. *Practical Grammar: Intended for the use of those who have little time for study*. London: J. Watson, 1847.

_____. *Principles of Secularism*. London: Holyoake and Co., 1859.

_____. *Public Performances of the Dead--A Review of American Spiritualism*. London: London Book Store, 1865.

_____. *Rationalism: A Treatise for the Times*. London: J. Watson, 1845.

_____. "The Reign of Time." The Baptist Tract Magazine 11 (October 1836): 341.

_____. Robert Owen--The Precursor of Social Progress. Manchester: Co-Operative Union Ltd., 1900.

_____. Rudiments of Public Speaking and Debate--or Hints on the Application of Logic. London: J. Watson, 1849.

_____. Secular Responsibility. London: Trubner, 1873.

_____. Secularism: The Affirmative Philosophy of the People. London: Holyoake & Co., 1854.

_____. Secularism a Religion Which Gives Heaven No Trouble. London: Watts & Co., 1882.

_____. Self Culture. Manuscript in Holyoake Collection. Bishopsgate Institute, 1850's.

_____. A Short and Easy Method With the Saints. London: Hetherington, 1843.

_____. Sixty Years of an Agitator's Life. 2 vols. London: T. Fisher Unwin, 1892.

_____. A Sketch of the Life and a Few of the Beauties of Pemberton--compiled and selected chiefly with a view of developing the causes which generated the Talent and Moral Greatness of this Extraordinary Man. London: J. Hobson, 1842.

_____. The Spirit of Bonner in the Disciples of Jesus or the Cruelty and Intolerance of Christianity Displayed in the Prosecution for Blasphemy, of Charles Southwell, Ed. of the "Oracle of Reason." London: Cleave & Hetherington, 1842.

_____. The Trial of George Jacob Holyoake--on an indictment for Blasphemy, before Mr. Justice Erskine, and a Common Jury at Gloucester--Aug, the 15, 1842. London: Printed for Anti-Persecution Union by T. Paterson, 1842.

_____. The Trial of Theism. London: Holyoake & Co., 1858.

_____. The Warpath of Opinion: Strange Things Seen Therein As Shown in the "Life of Bradlaugh" and "Memories" of Linton. Leicester: Cooperative Printing Society, Ltd., 1896.

_____. What Would Follow on the Effacement of Christianity? Buffalo: Office of the Freethinkers' Magazine, 1890.

_____. The Workman and the Suffrage--Letters to the Right Hon. Lord John Russell, M.P.--and the "Daily News." London: Holyoake & Co., 1859.

M'Innes, D. Modern Infidelity Tried on its Own Merits or A Reply to some of the Statements of Mr. G. J. Holyoake, in his discussion with the Rev. B. Grant, In Glasgow, October 1854. Glasgow: R. Robertson, 1856.

Mackintosh, John. The Logic of Atheism with Especial Reference to Mr. Holyoake's pretended Refutation of Paley. Newcastle-on-Tyne: Office of John Ross, 1850.

Martyn, Rev. J. M. The Forcible Feebles--or the Vaulting Weakness of Atheism, Being a Reply to the Potteries Secular Society's Review of "Mene Tekel." Hanley: Allbut & Daniel, 1853.

_____. "Mene Tekel" or Mr. Holyoake's Defeat in Hanley. Hanley: Allbut & Daniel, 1853.

Paterson, Thomas. The Devil's Looking Glass or Mirror of Infidelity. London: T. Paterson, 1848.

_____. Letters to Infidels on Charles Southwell's Manifestations of Friendship and the Pangs of Gratitude for the Late Deeply Lamented MQR of the "Movement." London: R. Paterson, 1846.

Potteries Secular Society. Libra or, the balances--being a Review of "Mene Tekel," exposing the unfairness and falsity of the Rev. J. M. Martyn's Report of Mr. Holyoake's Defeat in Hanley. Stoke-on-Trent: Geo. Turner, 1853.

Robertson, James. Secularists and Their Slanderers: or the "Investigator" Investigated. London: J. B. Bebbington, 1858.

Southwell, Charles. Another "Fourpenny Wilderness" in which may be found more nails for the coffin of Nonsense called Atheism, more Hints to Freethinkers, and a Reply to Geo. Jacob Holyoake's Examination of Charles Southwell's "Impossibilities of Atheism Demonstrated." London: J. Watson, 1852.

_____. The Impossibility of Atheism Demonstrated: with Hints to Nominal Atheists--in a Letter to the Freethinkers of Great Britain. London: J. Watson, 1852.

_____. Supernaturalism Exploded: In a Review of the famous Six Nights' Controversy between the Rev Brewin Grant, Christian, and Geo. Jacob Holyoake, Secularist. London: for the Secularist Association for the Diffusion of Useful Knowledge by J. Watson, 1853.

Sunday Closing. A Refutation of the Doctrines of Holyoake--(Commonly called Secularism) being an Answer to the letter Messrs. Witherington, Grimshaw, and Hilton. Bolton: J. Joyce, 1853.

A Tract for the Time--A Few Plain Thoughts--In Reply to the Arguments and Statements of Mr. Holyoake In Support of An Argument That There is no God. Stockton: J. Readman, 1851.

The Trial of Thomas Paterson for Blasphemy. London: H. Hetherington, 1844.

Watts, John, and "Iconoclast." Half Hours with Freethinkers. London: Watts & Co., 1864.

Williams, S. The Creed of Error: A Reply to Holyoake's "Logic of Death." London: Partridge & Oakey, 1851.

CONTEMPORARY FREETHOUGHT ADDRESSES, DEBATES, AND DISCUSSIONS

Atheism or Theism? Debate between "Iconoclast," The Accredited Champion of British Atheists and Others and William Honyman Gillespie, of Turbanehill. London: Houlston & Sons, 1872.

J. Barker's reply to George Jacob Holyoake on the origin, the character, and the tendency of Christianity. Lectures given at Halifax, February 14 and 15, 1848. Holyoake Collection. Bishopsgate Institute.

The Credibility and Morality of the Four Gospels. Five Nights' Discussion at Halifax between Rev. T. D. Matthias--Baptist Minister--and "Iconoclast." London: Farrah, Wilks, & Dunbar, 1860.

Christianity and Secularism. Report of a Public Discussion between the Rev. Brewin Grant, B.A. (Ed. of "The Bible and the People") and George Jacob Holyoake, Esq. (Ed. of "The Reasoner"). London: Ward & Co., 1853.

Christianity vs. Secularism--A Public Discussion in Newcastle-on-Tyne between the Rev. J. H. Rutherford and Mr. G. J. Holyoake, August 1, 3, 5, 1853. London: Ward & Co., 1854.

Cooper, Robert. Brewin Grant Refuted--Lectures to the Working Classes on Christianity and Secularism; Being a Review of the Arguments of the Rev. B. Grant and Rev. J. H. Hinton. London: J. Watson, 1853.

_____. A Popular Development of Atheism--Being a Reply to Mr. Knight's "Atheism Renounced." Lecture given at John Street Institution. London: J. Watson, 1853.

Discussion on Atheism--Report of a Public Discussion between the Rev.
  Brewin Grant, B. A. and C. Bradlaugh, South Place Chapel, June 22-
  27, 1875, "Is Atheism or is Christianity the True Secular Gospel,
  as tending to the improvement and happiness of mankind in this life
  by human efforts and material means?" London: Henry Hodge, 1875.

A Discussion on the Question "Has Man a Soul?" between The Rev. T.
  Lawson, of West Hartlepool and Charles Bradlaugh of London.
  Manchester: Tubbs, Brook, & Chrystal, 1861.

Discussion on Secularism--Report of a Public Discussion between the Rev.
  Brewin Grant (B.A.) and George Jacob Holyoake (Esq.) City Hall,
  Glasgow, October 2, 19. London: A. Hall, Virtue, & Co., 1854.

God, Man, and the Bible. Three Nights Discussion between the Rev.
  Joseph Baylee, D.D. and Charles Bradlaugh on 27-29/June/1860.
  London: Freethought Publishing Co., n.d.

Grant, Brewin. "Is Man Responsible for His Belief?" A Lecture
  Delivered in the City Hall, Glasgow, October 23rd, 1854. Glasgow:
  Robert Stack, 1854.

Hinton, J. H. A Lecture Delivered at the Royal British Institution--
  Cowper St., London, March 3, 1853, on the conclusion of the
  discussion between Mr. G. J. Holyoake and the Rev. Brewin Grant.
  London: Houlston and Stoneman, 1853.

Holyoake, G. J. Moral Errors which Endanger the Permanence of Co-
  Operative Societies. Paper read before the Political Economy
  Section of the Social Science Congress in Guildhall, London, 1862.
  Huddersfield: Henry Fielding, 1863.

_____. Three Lectures in Heywood in Answer to Mr. E. Grubb's
  Lectures Entitled--"Infidelity Unmasked." Heywood: A. Whitworth,
  1852.

_____. The Value of Biography in the Formation of Individual
  Character illustrated by The Life and Writings of Charles Reece
  Pemberton. A Lecture delivered May 12, 1844 to Branch 1 of London
  Communists. London: J. Watson, 1845.

_____. Working Class Representation: Its Conditions and
  Consequences--An Address to Electors of Birmingham at Town Hall,
  October 16, 1868. London: Bookstore 282 Strand, 1868.

Lamb, Mr. A. H. The Substance of a Lecture on the Being of a God
  (September 1, 1851) To Which are added Answers to Mr. Jacob
  Holyoake's Objections to Dr. Paley's Natural Theology. Middlesbro:
  J. Windross, 1851.

Pottinger, Rev. T. The Consequences of Atheism. Lecture given in Newcastle-on-Tyne. Newcastle-on-Tyne: John Ross, 1850.

Public Discussion on Teetotalism and the Maine Law: Between G. J. Holyoake and Dr. Frederic R. Lees. London: W. Tweedie, 1856.

Report of a Discussion on the Main Law, between G. J. Holyoake (London) and Mr. G. E. Lomax (Manchester) in Blackburn--November 16, 17, 1857. 2nd ed. Blackburn: F. J. Nichols, 1858.

The Report of the Four Nights Public Discussion at Bradford between George J. Holyoake, of London, ed. of the "Reasoner" and John Bowes of Manchester, ed. of the "Truth" on The Truth of Christianity and The Folly of Infidelity, The Free Agency of Man and The Formation of Character. London: E. Ward, W. Horsell, J. Watson, 1850.

A Report of the Public Discussion between G. J. Holyoake and David King. London: W. Horsell, Aldine Chambers, 1850.

Report of a Public Discussion Carried on By Henry Townley (Missionary) and George Jacob Holyoake. London: Ward & Co., 1852.

Satchwell and Christianity versus Holyoake and Atheistic Infidelity. Northampton: Mr. J. Taylor, 1847.

Scott, Rev. Thomas. Addressed to the Working Classes Popery not Christianity: or a Defence of Christianity against the attacks of Infidel Lecturers: with specific reference to Mr. Holyoake's Lecture "Artist' Room," Norwich, December 3, 1850. London: Jarrold & Sons, 1850.

Secularism, Scepticism, and Atheism--Verbatim Report of the Proceedings of a two Nights' Public Debate between G. J. Holyoake and C. Bradlaugh. London: Austin & Co., 1870.

Secularism: Unphilosophical, Immoral, and Anti-Social--Verbatim Report of a Three Nights' Debate between the Rev. Dr. McCann & Charles Bradlaugh, December 7, 14, 21, 1881. London: Watts & Co., n.d.

Substance of the Two Nights' Discussion . . . between Rev. Baylee and Frederick Hollick, Socialist Missionary on "The Genuineness, Authenticity, and Inspiration of The Bible." London: B. D. Cousins, 1839.

Turley, W. Mr. Holyoake and His Detractors--An Address to the Friends of Progress. London: W. Goddard, 1858.

Two Nights' Discussion between T. Cooper and C. Bradlaugh On the Being of a God as the maker and moral governor of the Universe. Hall of Science, February 1, 3, 1864. Bradlaugh Papers. Bishopsgate Institute.

"Was Jesus of Nazareth the Messiah?" A Three Nights' Discussion between Mr. Robert Roberts, Ed. of "Christadelphian" & Mr. Louis Stern, an Orthodox Jew, Birmingham, October 17-19, 1871. London: G. J. Stevenson, 1872.

"What is Christianity?" Report of a Public Discussion between David King of Birmingham, Evangelist, and Editor of the "British Harbinger"--and Charles Bradlaugh, of London, President of the National Secular Society and Editor of the "National Reformer." Birmingham: D. King, 1870.

Woodman, Rev. Woodville. The Doctrine of a Supreme Being Vindicated, and The Fallacy of Infidel Arguments Exposed and Refuted. Lecture. London: n.p., 1852.

SELECTED SECONDARY WORKS

Altholz, Josef L. (Ed.). The Mind and Art of Victorian England. Minneapolis: University of Minnesota Press, 1976.

Arnstein, Walter L. The Bradlaugh Case--A Study in Late Victorian Opinion and Politics. Oxford: Clarendon Press, 1965.

Bonner, Hypatia Bradlaugh. Charles Bradlaugh. 2 vols. London: T. Fisher Unwin, 1894.

_____. "The Warpath of Opinion"--A Reply. London: A. & H. B. Bonner, 1902.

Budd, Susan. "The Loss of Faith. Reasons for Unbelief among Members of the Secular Movement in England 1850-1950." Past and Present XXXVI (April 1967): 106-25.

_____. Varieties of Unbelief--Atheists and Agnostics in English Society 1850-1950. London: Heinemann Educational Books, Ltd., 1977.

Chadwick, Owen. The Victorian Church. 2 vols. London: Adam & Charles Black, 1966, 1970.

Cockshut, A. O. J. The Unbelievers--English Agnostic Thought 1840-1890. London: Collins, 1964.

Courtney, Janet. Freethinkers of the Nineteenth Century. London: Chapman & Hall, Ltd., 1920.

Currie, Robert; Gilbert, Alan; and Horsley, Lee. Churches and Churchgoers--Patterns of Church Growth in the British Isles Since 1700. Oxford: Clarendon Press, 1977.

Eros, John. "The Rise of Organized Freethought in Mid-Victorian England." Sociological Review, New Series II (July, 1954): 98-120.

Elliott-Binns, L. E. English Thought 1860-1900; The Theological Aspect. Greenwich, Conn.: Seabury Press, 1956.

Gay, John D. The Geography of Religion in England. London: Duckworth & Co., Ltd., 1971.

Gilbert, Alan D. Religion and Society in Industrial England--Church, Chapel and Social Change, 1740-1914. New York: Longman, 1976.

Goss, C. W. F. A Descriptive Bibliography of the Writings of G. J. Holyoake. London: Crowther & Goodman, Portspoken Press, 1908.

Grugel, Lee. Geo. Jacob Holyoake: A Study in the Evolution of a Victorian Radical. Philadelphia: Porcupine Press, 1976.

Inglis, Kenneth S. Churches and the Working Classes in Victorian England. London: Routledge and Kegan Paul, 1963.

Kitson Clark, George. Churchmen and the Condition of England 1832-1885: A Study in the Development of Social Ideas and Practice from the Old Regime to the Modern State. London: Methuen & Co., Ltd., 1973.

_____. The Making of Victorian England. Cambridge, Mass.: Harvard University Press, 1962.

Krantz, Charles K. "The British Secularist Movement: A Study in Militant Dissent." Ph.D. Dissertation, University of Rochester, 1964.

Livingstone, James C. The Ethics of Belief--An Essay on The Victorian Religious Conscience. Missoula, Montana: American Academy of Religion and Scholars Press, 1974.

McCabe, Joseph. Life and Letters of Geo. Jacob Holyoake. 2 vols. London: Watts & Co., 1908.

McGee, John Edwin. A Crusade for Humanity--The History of Organized Positivism in England. London: Watts & Co., 1931.

MacKay, Charles R. Life of Charles Bradlaugh, M.P. London: D. J. Gunn & Co., 1888.

Machin, G. I. T. Politics and the Churches in Great Britain 1832-1868. Oxford: Clarendon Press, 1977.

Meacham, Standish. "The Church in the Victorian City." *Victorian Studies* XI (March, 1968): 359-78.

Murphy, Howard. "The Ethical Revolt against Christian Orthodoxy in Early Victorian England." *American Historical Review* LX (July, 1955): 800-17.

Robertson, J. M. *A History of Free Thought in the Nineteenth Century*. 2 vols. New York: G. P. Putnam's, 1930.

Royle, E. "George Jacob Holyoake and the Secularist Movement in Britain, 1841-1861." Ph.D. Dissertation, Cambridge University, 1968.

_____, ed. *The Infidel Tradition From Paine to Bradlaugh*. London: Macmillan Press, Ltd., 1976.

_____. *Radical Politics 1790-1900, Religion and Unbelief*. London: Longman Group, Ltd., 1971.

_____. *Radicals, Secularists and Republicans--Popular Freethought in Britain, 1866-1915*. Manchester: University Press, 1980.

_____. *Victorian Infidels--The Origins of the British Secular Movement 1791-1866*. Manchester: University Press, 1974.

Smith, F. B. "The Atheist Mission, 1840-1900." In *Ideas and Institutions of Victorian Britain*, pp. 205-35. Edited by Robert Robson. London: G. Bell & Sons, Ltd., 1967.

Soloway, R. A. *Prelates and People--Ecclesiastical Social Thought in England 1783-1852*. London: Routledge & Kegan Paul, 1969.

Tribe, David H. *President Charles Bradlaugh, M.P.* London: Elek Books, 1971.

_____. *One Hundred Years of Free Thought*. London: Elek Books, Ltd., 1967.

Ward, William R. *Religion and Society in England 1790-1850*. London: B. T. Batsford, Ltd., 1972.

Wood, H. G. *Belief and Unbelief Since 1850*. Cambridge: University Press, 1955.

INDEX

"Anthony Collins," 35

Anti-Persecution Union, 15, 47, 76

Barker, Joseph, 48, 52, 61, 63, 138-141

Besant, Annie, 7, 27, 50, 235

Blasphemy laws, 78

Bradlaugh, Charles: changing interests, 235; conflict with Holyoake, 135-146; entry to Parliament, 6, 7, 157, 230; *Investigator* editor, 135; on blasphemy, 78; religious upbringing, 25-27

Carlile, Richard, 15, 25, 45-46

Church Census, 1851, 2

Chilton, William, 27, 30, 35, 46, 59, 66, 166, 205

Christianity: intellectual integrity of, 56-74; morality and, 42-49, 75-102; natural theology, 68-72; problem of evil, 62; science and, 59-61; scriptures, 63-65, 86-90

Church and State, 76-84

Cooper, Robert, 18, 105, 126-131, 207

Cooperative Movement, 6, 158

Deism, Deists, 15, 111, 234

Enlightenment, 9, 191, 238

Established Church, 76-85, 196, 221

Evans, Mary Ann (George Eliot), 2

Fleet Street House, 18, 126, 132-135, 148, 226-227

Freethought: affiliated "causes," 4, 47, 76, 139, 154-157, 231; "affirmativist" and "negativist" controversy, 161-173, 180-184; apologetics of, 221-222; community life, 209-218; decline of, 6, 237-238; definition of, 3, 148; dogma of, 202-206; journals of, 5; morality of, 195-200, 206; objectives of, 152-153; organizational efforts, 149-151, 159-173; phases of, 16-18; proselytizing efforts of, 220-228

Harmony Hall, 17, 111, 119-120, 148

Herald of Progress (1845-1846), 5, 16, 175

Holyoake, George Jacob: arrest of, 43-45; background in Owenite Socialism, 110; consistency of belief, 35, 114, 123, 139, 179; Cooperativism, 158; conflict with Bradlaugh, 135-146; conflict with Cooper, 126-131; conflict with Owen, 111-121; conflict with Southwell, 121-125; foreign associations of, 5, 36; on freewill, 96; on secular education, 214-215; on the truth of freethought, 105; pilgrimage within freethought, 123, 173-179, 235; publications of, 16, 43; religious upbringing, 22-25, 32, 42-44; Spurgeon and, 100

Holywell Street Case, 83

Investigator (1854-1859), 5, 18, 121-122, 126, 128-132, 162, 168

London Secular Society, 135-150

Malthusianism, 7, 139, 157, 179

Movement (1843-1845), 5, 16, 112, 162

National Reformer (1860-1890), 5, 16, 136, 138, 151, 162

National Secular Society, 6, 151, 230

Newman, Frances W., 2, 178, 235

New Moral World, 111, 116

Oath-swearing, 99, 137

Oracle of Reason (1841-1843), 5, 6, 16, 29, 46, 59, 68, 111, 112, 121, 162

Owenite Rational Society, 6, 16, 17, 29, 110, 111

Owen, Robert, 16, 111-121, 208

Paley, William, 69

Paterson, Thomas, 46, 61, 70, 168, 196, 219

Radical tradition, 15

<u>Reasoner</u> (1846-1861, 1865, 1871-1872), 5, 16, 64, 128-131, 138, 143, 162-163, 175

Ryall, Malthus Q., 29, 61, 67, 68

Secularism, 2, 4, 19, 20, 54, 122, 145-146, 160-162, 169, 175-180, 185, 188, 202-206. See also Freethought.

Socialism: Marxist, 7, 234; Owenite/Utopian, 5, 17, 110, 155, 208

Southwell, Charles, 16, 42-43, 46, 70, 110, 111-121, 121-125, 219, 235

Spurgeon, Charles, 100

Teetotalism, 157-158

Wilkes, John, 15

For Product Safety Concerns and Information please contact our EU representative GPSR@taylorandfrancis.com
Taylor & Francis Verlag GmbH, Kaufingerstraße 24, 80331 München, Germany